Sydney Omarr's

DAY-BY-DAY ASTROLOGICAL GUIDE FOR

GEMINI

May 21–June 20

2002

A SIGNET BOOK

SIGNET
Published by New American Library, a division of
Penguin Putnam Inc., 375 Hudson Street,
New York, New York 10014, U.S.A.
Penguin Books Ltd, 27 Wrights Lane,
London W8 5TZ, England
Penguin Books Australia Ltd, Ringwood,
Victoria, Australia
Penguin Books Canada Ltd, 10 Alcorn Avenue,
Toronto, Ontario, Canada M4V 3B2
Penguin Books (N.Z.) Ltd, 182–190 Wairau Road,
Auckland 10, New Zealand

Penguin Books Ltd, Registered Offices:
Harmondsworth, Middlesex, England

First published by Signet, an imprint of New American Library,
a division of Penguin Putnam Inc.

First Printing, June 2001
10 9 8 7 6 5 4 3 2 1

Copyright © Sydney Omarr, 2001
All rights reserved

Sydney Omarr is syndicated worldwide by
Los Angeles Times Syndicate.

REGISTERED TRADEMARK—MARCA REGISTRADA

Printed in the United States of America

Without limiting the rights under copyright reserved above, no part of
this publication may be reproduced, stored in or introduced into a
retrieval system, or transmitted, in any form, or by any means (electronic,
mechanical, photocopying, recording, or otherwise), without the prior written
permission of both the copyright owner and the above publisher of this
book.

BOOKS ARE AVAILABLE AT QUANTITY DISCOUNTS WHEN USED TO PROMOTE
PRODUCTS OR SERVICES. FOR INFORMATION PLEASE WRITE TO PREMIUM
MARKETING DIVISION, PENGUIN PUTNAM INC., 375 HUDSON STREET, NEW
YORK, NEW YORK 10014.

If you purchased this book without a cover you should be aware that this
book is stolen property. It was reported as "unsold and destroyed"
to the publisher and neither the author nor the publisher has received
any payment for this "stripped book."

2002
A BRAND-NEW YEAR—
A PROMISING NEW START

Enter Sydney Omarr's star-studded world of accurate day-by-day predictions for every aspect of your life. With expert readings and forecasts, you can chart a course to romance, adventure, good health, or career opportunities while gaining valuable insight into yourself and others. Offering a daily outlook for 18 full months, this fascinating guide shows you:

- The important dates in your life
- What to expect from an astrological reading
- How the stars can help you stay healthy and fit
- Your lucky lottery numbers
  And more!

Let this expert's sound advice guide you through a year of heavenly possibilities—for today and for every day of 2002!

SYDNEY OMARR'S DAY-BY-DAY ASTROLOGICAL GUIDE FOR

ARIES—March 21–April 19
TAURUS—April 20–May 20
GEMINI—May 21–June 20
CANCER—June 21–July 22
LEO—July 23–August 22
VIRGO—August 23–September 22
LIBRA—September 23–October 22
SCORPIO—October 23–November 21
SAGITTARIUS—November 22–December 21
CAPRICORN—December 22–January 19
AQUARIUS—January 20–February 18
PISCES—February 19–March 20

IN 2002

CHANCE TO WIN A PERSONALIZED HOROSCOPE FOR A FULL YEAR!

Enter the Sydney Omarr Horoscope Sweepstakes!

No purchase necessary. Details below. Open only to U.S. residents age 18 and up

Name _____

Address _____

City_____ State_____ Zip_____

Mail to:
Sydney Omarr Horoscope Sweepstakes
c/o Penguin Putnam Inc.
375 Hudson St., 5th floor
New York, NY 10014

All entries must be postmarked by August 31, 2001 and received by September 8, 2001.

1. NO PURCHASE NECESSARY TO ENTER OR WIN A PRIZE. To enter the Sydney Omarr Horoscope Sweepstakes, complete this official entry form or, on a 3" x 5" piece of paper, write your name and complete address. Mail your entry to: Sydney Omarr Horoscope Sweepstakes; c/o Penguin Putnam Inc.; 375 Hudson St., 5th floor; New York, NY 10014. Enter as often as you wish, but mail each entry in a separate envelope. No mechanically reproduced or computer generated entries allowed. All entries must be postmarked by 8/31/2001 and received by 9/8/2001 to be eligible. Not responsible for late, lost, damaged, incomplete, illegible, postage due or misdirected mail entries.

2. Winners will be selected from all eligible entries in a random drawing on or about 9/14/01, by Penguin Putnam Inc., whose decisions are final and binding. Odds of winning are dependent upon the number of entries received. Winners will be notified by mail and may be required to execute an affidavit of eligibility and release which must be returned within 14 days of notification or an alternate winner will be selected.

3. One (1) Grand Prize winner will receive a personalized one-year horoscope from an astrologer chosen by Sydney Omarr or Penguin Putnam Inc. One (1) Second Prize winner will receive a personalized one-month horoscope from an astrologer chosen by Sydney Omarr or Penguin Putnam Inc. Estimated aggregate value of Grand Prize and Second Prize: $250. If there is an insufficient number of entries, Penguin Putnam Inc. reserves the right not to award the prizes.

4. Sweepstakes open to residents of the U.S. 18 years of age or older, except employees and the immediate families of Penguin Putnam Inc., its affiliated companies, advertising and promotion agencies. Void in Puerto Rico, and wherever else prohibited by law. No cash substitutions, transfers or assignments of prizes are allowed. In event of unavailability, sponsor may substitute a prize of equal or greater value. Limit one prize per person, household or family. All Federal, State, and Local laws apply. Taxes, if any, are the sole responsibility of the prize winners. Winners consent to the use of their name and/or photos or likenesses for advertising purposes without additional compensation (except where prohibited). By accepting this prize, winners release Penguin Putnam Inc., its affiliated companies, advertising and promotion agencies from any and all liability for any loss, harm, injuries, damages, cost or expense arising out of participation in this Sweepstakes or the acceptance, use or misuse of the prize.

5. For the names of the prize-winners, send a self-addressed, stamped envelope after 9/28/01 to : SYDNEY OMARR HOROSCOPE SWEEPSTAKES WINNERS, Penguin Putnam Inc., 375 Hudson St., 5th floor, New York, NY 10014.

CONTENTS

Introduction: Your Cosmic Code	1
1. The Coming Trends of 2002!	3
2. Planning Ahead in 2002—Timing Your Life for Luck, Prosperity, and Love!	9
3. Teach Yourself Astrology	20
4. Crack the Astrology Code—Decipher Those Mysterious Glyphs on Your Chart	89
5. How Your Rising Sign Personalizes Your Horoscope	102
6. The Moon—Our Light Within	112
7. Astro-Mating—An Element-ary Guide to Love	127
8. Ask the Expert—Should You Have a Personal Reading?	135
9. The "In" Sites Online	141
10. The Sydney Omarr Yellow Pages	150
Your Gemini Home Pages—All About Your Life, Friends, Family, Work, and Style!	158
11. Are You True to Type?	160
12. "In Style" the Gemini Way	165
13. The Healthy Gemini	170
14. Gemini at Work!	172

15. Gemini Rich and Famous! 175
16. Gemini Pairs—How You Get Along with Every Other Sign 179
17. Astrological Outlook for Gemini in 2002 186
18. Eighteen Months of Day-by-Day Predictions—July 2001 to December 2002 188

INTRODUCTION

Your Cosmic Code

Are you ready for the excitement and challenges of the year 2002? We've cracked the mystery of the human genome, but there's another code that's been used to map the human personality since ancient times. Like your genetic imprint, your astrology chart is uniquely "you." It is a map of your moment in time, which has its own code, based on the position of the sun, moon, and planets at the time and place you were born. What is especially intriguing is that this system can offer specific, practical guidance, even when using only *one* of the elements of the code, your *sun sign*. Though you share that sun sign with others, there are many ways to use it every day to find a more fulfilling lifestyle. Your sun sign "map" can help you find success, attract love, look for a better job, have a healthier body, and even take the vacation of your dreams or decorate your home.

Just knowing the other person's sun sign can give you many clues to how to make your relationship a happy one. You can troubleshoot problems in advance and, if they crop up, find a way to make them work for you. In this year's edition of *Sydney Omarr's Guides,* you'll learn what's best for you and how your sign relates, positively and negatively, with every other sign under the sun.

"For every thing there is a season" could be the theme song of astrology. Will 2002 be the time to charge forward or proceed with caution, to change careers or stick with the job at hand, to fall in love? We'll deal in many ways with the question of timing—when are the potentially difficult times (which also present positive challenges), when can you expect delays and potential misunderstandings, when are the best times to take risks? You'll be able to get your life "on track" and chart your course with full knowledge of the shoals ahead.

For those who are new to astrology or would like to know more about it, there is basic information to give you an inside look at how astrology works. Then you can look up the other planets in your horoscope to find out how each contributes to your unique personality.

Astrologers have been quick to embrace the new technology of the twenty-first century, especially since sophisticated astrological computer programs have eliminated the tedious work of casting a chart and deliver beautiful chart printouts. Now anyone with access to the Internet can view their astrology chart at a free Internet site or buy the same programs professional astrologers use. We'll show you where to do this in chapters devoted especially to Internet resources. We'll also give you Sydney Omarr's updated "Yellow Pages" of the best places for books, tapes, and further astrological studies.

As we explore our inner cosmos via astrology, we are still searching for the same things that always have made life worth living: love, meaningful work, and fulfilling relationships. With Sydney Omarr's astonishingly accurate day-by-day forecasts, you can use your cosmic link to the universe to enhance every aspect of your life. So here's hoping you use your star power wisely and well for a productive and happy 2002!

CHAPTER 1

The Coming Trends of 2002!

We're at the beginning of a decisive decade, when many issues are coming to the forefront simultaneously: global expansion, territorial disputes, space travel, biotechnology breakthroughs, overpopulation, dangers of nuclear warfare, and environmental crises. Here are the key planets calling the shots and the trends to watch in 2002.

This year is a "bridge" year, when there are no dramatic shifts in the atmosphere (that comes next year). So it is more a time of consolidation, of taking stock and making plans for the future. The slow-moving planet Pluto is our guide to the hottest trends. Pluto brings about a heightened consciousness and transformation of matters related to the sign it is passing through. Now in Sagittarius, Pluto is emphasizing everything associated with this sign to prepare us philosophically and spiritually for things to come.

Perhaps the most pervasive sign of Pluto in Sagittarius is globalization in all its forms, which has become a main theme of the past few years. We are re-forming boundaries, creating new forms of travel that will definitely include space travel. At this writing, the $60 billion space station is under way, a joint venture between the United States, Russia, Japan, Europe, and Canada. It is scheduled for completion in 2006 and will be one of the brightest objects in the sky.

In true Sagittarius fashion, Pluto will shift our emphasis away from acquiring wealth to a quest for the meaning of it all, as upward strivers discover that money and power are not enough. Sagittarius is the sign of linking everything together; therefore the trend will be to find ways to interconnect on spiritual, philosophical, and intellectual levels.

Pluto in Sagittarius's spiritual emphasis has already filtered down to our home lives. Home altars and private sanctuaries are becoming a part of our personal environment. The oriental art of feng shui has moved westward, giving rise to a more harmonious, spiritual atmosphere in offices and homes, which also promotes luck and prosperity.

Sagittarians are known for their love of animals, and we have never been more pet-happy. Look for extremes related to animal welfare, such as vegetarianism, which will become even more popular and widespread as a lifestyle. As habitats are destroyed, the care, feeding, and control of wild animals will become a larger issue, especially where there are deer, bears, and coyotes in the back yard.

The Sagittarian love of the outdoors combined with Pluto's power has already promoted extreme sports, especially those that require strong legs, like rock climbing, trekking, or snowboarding. Rugged, sporty all-terrain vehicles continue to be popular, as are zippy little scooters which help us get around in a fun way. Expect the trend toward more adventurous travel and fitness or sports-oriented vacations to accelerate: exotic hiking trips to unexplored territories, mountain-climbing expeditions, spa vacations, and sports-associated resorts are part of this trend.

Publishing, which is associated with Sagittarius, has been transformed by the new electronic media, with an enormous variety of books available in print. The Internet bookstore will continue to prosper under Pluto in Sagittarius. It is fascinating that the online bookstore Amazon.com took the Sagittarius-influenced name of the fierce female tribe of archer-warriors who went to the extreme of removing their right breasts to better shoot their arrows.

Who's Lucky? Make Hay, Cancer and Leo!

Good fortune, expansion, and big money opportunities are associated with the movement of Jupiter, the planet that embodies the principle of expansion. Jupiter has a twelve-year cycle, staying in each sign for approximately one year.

When Jupiter enters a sign, the fields associated with that sign usually provide excellent opportunities. Areas of speculation associated with the sign Jupiter is passing through will have the hottest market potential—the ones that currently arouse excitement and enthusiasm.

The flip side of Jupiter is that there are no limits . . . you can expand off the planet under a Jupiter transit, which is why the planet is often called the "Gateway to Heaven." If something is going to burst—such as an artery—or overextend or go over the top in some way, it could happen under a supposedly "lucky" Jupiter transit . . . so be aware.

This year, Jupiter will finish its journey through Cancer in August, when it moves into Leo. So sun sign Cancers and Leos and those with strong Cancer or Leo influence in their horoscopes should have abundant growth opportunities during the year. On the other hand, those born under Capricorn and Aquarius, the signs which occur at the opposite time of year, may have to work harder for success.

Jupiter in Cancer should bring opportunities in home-related industries, child care, the food and shelter industries, cruises, maternal issues, shipping and boating, and water sports. Look for further expansion in home-based business and telecommuting. Combining mothering with an active career will be a key issue for Gen-X women, who'll have a tug of war between family and career.

After Jupiter moves into Leo in August, people will

be looking for more fun in life, more joy, and more opportunities to play. We'll all want to be young again, and chances are that plastic surgery will enjoy a big boom time. Bring on the divas, as larger-than-life personalities take center stage. Look for more self-aggrandizement and self-adornment in flamboyant fashions with plenty of color, style, and piles of gold jewelry. This is an influence which encourages extravagance, showing off, and enjoying the best things in life. On a more serious note, child-raising will very much be on our minds, since the sign of Leo rules children. How will we raise children in a workaholic era? Since this Jupiter encourages love affairs and casual sex, the pull of family ties and responsibilities could be one of the biggest challenges this year.

Saturn Puts on the Brakes in Gemini

Saturn keywords are focus, time, commitment, accomplishment, discipline, and restriction. If Jupiter gives you a handout, then Saturn hands you the bill. With Saturn, nothing's free; you work for what you get, so it's always a good idea to find the areas (or houses) of your horoscope where Saturn is passing through, to learn where to focus your energy on lasting value. With Saturn, you must be sure to finish what you start, be responsible, put in the hard work, and stick with it.

This year, Saturn finishes up its two-year transit of Gemini. The normally light-spirited Geminis have had to deal with the serious, sobering influence of Saturn, just after they enjoyed the expansive period of Jupiter in Gemini in 2000 and 2001. Geminis have to back up the risks they took then and will be required to deliver on promises made. It'll be a powerful challenge for changeable Geminis, who must now pay the piper.

In the world at large, Saturn in Gemini is sure to affect communications. Talk must be followed up by action now. We'll be concerned with Gemini issues of lower education and literacy, reforming the lower educational system. Since Gemini is an air sign, which rules the lungs, there will be further controversy and restriction surrounding smoking and the tobacco industry.

Uranus and Neptune in Aquarius— The High-Tech Signs

Uranus and Neptune are pushing us into the future as they continue their long stays in Aquarius. Uranus overthrows the worn-out status quo and points us toward the future. It rules the sign of Aquarius, so it has been in its most powerful position since 1995, and has created radical breakthroughs in technology, as well as a concern with issues that involve all humanity. It is now preparing to move into Pisces, a sign associated with spirituality, imagination, and creativity. Its coming influence should begin to show up this year, with some dramatic changes in the arts beginning this summer.

Our lust for techno-toys should make this a gadget-crazed time, especially as Jupiter enters playful Leo, reinforcing this trend. Interactive forms of amusement and communication will rival television for our leisure. In fact, television may be on its way out as we opt for more exciting forms of entertainment.

While Jupiter remains in Cancer, the first half of the year, look for more Cancer-related products and events in the news: home furnishings, housing, child care, food products and merchandising, and a surge in restaurants, futuristic cruise ships, and new concepts in living quarters. After Jupiter moves into Leo, it forms an uneasy relationship with Neptune and Uranus on the opposite side of the zodiac, which could engender conflicts between individuals and society at large, between what "I" want and what "they" want.

There will be concern about how technology is negatively affecting personal lives and creativity.

Where there is Neptune, look for imagination and creativity, and since this is the planet of deception and illusion, scams and scandals continue, especially in the high-tech area associated with Aquarius. Neptune is also associated with hospitals, which are acquiring a Neptunian glamour, as well as cutting-edge technology. The atmosphere of many hospitals is already changing from the intimidating sterile surgical environment of the past to that of a health-promoting spa, with alternative therapies such as massage, diet counseling, and aromatherapy available. New procedures in plastic surgery, also a Neptunian glamour field, and antiaging therapies should restore the bloom and the body of youth, as Jupiter in Leo glorifies the ever-young.

CHAPTER 2

Planning Ahead in 2002—Timing Your Life for Luck, Prosperity, and Love!

It's no secret that some of the most powerful and famous people, from Julius Caesar to financier J. P. Morgan, from Ronald Reagan to Cher, have consulted astrologers before they made their moves. If astrology helps the rich and famous stay on course through life's ups and downs, why not put it to work for you?

Take control of your life by coordinating your schedule with the cosmos. For instance, if you know the dates that the mischievous planet Mercury will be creating havoc with communications, you'll back up that vital fax with a duplicate by Express Mail; you'll read between the lines of contracts and put off closing that deal until you have double-checked all the information. When Venus is in your sign, making you the romantic flavor of the month, you'll be at your most attractive. That would be a great time to update your wardrobe, revamp your image, or ask someone you'd like to know better to dinner. Venus helps you make that sales pitch and win over the competition.

To find out for yourself if there's truth to the saying "Timing is everything," mark your own calendar for love, career moves, vacations, and important events, using the following information and the tables in this chapter and the one titled "Look Up Your Planets," as well as the moon sign listings under your daily forecast. Here are the happenings to note on your agenda:

- Dates of your sun sign (high-energy period)
- The month previous to your sun sign (low-energy period)
- Dates of planets in your sign this year
- Full and new moons
  (Pay special attention when these fall in your sun sign.)
- Eclipses
- Moon in your sun sign every month, as well as moon in the opposite sign (listed in daily forecast)
- Mercury retrogrades
- Other retrograde periods

Your Personal Power Time

Every birthday starts a cycle of solar energy for you. You should feel a new surge of vitality as the powerful sun enters your sign. This is the time when predominant energies are most favorable to you. So go for it! Start new projects; make your big moves. You'll get the recognition you deserve now, when everyone is attuned to your sun sign. Look in the tables in this book to see if other planets will also be passing through your sun sign at this time. Venus (love, beauty), Mars (energy, drive), or Mercury (communication, mental sharpness) reinforce the sun and give an extra boost to your life in the areas they affect. Venus will rev up your social and love life, making you seem especially attractive. Mars gives you extra energy and drive. Mercury fuels your brain power and helps you communicate. Jupiter signals an especially lucky period of expansion.

There are two "down" times related to the sun. During the month before your birthday period, when you are winding up your annual cycle, you could be feeling especially vulnerable and depleted, so get extra rest, watch your diet, and don't overstress yourself. Use this time to gear up for a big "push" when the sun enters your sign.

Another "down" time is when the sun is in the opposite sign from your sun sign (six months from your birthday) and the prevailing energies are very different from yours. You may feel at odds with the world, and things might not come easily. You'll have to work harder for recognition, because people are not on your wavelength. However, this could be a good time to work on a team, in cooperation with others or behind the scenes.

How to Use the Moon's Phase and Sign

Working with the phases of the moon is as easy as looking up at the night sky. During the new moon, when both the sun and the moon are in the same sign, it's the best time to begin new ventures, especially the activities that are favored by that sign. You'll have powerful energies pulling you in the same direction. You'll be focused outward, toward action and doing. Postpone breaking off, terminating, deliberating, or reflecting, activities that require introspection and passive work.

Get your project under way during the first quarter, then go public at the full moon, a time of high intensity, when feelings come out into the open. This is your time to shine—to express yourself. Be aware, however, that because pressures are being released, other people are also letting off steam and confrontations are possible. So try to avoid arguments. Traditionally, astrologers often advise against surgery at this time, which could produce heavier bleeding.

During the last quarter of the new moon, you'll be most controlled. This is a winding-down phase, a time to cut off unproductive relationships and do serious thinking and inward-directed activities.

You'll feel some new and full moons more strongly than others, especially those new moons that fall in your sun sign and full moons in your opposite sign. Because that full moon happens at your low-energy time of year, it is likely to be an especially stressful time in a relationship, when any hidden problems or unexpressed emotions could surface.

Full and New Moons in 2002

New Moon in Capricorn—January 13
Full Moon in Leo—January 28
New Moon in Aquarius—February 12
Full Moon in Virgo—February 27
New Moon in Pisces—March 13
Full Moon in Libra—March 28
New Moon in Aries—April 12
Full Moon in Scorpio—April 27
New Moon in Taurus—May 12
Full Moon in Sagittarius (lunar eclipse)—May 26
New Moon in Gemini (solar eclipse)—June 10
Full Moon in Capricorn (lunar eclipse)—June 24
New Moon in Cancer—July 10
Full Moon in Aquarius—July 24
New Moon in Leo—August 8
Full Moon in Aquarius (second time)—August 22
New Moon in Virgo—September 6
Full Moon in Pisces—September 21
New Moon in Libra—October 6
Full Moon in Aries—October 21
New Moon in Scorpio—November 4
Full Moon in Taurus (lunar eclipse)—November 19
New Moon in Sagittarius (solar eclipse)—December 4
Full Moon in Gemini—December 19

Moon Sign Timing

To forecast the daily emotional "weather," to determine your monthly high and low days, or to synchronize your activities with the cycles and the sign of the moon, take note of the moon's daily sign under your daily forecast at the end of the book. Here are some of the activities favored and moods you are likely to encounter under each sign.

Moon in Aries

Get moving! The new moon in Aries is an ideal time to start new projects. Everyone is pushy, raring to go, and rather impatient and short-tempered. Leave details and follow-up for later. Competitive sports or martial arts are great ways to let off steam. Quiet types could use some assertiveness, but it's a great day for dynamos. Be careful not to step on too many toes.

Moon in Taurus

It's time to do solid, methodical tasks. This is the time to tackle follow-through or backup work. Lay the foundations for success. Make investments, buy real estate, do appraisals, and do some hard bargaining. Attend to your property—get out in the country. Spend some time in your garden. Enjoy creature comforts, music, a good dinner, and sensual lovemaking. Forget starting a diet.

Moon in Gemini

Talk means action today. Telephone, write a letter, fax! Make new contacts; stay in touch with steady customers. You can handle lots of tasks at once. A great day for mental activity of any kind. Don't try to pin people down—they, too, are feeling restless. Keep it light. Flirtations and socializing are good. Watch gossip—and don't give away secrets.

Moon in Cancer

This is a moody, sensitive, emotional time. People respond to personal attention and mothering. Stay at home; have a family dinner; call your mother. Nostalgia, memories, and psychic powers are heightened. You'll want to hang on to people and things (don't clean out your closets now). You could have some shrewd insights into what others really need and want now. Pay attention to dreams, intuition, and gut reactions.

Moon in Leo

Everybody is in a much more confident, warm, generous mood. It's a good day to ask for a raise, show what you can do, or dress like a star. People will respond to flattery; enjoy a bit of drama and theater. You may be extravagant—treat yourself royally, and show off a bit (but don't break the bank!). Be careful that you don't promise more than you can deliver!

Moon in Virgo

Do practical, down-to-earth chores. Review your budget. Make repairs. Be an efficiency expert. Not a day to ask for a raise. Have a health checkup. Revamp your diet. Buy vitamins or health food. Make your home spotless. Take care of details and piled-up chores. Reorganize your work and life so they run more smoothly and efficiently. Save money. Be prepared for others to be in a critical, faultfinding mood.

Moon in Libra

Attend to legal matters. Negotiate contracts. Arbitrate. Do things with your favorite partner. Socialize.

Be romantic. Buy a special gift, a beautiful object. Decorate yourself or your surroundings. Buy new clothes. Throw a party. Have an elegant, romantic evening. Smooth over any ruffled feathers. Avoid confrontations. Stick to civilized discussions.

Moon in Scorpio

This is a day to do things with passion. You'll have excellent concentration and focus. Try not to get too intense emotionally, however, and avoid sharp exchanges with loved ones. Others may tend to go to extremes, get jealous, and overreact. Great for troubleshooting, problem-solving, research, scientific work—and making love. Pay attention to psychic vibes.

Moon in Sagittarius

A great time for travel. Have philosophical discussions. Set long-range career goals. Work out, do sports, or buy athletic equipment. Others will be feeling upbeat, exuberant, and adventurous. Risk taking is favored—you may feel like taking a gamble, betting on the horses, visiting a local casino, or buying a lottery ticket. Teaching, writing, and spiritual activities also get the green light. Relax outdoors. Take care of animals.

Moon in Capricorn

You can accomplish a lot today, so get on the ball! Issues concerning your basic responsibilities, duties, family and parents could crop up. You'll be expected to deliver on promises now. Weed out the dead wood from your life. Get a dental checkup.

Moon in Aquarius

A great day for doing things with groups—clubs, meetings, outings, politics, and parties. Campaign for your candidate. Work for a worthy cause. Deal with larger issues that affect humanity: the environment and metaphysical questions. Buy a computer or an electronic gadget. Watch TV. Wear something outrageous. Try something you've never done before. Present an original idea. Don't stick to a rigid schedule—go with the flow. Take a class in meditation, mind control, or yoga.

Moon in Pisces

This can be a very creative day, so let your imagination work overtime. Film, theater, music, or ballet could inspire you. Spend some time alone, resting and reflecting, reading or writing poetry. Daydreams can also be profitable. Help those less fortunate or lend a listening ear to someone who may be feeling blue. Don't overindulge in self-pity or escapism, however. People are especially vulnerable to substance abuse now. Turn your thoughts to romance and someone special.

When the Planets Go Backward

All the planets, except for the sun and moon, have times when they appear to move backward—or retrograde—in the sky, or so it seems from our point of view on earth. At these times, planets do not work as they normally do, so it's best to "take a break" from that planet's energies in our life and do some work on an inner level.

Mercury Retrograde

Mercury goes retrograde most often, and its effects can be especially irritating. When it reaches a short distance ahead of the sun three times a year, it seems to move backward from our point of view. Astrologers often compare retrograde motion to the optical illusion that occurs when we ride on a train that passes another train traveling at a different speed—the second train appears to be moving in reverse.

What this means to you is that the Mercury-ruled areas of your life—analytical thought processes, communications, and scheduling—are subject to all kinds of confusion. Be prepared. People will change their minds, or renege on commitments. Communications equipment can break down. Schedules must be changed on short notice. People are late for appointments or don't show up at all. Traffic is terrible. Major purchases malfunction, don't work out, or get delivered in the wrong color. Letters don't arrive or are delivered to the wrong address. Employees will make errors that have to be corrected later. Contracts don't work out or must be renegotiated.

Since most of us can't put our lives on "hold" for nine weeks every year (three Mercury retrograde periods), we should learn to tame the trickster and make it work for us. The key is in the prefix "re-." This is the time to go back over things in your life. Reflect on what you've done during the previous months. Look for deeper insights, spot errors you've missed, and take time to review and reevaluate what has happened. This time is very good for inner spiritual work and meditations. *Re*st and *re*ward yourself—it's a good time to take a vacation, especially if you revisit a favorite place. *Re*organize your work and finish up projects that are backed up. Clean out your desk and closets. Throw away what you can't *re*cycle. If you must sign contracts or agreements, do so with a contingency clause that lets you *re*evaluate the terms later.

Postpone major purchases or commitments. Don't get married (unless you're *re*marrying the same person). Try not to rely on other people keeping appointments, contracts, or agreements to the letter—have several alternatives. Double-check and read between the lines. Don't buy anything connected with communications or transportation (if you must, be sure to cover yourself). Mercury retrograding through your sun sign will intensify its effect on your life.

If Mercury was retrograde when you were born, you may be one of the lucky people who don't suffer the frustrations of this period. If so, your mind probably works in a very intuitive, insightful way.

The sign Mercury is retrograding through can give you an idea of what's in store—as well as the sun signs that will be especially challenged.

MERCURY RETROGRADE PERIODS IN 2002
Mercury has three retrograde periods this year: from January 18 to February 8, from May 15 to June 8, and from September 14 to October 6.

Venus Retrograde

Retrograding Venus can cause your relationships to take a backward step, or it can make you extravagant and impractical. Shopping till you drop and buying what you cannot afford are trip-ups at this time. It's *not* a good time to redecorate—you'll hate the color of the walls later. Postpone getting a new hairstyle and try not to fall in love either. But if you wish to make amends in an already troubled relationship, make peaceful overtures at this time. (Note: there is no Mars retrograde period this year.)

VENUS RETROGRADE PERIOD IN 2002
Venus retrogrades from October 10 to November 21.

When Other Planets Retrograde

The slower-moving planets stay retrograde for months at a time (Saturn, Jupiter, Neptune, Uranus, and Pluto). When Saturn is retrograde, it's an uphill battle with self-discipline. You may feel more like hanging out at the beach than getting things done. Neptune retrograde promotes a dreamy escapism from reality, whereas Uranus retrograde may mean setbacks in areas where there have been sudden changes. Think of this as an adjustment period, a time to think things over and allow new ideas to develop. Pluto retrograde is a time to work on establishing proportion and balance in areas where there have been recent dramatic transformations.

When the planets start moving forward again, there's a shift in the atmosphere. Activities connected with each planet start moving ahead, and plans that were stalled get rolling. Make a special note of those days on your calendar and proceed accordingly.

Other Retrogrades in 2002

Jupiter is retrograde from November 2, 2001, until March 1, 2002. It turns retrograde again on December 4, 2002.

Saturn retrogrades from February 7 to October 11.
Uranus retrogrades from June 6 to November 3.
Neptune retrogrades from May 13 to October 20.
Pluto retrogrades from March 20 to August 16.

CHAPTER 3

Teach Yourself Astrology

Astrology is a powerful tool of inner transformation that can help you access your personal potential, to understand others, and to interpret events in your life and in the world at large. You don't have to be an expert in astrology to put it to work for you. In this chapter, we'll demystify the horoscope chart and walk you through the basic concepts, so you'll know a sign from a house and what the planets mean. Perhaps from here, you'll upgrade your knowledge with a computer program that calculates charts for everyone you know in a nanosecond, or you'll join an astrology class in your city, or you'll want to explore different techniques of astrology and go on to the asteroids and the fixed stars. The sky's the limit, literally. So let's take off!

The Basics: Signs, Houses, Constellations, and the Zodiac

Everyone knows what a sign is ... or do they? A *sign* is literally a 30-degree portion of the zodiac, a circular belt of the sky. That is what is meant by a "sign of the zodiac." Things happen within a sign, but a sign does not *do* anything itself—that's the job of the planets. Each sign is simply a portion of celestial real estate and has certain unique characteristics described by four things: an *element* (earth, air, fire, water), a *quality* or mode (cardinal (active), fixed, mutable), by a *polarity* (masculine/feminine, yin/yang) and finally by a *position* in the sequence of zodiac signs.

The *signs* are named after *constellations,* patterns of stars on the zodiac which originally lit up the twelve divisions, like billboards. However, over the centuries, the constellations have shifted from our point of view here on earth. So the constellation which once marked a particular sign may now be in the territory of another sign. (Most Western astrologers use the twelve-equal-part division of the zodiac; however, there are some methods of astrology that still do use the constellations instead of the signs.) However, the *names* of the signs remain the same as their original placemarkers.

Most people think of themselves in terms of their *sun sign,* which refers to the sign the sun seems to be passing through at a given moment, from our point of view here on earth. (Of course, we are the ones that are traveling around the sun.) For instance, "I'm an Aries" means that the sun was passing through Aries territory at your birth. However, there are nine other planets (plus asteroids, fixed stars, and sensitive points) which also form our total astrological personality, and some or many of these will be located in other signs. No one is completely "Aries," with all their astrological components in one sign! (Please note that, in astrology, the sun and moon are usually referred to as "planets," though of course they're not.)

Defining the Signs

What makes Aries the sign of go-getters and Taureans savvy with money? And Geminis talk a blue streak and Sagittarians footloose? Descriptions of the signs are not accidental; they are characterized by different combinations of four concepts we have already mentioned: the sign's element, quality, polarity, and position in the sequence of the zodiac.

Take the element of fire: it's associated with passion, heat. Then have it work in an active, energetic way. Give it a jolt of positive energy and place it first in line. And doesn't that sound like the active, me-first, driving, hotheaded, energetic Aries?

Then take the element of earth: it's practical, sensual, where things grow. Make it work in a fixed, stable way or mode. Give it the kind of energy that reacts to its surroundings, that settles in. Make it the consolidating force, coming right after the passionate beginning of Aries. Now you've got a good idea of how sensual, earthy Taurus operates.

Another way to grasp the idea is to pretend you're doing a magical puzzle based on the numbers that can divide into 12 (the total number of signs): 4, 3, and 2. There are 4 "building blocks" or elements, 3 ways a sign operates (qualities or modes), and 2 polarities. These alternate, in turn, around the zodiac, with a different combination coming up for each sign.

THE FOUR ELEMENTS

Here's how they add up. The *four elements* describe the physical concept of the sign. Is it fiery (dynamic), earthy (practical), airy (mental), or watery (emotional)? Divide the 12 signs by the 4 elements and you get 3 zodiac signs of each element: fire (Aries, Leo, Sagittarius); earth (Taurus, Virgo, Capricorn); air (Gemini, Libra, Aquarius); and water (Cancer, Scorpio, Pisces). These are the same elements that make up our planet: earth, air, fire, and water. But astrology uses the elements as *symbols* which link your body and psyche to the rhythms of the cosmos. If major planets in a horoscope are passing through fire signs, the person will be likely to have a warm, enthusiastic personality, able to fire up or motivate others. These are people who make ideas catch fire and spring into existence, but they also have hot tempers. Those with major planets in earth signs are the builders of the zodiac who follow through after the initiative of fire signs to make things happen. These people are solid, practical realists who enjoy material things and sensual pleasures. They are interested in ideas that can be used to achieve concrete results. With major planets in air signs, a person will be more mental, a good communicator. Following the consolidating earth signs, air people reach out to inspire others through the use of words, social contacts, discussion, and debate. Water sign people complete each four-element series, adding the ingredients of emotion, compassion, and imagination. These people are nonverbal communicators who attune themselves to their surroundings and react through the medium of feelings.

THE THREE QUALITIES

The second consideration when defining a sign is how it will operate. Will it take the initiative, or move slowly and deliberately, or adapt easily? Its *quality* (or modality) will tell. There are 3 qualities; therefore, after dividing 3 into 12 signs, it follows that there will be 4 signs of each quality: cardinal, fixed, and mutable.

Cardinal signs begin each season (Aries, Cancer, Libra, Capricorn). People with major planets in cardinal signs tend to be doers. They're active, always involved in projects. They are usually on the fast track to success, impatient to get things under way. Those with major planets in *fixed signs* (Taurus, Leo, Scorpio, Aquarius) move steadily and are always in control. Since these signs happen in the middle of a season, after the initial character of the season is established, it follows that people with major planets in fixed signs would tend to be more centered; they move more deliberately and do things more slowly but thoroughly. The fixed signs fall in parts of your horoscope where you take root and integrate your experiences. *Mutable signs* (Gemini, Virgo, Sagittarius, Pisces) embody the principle of distribution. Planets in these signs will break up the cycle, preparing the way for a change by distributing the energy to the next group. People with predominantly mutable planets are likely to be flexible, adaptable, and communicative. They can move in many directions easily, darting around obstacles.

THE TWO POLARITIES

In addition to an element and a quality, each sign has a *polarity,* either a positive or negative electrical charge that generates energy around the zodiac, like a giant battery. Polarity refers to opposites, which you could also define as masculine/feminine, yin/yang, active/reactive. In their zodiac positions, the six fire and air signs are positive, active, masculine, and yang in polarity. Therefore, planets in these signs will express their energy openly, expanding outward. The six earth and water signs are reactive, negative, and yin—in other words, nurturing and receptive in polarity, which allows the energy to develop and take shape.

All positive energy would be like a car without brakes. All negative energy would be like a stalled vehicle, going nowhere. So both polarities are needed in balanced proportion, to keep the zodiac in a state of equilibrium.

THE ORDER OF THE SIGNS

The specific order of the signs is vital to the balance of the zodiac and the transmission of energy around the cycle. Though each sign is quite different from its neighbors on either side, each seems to grow out of its predecessor like links in a chain, transmitting a synthesis of energy accumulated along the chain to the following sign, beginning with the fire-powered, active, positive, cardinal sign of Aries and ending with watery, mutable, reactive Pisces.

Houses of the Horoscope—
Where the Action Is

We come to the concept of *houses* as we set up a specific horoscope, which is a map of the heavens at a given moment in time. Picture the horoscope chart as a wheel with twelve spokes. In between each of the "spokes" is a section called a *house*. The wheel is stationary, however . . . the houses are always in the same place. Each house represents a different area of life and is influenced or "ruled" by a sign and a planet that are associated with that house. But besides the house's given "rulers," it is colored by the sign which is passing over the spoke (or cusp) at the moment when the horoscope chart is cast. In other words, the first house is naturally ruled by Aries and Mars; however, if Capricorn was the sign passing over the house at the time the chart was cast, it would have a Capricorn influence.

Numerically, the house order begins at the left center spoke (or the 9 position if you were reading a clock) and is read counterclockwise around the chart.

The First House—Home of Aries and the Planet Mars

This is the house of "firsts"—the first impression you make, how you initiate matters, the image you choose to project. This is where you advertise yourself, where you project your personality. Planets that fall here will intensify the way you come across to others. Often the first house will project an entirely different type of energy from the sun sign. For instance, a Capricorn with Leo in the first house will come across as much more flamboyant than the average Capricorn. The sign on the cusp of this house is known as your *ascendant,* or *rising sign.*

The Second House—Home of Taurus and Venus

Here is your contact with the material world. In this house are your attitudes about money, possessions, finances, whatever belongs to you, and what you own, as well as your earning and spending capacity. On a deeper level, this house reveals your sense of self-worth, the inner values that draw wealth in various forms.

The Third House—Home of Gemini and Mercury

This house describes how you communicate with others—are you understood? Here you reach out to others nearby and interact with the immediate environment. This is how your thinking process works, the way you express your thoughts. In relationships, here are your first experiences with brothers and sisters, and how you handle people close to you, such as your neighbors or pals. It's also where you take short trips, write letters, or use the telephone. It shows how your mind works in terms of left-brain logical and analytical functions.

The Fourth House—Home of Cancer and the Moon

This house shows how you are nurtured and made to feel secure—your roots! Located at the bottom of the chart, the fourth house, like the home, shows the foundation of life, your deepest psychological underpinnings. Here is where you have the deepest confrontation with who you are, and how you make yourself feel secure. It shows your early home environment and the circumstances at the end of your life—your final "home"—as well as the place you call home now. Astrologers look here for information about the primary nurturers in your life.

The Fifth House—Home of Leo and the Sun

This is how you express yourself creatively—your idea of play. The Leo house is where the creative potential develops, where you show off your talents. It is also where you procreate, in the sense that your children are outgrowths of your creative ability. It most represents your inner childlike self, the part of you which finds joy in play. If inner security has been established by the time you reach this house, you are now free to have fun, romance, and love affairs—to give of yourself. This is also the place astrologers look for the playful kind of love affairs, flirtations, and brief romantic encounters (rather than long-term commitments).

The Sixth House—Home of Virgo and Mercury

Here is your "care and maintenance" department. It shows how you function in daily life, where you get things done, and where you determine how you look after others and fulfill service duties, such as taking care of pets. Here are your daily survival, your "job" (as opposed to your career, which is the domain of the tenth house), your diet, and your health and fitness regimens. Here is where you take care of your body and organize yourself to perform efficiently.

The Seventh House—Home of Libra and Venus

This house shows your attitude toward partners and those with whom you enter commitments, contracts, or agreements. This house has to do with your relationships—your close, intimate, one-on-one relationships (even your open enemies—those you "face off" with). Open hostilities, lawsuits, divorces, and marriages happen here. If the first house represents the "I," the seventh or opposite house represents the "not-I"—the complementary partner you attract by the way you come across. If you are having trouble with partnerships, consider what you are attracting by the interaction of your first and seventh house.

The Eighth House—Home of Scorpio and Pluto (also Mars)

This refers to how you merge with something or someone, and how you handle power and control. This is one of the most mysterious and powerful houses, where your energy transforms itself from "I" to "we." As you give up your personal power and control by uniting with something or someone, two kinds of energies merge and become something greater, leading to a regeneration of the self on a higher level. Here are your attitudes toward sex, shared resources, and taxes (what you share with the government). Because this house involves what belongs to others, you face issues of control and power struggles, or undergo a deep psychological transformation as you bond with another. Here you transcend yourself with dreams, drugs, and occult or psychic experiences that reflect the collective unconscious.

The Ninth House—Home of Sagittarius and Jupiter

Here is where you search for wisdom and higher knowledge—your belief system. While the third house represents the "lower mind," its opposite on the wheel, the ninth house, is the "higher mind." This is where you ask the "big" questions like "Why are we here?" The ninth house shows what you believe in. After the third house has explored what was close at hand, the ninth stretches out to broaden you with higher education and travel. Here you stretch spiritually with religious activity. Since you are concerned with how everything is related, you tend to take risks, break rules, and push boundaries. Here is where you express your ideas in a book or extensive thesis, where you pontificate, philosophize, or preach.

The Tenth House—Home of Capricorn and Saturn

Here is your public image and how you handle authority. Located directly overhead at the "high noon" position on the horoscope wheel, this house is associated with high-profile activities, where the world sees you. It deals with your career (but not your routine "job"), and your reputation. Here is where you go public and take on responsibilities (as opposed to the fourth house, where you stay home). This will affect the career you choose and your "public relations." This house is also associated with your father or the main authority figure in your life.

The Eleventh House—Home of Aquarius and Uranus

Here is your support system, how you relate to society and your goals. In this house, you extend your identity to belong to a group, a team, a club, a goal, or a belief system. You worry about being popular, winning the election, or making the team; you define what you really want, the kinds of friends you have, your political affiliations, and the kinds of groups you'll belong to. Here is where you become concerned with "what other people think," or you rebel against society. Here is where you could become a socially conscious humanitarian—or a party-going social butterfly. It's where you look to others to stimulate you and discover your kinship to the rest of humanity. The sign on the cusp of this house can help you understand what you gain and lose from friendships.

The Twelfth House—Home of Pisces and Neptune

Here is where the boundaries between yourself and others become blurred, where you become self-less. In your trip around the zodiac, you've gone from the "I" of self-assertion in the first house to the final house, symbolizing the dissolution that happens before rebirth. It's where accumulated experiences are processed in the unconscious. Spiritually oriented astrologers look to this house for evidence of past lives and karma. Places where we go for solitude or to do spiritual or reparatory work belong here, such as retreats, religious institutions, or hospitals. Here are also institutions such as prisons where we withdraw from society or are forced to withdraw because of antisocial behavior. Selfless giving through charitable acts is part of this house, as is helpless receiving or dependence on charity.

In your daily life, the twelfth house reveals your deepest intimacies, your best-kept secrets, especially those you hide from yourself, repressed deep in the unconscious. It is where we surrender a sense of a separate self to a deep feeling of wholeness, such as selfless service in religion or any activity that involves merging with the greater whole. Many sports stars have important planets in the twelfth house that enable them to play in the "zone," finding an inner, almost mystical, strength that transcends their limits.

The Planets Power Up Your Houses

Houses are stronger or weaker depending on how many planets are inhabiting them. If there are many planets occupying a given house, it follows that the activities of that house will be emphasized in your life. If the planet that rules the house naturally is also located there, this too adds power to the house.

Mapping Your Planets

The ten major planets (including the sun and moon) are the doers in your chart. The planets cause things to happen. They will play starring or supporting roles, depending on their positions in your horoscope. A planet in the first house, particularly one that's close to your rising sign, is sure to be a featured player. Planets that are grouped together usually operate together like a team, playing off each other, rather than expressing their energy singularly. A planet that stands alone, away from the others, is usually outstanding and sometimes calls the shots.

The best place for a planet is in the sign or signs it rules; the next best is in a sign where it is *exalted,* or especially harmonious. On the other hand, there are signs where a planet has to work harder to play its role. These are called the planet's *detriment* and *fall.* The sign opposite a planet's rulership, which embodies the opposite area of life, is its *detriment.* The sign opposite its exaltation is its *fall.* Though these terms may suggest unfortunate circumstances for the planet, that is not always true. In fact, a planet that is debilitated can actually be more complete, because it must stretch itself to meet the challenges of living in a more difficult sign. Like world leaders who've had to struggle for greatness, this planet may actually develop more strength and character.

Here's a list of the best places for each planet to be. Note that, as Uranus, Neptune, and Pluto were discovered, they replaced the traditional rulers of signs which best complemented their energies.

ARIES—Mars.
TAURUS—Venus, in its most sensual form.
GEMINI—Mercury in its communicative role.
CANCER—the moon.
LEO—the sun.

- VIRGO—Also Mercury, this time in its more critical capacity.
- LIBRA—Also Venus, in its more aesthetic, judgmental form.
- SCORPIO—Pluto, replacing the sign's original ruler, Mars.
- SAGITTARIUS—Jupiter.
- CAPRICORN—Saturn.
- AQUARIUS—Uranus, replacing Saturn, its original ruler.
- PISCES—Neptune, replacing Jupiter, its original ruler.

A person who has many planets in exalted signs is lucky indeed, for here is where the planet can accomplish the most and be its most influential and creative.

- SUN—Exalted in Aries, where its energy creates action.
- MOON—Exalted in Taurus, where instincts and reactions operate on a highly creative level.
- MERCURY—Exalted in Aquarius, where it can reach analytical heights.
- VENUS—Exalted in Pisces, a sign whose sensitivity encourages love and creativity.
- MARS—Exalted in Capricorn, a sign that puts energy to work productively.
- JUPITER—Exalted in Cancer, where it encourages nurturing and growth.
- SATURN—At home in Libra, where it steadies the scales of justice and promotes balanced, responsible judgment.
- URANUS—Powerful in Scorpio, where it promotes transformation.
- NEPTUNE—Especially favored in Cancer, where it gains the security to transcend to a higher state.
- PLUTO—Exalted in Pisces, where it dissolves the old cycle, to make way for transition to the new.

The Sun and the Moon

Since the sun is always the first consideration, it is important to treat it as the star of the show. It is your conscious ego and it is always center stage, even when sharing a house or a sign with several other planets. This is why sun sign astrology works for so many people.

The sun rules the sign of Leo, gaining strength through the pride, dignity, and confidence of the fixed-fire personality. It is exalted in "me-first" Aries. In its detriment, Aquarius, the sun-ego is strengthened through group participation and social consciousness, rather than through self-centeredness. (Note how many Aquarius people are involved in politics, social work, and public life. They are following the demands of their sun sign to be spokesperson for a group.) In its fall, Libra, the sun needs the strength of a partner—an "other"—to enhance its own balance and self-expression.

As the sun represents your outer light, the moon represents the inner "you," your deep emotional nature. We go into more detail about the moon and its influence in your life and moods in a separate chapter in this book. Read it for details about this all-important planet.

Each of the other eight planets is colored by the sign it is passing through. For example, Mercury, the planet that rules the way you communicate, will express itself in a dynamic, headstrong way if it was passing through the sign of Aries when you were born. You will speak differently if it was passing through the slower, more patient sign of Taurus. And so on through the list. Here's a rundown of the planets and how they behave in every sign.

The Personal Planets—Mercury, Venus, and Mars

These planets work in your immediate personal life.

Mercury affects how you communicate and how your mental processes work. Are you a quick study who grasps information rapidly, or do you learn more slowly and thoroughly? How is your concentration? Can you express yourself easily? Are you a good writer? All these questions can be answered by your Mercury placement.

Venus shows what you react to. What turns you on? What appeals to you aesthetically? Are you charming to others? Are you attractive to look at? Your taste, your refinement, your sense of balance and proportion are all Venus-ruled.

Mars is your outgoing energy, your drive and ambition. Do you reach out for new adventures? Are you assertive? Are you motivated? Self-confident? Hot-tempered? How you channel your energy and drive is revealed by your Mars placement.

Mercury Communicates

Since Mercury never travels far from the sun, read Mercury in your sun sign, then the signs preceding and following it. Then decide which reflects the way your mind works.

Mercury in Aries

Your mind is very active and assertive. You never hesitate to say what you think or shy away from a battle. In fact, you may relish a verbal confrontation. Tact is not your strong point, so you may have to learn not to trip over your tongue.

Mercury in Taurus

Though you may be a slow learner, you have good concentration and mental stamina. You want to make your ideas really happen. You'll attack a problem methodically and consider every angle thoroughly, never jumping to conclusions. You'll stick with a subject until you master it.

Mercury in Gemini

A wonderful communicator with great facility for expressing yourself both verbally and in writing. You talk and talk, love gathering all kinds of information. You probably finish other people's sentences and talk with hand gestures. You can talk to anybody anytime and probably have phone and e-mail bills to prove it. You read anything from sci-fi to Shakespeare and might need an extra room just for your book collection. Though you learn fast, you may lack focus and discipline. Watch a tendency to jump from subject to subject.

Mercury in Cancer

You rely on intuition more than logic. Your mental processes are usually colored by your emotions, so you may seem shy or hesitant to voice your opinions. However, this placement gives you the advantage of great imagination and empathy in the way you communicate with others.

Mercury in Leo

You are enthusiastic and very dramatic in the way you express yourself. You like to hold the attention of groups and could be a great public speaker. Your mind thinks big, so you'd prefer to deal with the overall picture rather than with the details.

Mercury in Virgo

This is one of the best places for Mercury. It should give you critical ability, attention to details, and thorough analysis. Your mind focuses on the practical side of things. This type of thinking is very well suited to being a teacher or an editor.

Mercury in Libra

You're either a born diplomat who smoothes over ruffled feathers or a talented debater. However, since you're forever weighing the pros and cons of a situation, you may vacillate when making decisions.

Mercury in Scorpio

This is an investigative mind which stops at nothing to get the answers. You may have a sarcastic, stinging wit or a gift for the cutting remark. There's always a grain of truth to your verbal sallies, thanks to your penetrating insight.

Mercury in Sagittarius

You're a super salesman with a tendency to expound. Though you are very broad-minded, you can be dogmatic when it comes to telling others what's good for them. You won't hesitate to tell the truth as you see it, so watch a tendency toward tactlessness. On the plus side, you have a great sense of humor. This position of Mercury is often considered by astrologers to be at a disadvantage because Sagittarius opposes Gemini, the sign Mercury rules, and squares off with Virgo, another Mercury-ruled sign. What often happens is that Mercury in Sagittarius oversteps its bounds and loses sight of the facts in a situation. Do a reality check before making promises that you may not be able to keep.

Mercury in Capricorn

This placement endows good mental discipline. You have a love of learning and a very orderly approach to your subjects. You will patiently plod through the facts and figures until you have mastered the tasks. You grasp structured situations easily, but may be short on creativity.

Mercury in Aquarius

With Uranus and Neptune in Aquarius now energizing your Mercury, you're sure to be on the cutting edge of new ideas. An independent, original thinker, you'll have more far-out ideas than the average person and be quick to check out any unusual opportunities. Your opinions are so well researched and grounded, in fact, that once your mind is made up, it is difficult to change.

Mercury in Pisces

You have the psychic intuitive mind of a natural poet. Learn to make use of your creative imagination. You may think in terms of helping others, but check a tendency to be vague and forgetful of details.

Venus Relates

Venus tells how you relate to others and to your environment. It shows where you receive pleasure, what you love to do. Find your Venus placement on the chart on pages 68–75 by looking for the year of your birth in the left-hand column. Then follow the line of that year across the page until you reach the time period of your birthday. The sign heading that column will be your Venus. If you were born on a day when Venus was changing signs, check the signs preceding or following that day to determine if that feels more like your Venus nature.

Venus in Aries

You can't stand to be bored, confined, or ordered around. But a good challenge, maybe even a rousing row, turns you on. Don't you pick a fight now and then just to get someone stirred up? You're attracted by the chase, not the catch, which could cause some problems in your love life, if the object of your affection becomes too attainable. You love someone who keeps you on your toes. You like to wear red and be first with the latest fashion. You'll spot a trend before anyone else.

Venus in Taurus

All your senses work in high gear. You love to be surrounded by glorious tastes, smells, textures, sounds, and visuals. Austere minimalism is not your style. Neither is being rushed. You like time to enjoy your pleasures. Soothing surroundings with plenty of creature comforts are your cup of tea. You like to feel secure in your nest, with no sudden jolts or surprises. You like familiar objects—in fact, you may hate to let anything or anyone go.

Venus in Gemini

You are a lively, sparkling personality who thrives in a situation that affords a constant variety and a frequent change of scenery. A varied social life is important to you, with plenty of stimulation and a chance to engage in some light flirtation. Commitment may be difficult, because playing the field is so much fun.

Venus in Cancer

An atmosphere where you feel protected, coddled, and mothered is best for you. You love to be surrounded by children in a cozy, homelike situation. You are attracted to those who are tender and nurturing, who make you feel secure and well provided for. You may be quite secretive about your emotional life or attracted to clandestine relationships.

Venus in Leo

First-class attention in large doses turns you on, and so do the glitter of real gold and the flash of mirrors. You like to feel like a star at all times, surrounded by your admiring audience. The side effect is that you may be attracted to flatterers and tinsel, while the real gold requires some digging.

Venus in Virgo

Everything neatly in its place? On the surface, you are attracted to an atmosphere where everything is in perfect order, but underneath are some basic, earthy urges. You are attracted to those who appeal to your need to teach, be of service, or play out a Pygmalion fantasy. You are at your best when you are busy doing something useful, helping someone improve.

Venus in Libra

"Elegance" and "harmony" are your key words. You can't abide an atmosphere of contention. Your taste tends toward the classic, with light harmonies of color— nothing clashing, trendy, or outrageous. You love doing things with a partner and should be careful to pick one who is decisive, but patient enough to let you weigh the pros and cons. And steer clear of argumentative types. It helps a lot if your partner is attractive and stylish, as well as charming, and appreciates the finer things in life.

Venus in Scorpio

Hidden mysteries intrigue you. In fact, anything that is too open and aboveboard is a bit of a bore. You surely have a stack of whodunits by the bed, along with an erotic magazine or two. You like to solve puzzles, and may also be fascinated with the occult, crime, or scientific research. Intense, all-or-nothing situations add spice to your life, and you love to ferret out the secrets of others. But you could get burned by your flair for living dangerously. The color black, spicy food, dark wood furniture, and heady perfume all get you in the right mood.

Venus in Sagittarius

If you are not actually a world traveler, your surroundings are sure to reflect your love of faraway places. You like a casual outdoor atmosphere and a dog or two to pet. There should be plenty of room for athletic equipment and suitcases. You're attracted to kindred souls who love to travel and who share your freedom-loving philosophy of life. Athletics, spiritual, or New Age pursuits could be other interests.

Venus in Capricorn

No fly-by-night relationships for you! You want substance in life and you are attracted to whatever will help you get where you are going. Status objects turn you on. And so do those who have a serious, responsible, businesslike approach, or who remind you of a beloved parent. It is characteristic of this placement to be attracted to someone of a different generation. Antiques, traditional clothing, and dignified behavior favor you.

Venus in Aquarius

This Venus wants to make friends more than to make love. You like to be in a group, particularly one pushing a worthy cause. In fact, fame of one sort or another is fascinating to you. You feel quite at home surrounded by people, but may remain detached from any intense commitment. Original ideas and unpredictable people attract you. You don't like everything to be planned out in advance, preferring spontaneity and delightful surprises.

Venus in Pisces

Venus is exalted in Pisces, which makes this one of the more desirable Venuses to have. This Venus loves to give of the self, and you'll find plenty of takers. Stray animals and people appeal to your heart and your pocketbook, but be careful to look at their motives realistically once in a while. You are extremely vulnerable to sob stories of all kinds. Fantasy, theater, and psychic or spiritual activities also speak to you.

Mars Moves and Shakes

Mars shows how you pursue your goals, whether you have energy to burn or proceed at a slow, steady pace. Or are you nervous, restless, unable to sit still? Mars will also show how you get angry. Will you explode, do a slow burn, or hold everything inside, then get revenge later?

To find your Mars, turn to the chart on pages 76–87. Then find your birth year in the left-hand column and trace the line across horizontally until you come to the column headed by the month of your birth. There you will find an abbreviation of your Mars sign. If the description of your Mars sign doesn't ring true, read the description of the signs preceding and following it. You may have been born on a day when Mars was changing signs, and your Mars would then be in the adjacent sign.

Mars in Aries

In the sign it rules, Mars shows its brilliant fiery nature. You have an explosive temper and can be quite impatient, but on the other hand, you possess tremendous courage, energy, and drive. You'll let nothing stand in your way as you race to be first! Obstacles are met head-on and broken through by force. However, situations that require patience and persistence could make you explode in rage. You're a great starter, but not necessarily there at the finish.

Mars in Taurus

Slow, steady, concentrated energy gives you staying power. You've got great stamina and you never give up. Your tactic is to wear away obstacles with your persistence. Often you come out a winner because you've had the patience to hang in there. When angered, you do a slow burn.

Mars in Gemini

You can't sit still for long. This Mars craves variety. You often have two or more things going on at once. It's all an amusing game to you. Your life can get very complicated, which only adds spice and stimulation. What drives you into a nervous, hyper state? Boredom, sameness, routine, and confinement. You can do wonderful things with your hands, and you have a way with words.

Mars in Cancer

You rarely attack head-on. Instead, you'll keep things to yourself, make plans in secret, and always cover your actions. This might be interpreted by some as manipulative, but it's really your method of self-protection. You get furious when anyone knows too much about you, though you do like to know all about others. Your mothering and feeding instincts can be put to good use, if you work in food, hotel, or child-care-related businesses. You may have to overcome your fragile sense of security, which prompts you not to take risks and to get physically upset when criticized. Don't take things so personally!

Mars in Leo

You have a very dominant personality that takes center stage. Modesty is not one of your stellar traits, nor is taking a back seat, ever. You prefer giving the orders and have been known to make a dramatic scene if they are not obeyed. Properly used, this Mars confers leadership ability, endurance, and courage.

Mars in Virgo

You are the faultfinder of the zodiac, who notices every detail. Mistakes of any kind make you nervous, and you are sure you can do the job better than anyone else. You may worry, even if everything is going smoothly. Though you might not express anger directly, you sure can nag. You have definite likes and dislikes. You are certainly more industrious and detail-oriented than other signs. Your Mars energy is often most positively expressed in some kind of teaching role.

Mars in Libra

This Mars will have a passion for beauty, justice, and art. Generally, you will avoid confrontations at all costs. You prefer to spend your energy finding diplomatic solutions or weighing pros and cons. Your other techniques are passive aggression or exercising your well-known charm to get people to do what you want.

Mars in Scorpio

This is a powerful placement, so intense that it demands careful channeling into worthwhile activities. Otherwise, you could become obsessed with your sexuality or might use your need for power and control to manipulate others. You are strong-willed, shrewd, and very private about your affairs, and you'll usually have a secret agenda behind your actions. Your great stamina, focus, and discipline would be excellent assets for careers in the military or medical fields, especially research or surgery. When angry, you don't get mad—you get even!

Mars in Sagittarius

This expansive Mars often propels people into sales, travel, athletics, or philosophy. Your energies function well when you are on the move. You have a hot temper and are inclined to say what you think before you consider the consequences. You shoot for high goals and talk endlessly about them, but you may be weak on groundwork. This Mars needs a solid foundation. Watch a tendency to take unnecessary risks.

Mars in Capricorn

This is an ambitious Mars with an excellent sense of timing. You have an eye for those who can be useful to you, and you may dismiss people ruthlessly when you're angry. But you drive yourself hard and deliver full value. This is a good placement for an executive. You'll aim for status and a high material position in life, and keep climbing despite the odds. A great Mars to have!

Mars in Aquarius

This is the most rebellious Mars. You seem to have a drive to assert yourself against the status quo. You may enjoy provoking people, shocking them out of traditional views. Or this placement could express itself in an offbeat sex life. Somehow you often find yourself in unconventional situations. You enjoy being a leader of an active avant-garde group, which pursues forward-looking studies, politics, or goals.

Mars in Pisces

This Mars is a good actor who knows just how to appeal to the sympathies of others. You create and project wonderful fantasies or use your sensitive antennae to crusade for those less fortunate. You get what you want through creating a veil of illusion and glamour. This is a good Mars for someone in the creative fields—a dancer, performer, or photographer—or for someone in motion pictures. Many famous film stars have this placement. Watch a tendency to manipulate by making others feel sorry for you.

Jupiter Expands

Jupiter is the planet in your horoscope that makes you want *more*. This big, bright, swirling mass of gases is associated with abundance, prosperity, and the kind of windfall you get without too much hard work. You're optimistic under Jupiter's influence, when anything seems possible. You'll travel, expand your mind with higher education, and publish to share your knowledge widely. But a strong Jupiter has its downside, too, because Jupiter's influence is neither discriminating nor disciplined. It represents the principle of growth without judgment, and could result in extravagance, weight gain, laziness, and carelessness, if not kept in check.

Be sure to look up your Jupiter in the tables in this book. When the current position of Jupiter is favorable, you may get that lucky break. This is a great time to try new things, take risks, travel, or get more education. Opportunities seem to open up easily, so take advantage of them.

Once a year, Jupiter changes signs. That means you are due for an expansive time every twelve years, when Jupiter travels through your sun sign. You'll also have "up" periods every four years, when Jupiter is in the same element as your sun sign.

Jupiter in Aries

You are the soul of enthusiasm and optimism. Your luckiest times are when you are getting started on an exciting project or selling an ideal that you really believe in. You may have to watch a tendency to be arrogant with those who do not share your enthusiasm. You follow your impulses, often ignoring budget or other commonsense limitations. To produce real, solid benefits, you'll need patience and follow-through wherever this Jupiter falls in your horoscope.

Jupiter in Taurus

You'll spend on beautiful material things, especially those that come from nature—items made of rare woods, natural fabrics, or precious gems, for instance. You can't have too much comfort or too many sensual pleasures. Watch a tendency to overindulge in good food, or to overpamper yourself with nothing but the best. Spartan living is not for you! You may be especially lucky in matters of real estate.

Jupiter in Gemini

You are the great talker of the zodiac, and you may be a great writer, too. But restlessness could be your weak point. You jump around, talk too much, and could be a jack-of-all-trades. Keeping a secret is especially difficult, so you'll also have to watch a tendency to spill the beans. Since you love to be at the center of a beehive of activity, you'll have a vibrant social life. Your best opportunities will come through your talent for language—speaking, writing, communicating, and selling.

Jupiter in Cancer

You are luckiest in situations where you can find emotional closeness or deal with basic security needs, such as food, nurturing, or shelter. You may be a great collector and you may simply love to accumulate things—you are the one who stashes things away for a rainy day. You probably have a very good memory and love children—in fact, you may have many children to care for. The food, hotel, child-care, and shipping businesses hold good opportunities for you.

Jupiter in Leo

You are a natural showman who loves to live in a larger-than-life way. Yours is a personality full of color that always finds its way into the limelight. You can't have too much attention or applause. Show biz is a natural place for you, and so is any area where you can play to a crowd. Exercising your flair for drama, your natural playfulness, and your romantic nature brings you good fortune. But watch a tendency to be overly extravagant or to monopolize center stage.

Jupiter in Virgo

You actually love those minute details others find boring. To you, they make all the difference between the perfect and the ordinary. You are the fine craftsman who spots every flaw. You expand your awareness by finding the most efficient methods and by being of service to others. Many will be drawn to medical or teaching fields. You'll also have luck in publishing, crafts, nutrition, and service professions. Watch out for a tendency to overwork.

Jupiter in Libra

This is an other-directed Jupiter that develops best with a partner, for the stimulation of others helps you grow. You are also most comfortable in harmonious, beautiful situations, and you work well with artistic people. You have a great sense of fair play and an ability to evaluate the pros and cons of a situation. You usually prefer to play the role of diplomat rather than adversary.

Jupiter in Scorpio

You love the feeling of power and control, of taking things to their limit. You can't resist a mystery, and your shrewd, penetrating mind sees right through to the heart of most situations and people. You have luck in work that provides for solutions to matters of life and death. You may be drawn to undercover work, behind-the-scenes intrigue, psychotherapy, the occult, and sex-related ventures. Your challenge will be to develop a sense of moderation and tolerance for other beliefs. This Jupiter can be fanatical. You may have luck in handling other people's money—insurance, taxes, and inheritance can bring you a windfall.

Jupiter in Sagittarius

Independent, outgoing, and idealistic, you'll shoot for the stars. This Jupiter compels you to travel far and wide, both physically and mentally, via higher education. You may have luck while traveling in an exotic place. You also have luck with outdoor ventures, exercise, and animals, particularly horses. Since you tend to be very open about your opinions, watch a tendency to be tactless and to exaggerate. Instead, use your wonderful sense of humor to make your point.

Jupiter in Capricorn

Jupiter is much more restrained in Capricorn, the sign of rules and authority. Here, Jupiter can make you overwork and heighten any ambition or sense of duty you may have. You'll expand in areas that advance your position, putting you farther up the social or corporate ladder. You are lucky working within the establishment in a very structured situation, where you can show off your ability to organize and reap rewards for your hard work.

Jupiter in Aquarius

This is another freedom-loving Jupiter, with great tolerance and originality. You are at your best when you are working for a humanitarian cause and in the company of many supporters. This is a good Jupiter for a political career. You'll relate to all kinds of people on all social levels. You have an abundance of original ideas, but you are best off away from routine and any situation that imposes rigid rules. You need mental stimulation!

Jupiter in Pisces

You are a giver whose feelings and pocketbook are easily touched by others, so choose your companions with care. You could be the original sucker for a hard-luck story. Better find a worthy hospital or charity to appreciate your selfless support. You have a great creative imagination and may attract good fortune in fields related to oil, perfume, pharmaceuticals, petroleum, dance, footwear, and alcohol. But beware of overindulgence in alcohol—focus on a creative outlet instead.

Saturn Brakes

Jupiter speeds you up with *lucky breaks,* then along comes Saturn to slow you down with the *disciplinary brakes.* Saturn has unfairly been called a malefic planet, one of the bad guys of the zodiac. On the contrary, Saturn is one of our best friends, the kind who tells you what you need to hear, even if it's not good news. Under a Saturn transit, we grow up, take responsibility for our lives, and emerge from whatever test this planet has in store, far wiser, more capable, and more mature.

When Saturn hits a critical point in your horoscope, you can count on an experience that will make you slow up, pull back, and reexamine your life. It is a call to eliminate what is not working and to shape up. By the end of its twenty-eight-year trip around the zodiac,

Saturn will have tested you in all areas of your life. The major tests happen in seven-year cycles, when Saturn passes over the *angles* of your chart—your rising sign, midheaven, descendant, and nadir. This is when the real life-changing experiences happen. But you are also in for a testing period whenever Saturn passes a *planet* in your chart or stresses that planet from a distance. Therefore, it is useful to check your planetary positions with the timetable of Saturn to prepare in advance, or at least to brace yourself.

When Saturn returns to its location at the time of your birth, at approximately age twenty-eight, you'll have your first Saturn return. At this time, a person usually takes stock or settles down to find his mission in life and assumes full adult duties and responsibilities.

Another way Saturn helps us is to reveal the karmic lessons from previous lives and give us the chance to overcome them. So look at Saturn's challenges as much-needed opportunities for self-improvement. Under a Jupiter influence, you'll have more fun, but Saturn gives you solid, long-lasting results.

Look up your natal Saturn in the tables in this book for clues on where you need work.

Saturn in Aries

Saturn here puts the brakes on Aries's natural drive and enthusiasm. You don't let anyone push you around and you know what's best for yourself. Following orders is not your strong point, and neither is diplomacy. You tend to be quick to go on the offensive in relationships, attacking first, before anyone attacks you. Because no one quite lives up to your standards, you often wind up doing everything yourself. You'll have to learn to cooperate and tone down self-centeredness.

Saturn in Taurus

A big issue is taking control of your cash flow. There will be lean periods that can be frightening, but you have the patience and endurance to stick them out and the methodical drive to prosper in the end. Learn to take a philosophical attitude like Ben Franklin, who had this placement and who said, "A penny saved is a penny earned."

Saturn in Gemini

You are a serious student of life, who may have difficulty communicating or sharing your knowledge. You may be shy, speak slowly, or have fears about communicating, like Eleanor Roosevelt. You dwell in the realms of science, theory, or abstract analysis, even when you are dealing with the emotions, like Sigmund Freud, who also had this placement.

Saturn in Cancer

Your tests come with establishing a secure emotional base. In doing so, you may have to deal with some very basic fears centering on your early home environment. Most of your Saturn tests will have emotional roots in those early childhood experiences. You may have difficulty remaining objective in terms of what you try to achieve, so it will be especially important for you to deal with negative feelings such as guilt, paranoia, jealousy, resentment, and suspicion. Galileo and Michaelangelo also navigated these murky waters.

Saturn in Leo

This is an authoritarian Saturn, a strict, demanding parent who may deny the pleasure principle in your zeal to see that rules are followed. Though you may feel guilty about taking the spotlight, you are very ambitious and loyal. You have to watch a tendency toward rigidity, also toward overwork and holding back affection. Joseph Kennedy and Billy Graham share this placement.

Saturn in Virgo

This is a cautious, exacting Saturn, intensely hard on yourself. Most of all, you give yourself the roughest time with your constant worries about every little detail, often making yourself sick. You may have difficulties setting priorities and getting the job done. Your tests will come in learning tolerance and understanding of others. Charles de Gaulle, Mae West, and Nathaniel Hawthorne had this meticulous Saturn.

Saturn in Libra

Saturn is exalted here, which makes this planet an ally. However, there are very likely to be commitment issues. You must learn to stand solidly on your own before you can have a successful relationship. You may choose very serious, older partners in life. You are extremely cautious as you deliberate every involvement—with good reason. It is best that you find an occupation that makes good use of your sense of duty and honor. Steer clear of fly-by-night situations. Both Khrushchev and Mao Tse-tung had this placement, too.

Saturn in Scorpio

You have great staying power. This Saturn tests you in situations involving control of others. You may feel drawn to some kind of intrigue or undercover work, like J. Edgar Hoover. Or there may be an air of mystery surrounding your life and death, like Marilyn Monroe and Robert Kennedy, who had this placement. There are lessons to be learned from your sexual involvements. Often sex is used for manipulation or is somehow out of the ordinary. The Roman emperor Caligula and the transvestite Christine Jorgensen are extreme cases.

Saturn in Sagittarius

Your challenges and lessons will come from tests of your spiritual and philosophical values, as happened to Martin Luther King and Gandhi. You are high-minded and sincere with this reflective, moral placement. Uncompromising in your ethical standards, you could become a benevolent despot.

Saturn in Capricorn

With the help of Saturn at maximum strength, your judgment will improve with age. And like Spencer Tracy's screen image, you'll be the gray-haired hero with a strong sense of responsibility. You advance in life slowly but steadily, always with a strong hand at the helm and an eye for the advantageous situation. Like Pat Robertson, you're likely to stand for conservative values. Negatively, you may be a loner, prone to periods of melancholy.

Saturn in Aquarius

Your tests come from relationships with groups. Do you care too much about what others think? Do you feel like an outsider, as Greta Garbo did? You may fear being different from others and therefore demean your own unique, forward-looking gifts, or like Lord Byron and Howard Hughes, take the opposite tack and rebel in the extreme. However, others with this placement have been able to apply discipline to accomplish great humanitarian goals, as Albert Schweitzer did.

Saturn in Pisces

Your fear of the unknown and the irrational may lead you to the safety and protection of an institution. You may go on the run like Jesse James, who had this placement, to avoid looking too deeply inside. Or you might go in the opposite, more positive direction and develop a disciplined psychoanalytic approach, which puts you more in control of your feelings. Some of you will take refuge in work with hospitals, charities, or religious institutions. Queen Victoria, who had this placement, symbolized an era when institutions of all kinds were sustained. Discipline applied to artistic work, especially poetry and dance, or spiritual work, such as yoga or meditation, might be helpful.

Uranus, Neptune, and Pluto Affect Your Whole Generation

These three planets remain in signs such a long time that a whole generation bears the imprint of the sign. Mass movements, great sweeping changes, fads that characterize a generation, even the issues of the conflicts and wars of the time are influenced by the "outer three." When one of these distant planets changes signs, there is a definite shift in the atmosphere, the feeling of the end of an era.

Since these planets are so far away from the sun—too distant to be seen by the naked eye—they pick up signals from the universe at large. These planetary receivers literally link the sun with distant energies, and then perform a similar function in your horoscope by linking your central character with intuitive, spiritual, transformative forces from the cosmos. Each planet has a special domain and will reflect this in the area of your chart where it falls.

Uranus Wakes You Up

There is nothing ordinary about this quirky green planet that seems to be traveling on its side, surrounded by a swarm of moons. Is it any wonder that astrologers assigned it to Aquarius, the most eccentric and gregarious sign? Uranus seems to wend its way around the sun, marching to its own tune.

Uranus's energy is electrical, happening in sudden flashes. It is not influenced by karma or past events, nor does it regard tradition, sex, or sentiment. The Uranian key words are "surprise" and "awakening." Uranus wakes you up, jolts you out of your comfortable rut. Suddenly, there's that flash of inspiration, that bright idea, a totally new approach that revolutionizes whatever you're doing. A Uranus event takes you by surprise, happens from out of the blue, for better or for worse. The Uranus place in your life is where you wake up to your own special qualities and become your own person, leaving the structures of Saturn behind.

Look up the sign of Uranus at the time of your birth. Then place it in the appropriate house in your chart and see where you follow your own tune.

Uranus in Aries

BIRTH DATES:
March 31, 1927–November 4, 1927
January 13, 1928—June 6, 1934
October 10, 1934—March 28, 1935

Your generation is original, creative, pioneering. It developed the computer, the airplane, and the cyclotron. You let nothing hold you back from exploring the unknown and have a powerful mixture of fire and electricity behind you. Women of your generation were among the first to be liberated. You were the unforgettable style setters. You have a surprise in store for everyone. Like Yoko Ono, Grace Kelly, and Jacqueline Onassis, your life may be jolted by sudden and violent changes.

Uranus in Taurus

BIRTH DATES:
June 6, 1934–October 10, 1934
March 28, 1935–August 7, 1941
October 5, 1941–May 15, 1942

World War II began during your generation. You are probably self-employed or would like to be. You have original ideas about making money, and you brace yourself for sudden changes of fortune. This Uranus can cause shakeups, particularly in finances, but it can also make you a born entrepreneur.

Uranus in Gemini

BIRTH DATES:
August 7, 1941–October 5, 1941
May 15, 1942–August 30, 1948
November 12, 1948–June 10, 1949

You were the first children to be influenced by television. Now, in your adult years, your generation stocks up on answering machines, cordless phones, car phones, computers, and fax machines—any new way you can communicate. You have an inquiring mind, but your interests may be rather short-lived. This Uranus can be easily fragmented if there is no structure and focus.

Uranus in Cancer

BIRTH DATES:
August 30, 1948–November 12, 1948
June 10, 1949–August 24, 1955
January 28, 1956–June 10, 1956

This generation came at a time when divorce was becoming commonplace, so your home image is unconventional. You may have an unusual relationship with your parents; you may have come from a broken home or an unconventional one. You'll have unorthodox ideas about parenting, intimacy, food, and shelter. You may also be interested in dreams, psychic phenomena, and memory work.

Uranus in Leo

BIRTH DATES:
August 24, 1955–January 28, 1956
June 10, 1956–November 1, 1961
January 10, 1962–August 10, 1962

This generation understands how to use electronic media. Many of your group are now leaders in the high-tech industries, and you also understand how to use the new media to promote yourself. Like Isadora Duncan, you may have a very eccentric kind of charisma and a life that is sparked by unusual love affairs. Your children, too, may have traits that are out of the ordinary. Where this planet falls in your chart, you'll have a love of freedom, be a bit of an egomaniac, and show the full force of your personality in a unique way, like tennis great Martina Navratilova.

Uranus in Virgo

BIRTH DATES:
November 1, 1961–January 10, 1962
August 10, 1962–September 28, 1968
May 20, 1969–June 24, 1969

You'll have highly individual work methods, and many will be finding newer, more practical ways to use computers. Like Einstein, who had this placement, you'll break the rules brilliantly. Your generation came at a time of student rebellions, the civil rights movement, and the general acceptance of health foods. Chances are, you're concerned about pollution and cleaning up the environment. You may also be involved with nontraditional healing methods. Heavyweight champ Mike Tyson has this placement.

Uranus in Libra

BIRTH DATES:
September 28, 1968–May 20, 1969
June 24, 1969–November 21, 1974
May 1, 1975–September 8, 1975

Your generation will be always changing partners. Born during the era of women's liberation, you may have come from a broken home and have no clear image of what a marriage entails. There will be many sudden splits and experiments before you settle down. Your generation will be much involved in legal and political reforms and in changing artistic and fashion looks.

Uranus in Scorpio

BIRTH DATES:
November 21, 1974–May 1, 1975
September 8, 1975–February 17, 1981
March 20, 1981–November 16, 1981

Interest in transformation, meditation, and life after death signaled the beginning of New Age consciousness. Your generation recognizes no boundaries, no limits, and no external controls. You'll have new attitudes toward death and dying, psychic phenomena, and the occult. Like Mae West and Casanova, you'll shock 'em sexually, too.

Uranus in Sagittarius

BIRTH DATES:
February 17, 1981–March 20, 1981
November 16, 1981–February 15, 1988
May 27, 1988–December 2, 1988

Could this generation be the first to travel in outer space? An earlier generation with this placement included Charles Lindbergh—at that time, the first Zeppelins and the Wright Brothers were conquering the skies. Uranus here forecasts great discoveries, mind expansion, and long-distance travel. Like Galileo and Martin Luther, this generation will formulate new theories about the cosmos and man's relation to it.

Uranus in Capricorn

BIRTH DATES:
December 20, 1904–January 30, 1912
September 4, 1912–November 12, 1912
February 15, 1988–May 27, 1988
December 2, 1988–April 1, 1995
June 9, 1995–January 12, 1996

This generation will challenge traditions with the help of electronic gadgets. During the mid-1990s, we got organized with the help of technology put to practical use. Home computers and handheld devices became widely used. Great leaders, who were movers and shakers of history, like Julius Caesar and Henry VIII, were born under this placement.

Uranus in Aquarius

BIRTH DATES:
January 30, 1912–September 4, 1912
November 12, 1912–April 1, 1919
August 16, 1919–January 22, 1920
April 1, 1995–June 9, 1995
January 12, 1996–March 10, 2003

The last generation with this placement produced great innovative minds such as Leonard Bernstein and Orson Welles. Babies who are born now will become another radical breakthrough generation, much concerned with global issues that involve all humanity. Intuition, innovation, and sudden changes will continue to surprise everyone while Uranus is in its home sign.

Uranus in Pisces

BIRTH DATES:
April 1, 1919–August 16, 1919
January 22, 1920–March 31, 1927
November 4, 1927–January 12, 1928
March 10, 2003–May 28, 2010

Uranus in Pisces previously focused attention on the rise of electronic entertainment—radio and the cinema—and the secretiveness of Prohibition. This produced a generation of idealists exemplified by Judy Garland's theme, "Somewhere Over the Rainbow." Coming up next year will be the dramatic return of Uranus to Pisces, which should spark a wonderful spurt of creativity and innovation in the arts.

Neptune Takes You out of This World

Under Neptune's influence, you see what you want to see. But Neptune also encourages you to create, letting your fantasies and daydreams run free. Neptune is often maligned as the planet of illusions, drugs, and alcohol, where you can't bear to face reality. But it also embodies the energy of glamour, subtlety, mystery, and mysticism, and governs anything that takes you beyond the mundane world, including out-of-body experiences.

Neptune acts to break through your ordinary perceptions and take you to another level of reality, where you experience either confusion or ecstasy. Neptune's force can pull you off-course, the way this planet affects its neighbor, Uranus, but only if you allow this to happen. Those who use Neptune wisely can translate their daydreams into poetry, theater, design, or inspired moves in the business world, avoiding the tricky "con artist" side of this planet.

Find your Neptune listed below:

Neptune in Cancer

BIRTH DATES:
July 19, 1901–December 25, 1901
May 21, 1902–September 23, 1914
December 14, 1914–July 19, 1915
March 1916–May 2, 1916

Dreams of the homeland, idealistic patriotism, and glamorization of the nurturing assets of women characterized this time. You who were born here have unusual psychic ability and deep insights into the basic needs of others.

Neptune in Leo

BIRTH DATES:
September 23, 1914–December 14, 1914
July 19, 1915–March 19, 1916
May 2, 1916–September 21, 1928
February 19, 1929–July 24, 1929

Neptune here brought us the glamour and high living of the 1920s and the big spenders of that time. The Neptunian temptations of gambling, seduction, theater, and lavish entertaining distracted us from the realities of the age. Those born in this generation also made great advances in the arts.

Neptune in Virgo

BIRTH DATES:
September 21, 1928–February 19, 1929
July 24, 1929–October 3, 1942
April 17, 1943–August 2, 1943

Neptune in Virgo encompassed the Great Depression and World War II, while those born at this time later spread the gospel of health and fitness. This generation's devotion to spending hours at the office inspired the term "workaholic."

Neptune in Libra

BIRTH DATES:
October 3, 1942–April 17, 1943
August 2, 1943–December 24, 1955
March 12, 1956–October 19, 1956
June 15, 1957–August 6, 1957

Neptune in Libra produced the romantic generation who would later be extremely concerned with relating. As this generation matured, there was a new trend toward marriage and commitment. Racial and sexual equality become important issues, as they redesigned traditional relationship roles to suit modern times.

Neptune in Scorpio

BIRTH DATES:
December 24, 1955–March 12, 1956
October 19, 1956–June 15, 1957
August 6, 1957–January 4, 1970
May 3, 1970–November 6, 1970

Neptune in Scorpio ushered in a generation that would become interested in transformative power. Born in an era that glamorized sex, drugs, rock and roll, and Eastern religion, they matured in a more sobering time of AIDS, cocaine abuse, and New Age spirituality. As they evolve, they will become active in healing the planet from the results of the abuse of power.

Neptune in Sagittarius

BIRTH DATES:
January 4, 1970–May 3, 1970
November 6, 1970–January 19, 1984
June 23, 1984–November 21, 1984

Neptune in Sagittarius was the time when space and astronaut travel became a reality. The Neptune influence glamorized new approaches to mysticism, religion, and mind expansion. This generation will take a new approach to spiritual life, with emphasis on visions, mysticism, and clairvoyance.

Neptune in Capricorn

BIRTH DATES:
January 19, 1984–June 23, 1984
November 21, 1984–January 29, 1998

Neptune in Capricorn brought a time when delusions about material power were first glamorized, then dashed on the rocks of reality. It was also a time when the psychic and occult worlds spawned a new category of business enterprise, and sold services on television.

Neptune in Aquarius

BIRTH DATES:
January 29, 1998–April 4, 2111

This should continue to be a time of breakthroughs, when the creative influence of Neptune reaches a universal audience. This is a time of dissolving barriers, of globalization, when we truly become one world. Computer technology used for the creative arts, innovative drug therapies, and high-tech "highs" such as trance music are recent manifestations.

Pluto Transforms You

Pluto is a mysterious little planet with a strange elliptical orbit that occasionally runs inside the orbit of its neighbor Neptune. Because of its eccentric path, the length of time Pluto stays in any given sign can vary from thirteen to thirty-two years. It has covered only seven signs in the past century. Though it is a tiny planet, its influence is great. When Pluto zaps a strategic point in your horoscope, your life changes dramatically.

This little planet is the power behind the scenes; it affects you at deep levels of consciousness, causing events to come to the surface that will transform you and your generation. Nothing escapes, or is sacred, with this probing planet. The Pluto place in your horoscope is where you have invisible power (Mars governs the visible power), where you can transform, heal, and affect the unconscious needs of the masses. Pluto tells how your generation projects power, what makes it seem "cool" to others. And when Pluto changes signs, there's a whole new concept of what's cool.

Pluto in Gemini

BIRTH DATES:
Late 1800s–May 26, 1914

This was a time of mass suggestion and breakthroughs in communications, when many brilliant writers, such as Ernest Hemingway and F. Scott Fitzgerald, were born. Henry Miller, D. H. Lawrence, and James Joyce scandalized society by using explicit sexual images and language in their literature. "Muckraking" journalists exposed corruption. Pluto-ruled Scorpio President Theodore Roosevelt said, "Speak softly, but carry a big stick." This generation had an intense need to communicate and made major breakthroughs in knowledge. A compulsive restlessness and a thirst for a variety of experiences characterizes many of this generation.

Pluto in Cancer

BIRTH DATES:
May 26, 1914–June 14, 1939

Dictators and mass media rose up to wield emotional power over the masses. Women's rights was a popular issue. Deep sentimental feelings, acquisitiveness, and possessiveness characterized these times and people. The great Hollywood stars who embodied the American image were born during this period: Grace Kelly, Esther Williams, Frank Sinatra, Lana Turner, etc.

Pluto in Leo

BIRTH DATES:
June 14, 1939–August 19, 1957

The performing arts played on the emotions of the masses. Mick Jagger, John Lennon, and rock and roll were born at this time. So were "baby boomers" like Bill and Hillary Clinton. Those born here tend to be self-centered, powerful, and boisterous. This generation does its own thing, for better or for worse.

Pluto in Virgo

BIRTH DATES:
August 19, 1957–October 5, 1971
April 17, 1972–July 30, 1972

This is the "yuppie" generation that sparked a mass movement toward fitness, health, and career. A much more sober, serious, driven generation than the fun-loving Pluto in Leos. During this time, machines were invented to process detail work efficiently. Inventions took a practical turn, as answering machines, fax machines, car phones, and home office equipment contributed to transform the workplace.

Pluto in Libra

BIRTH DATES:
October 5, 1971–April 17, 1972
July 30, 1972–August 28, 1984

A mellower generation concerned with partnerships, working together, and finding diplomatic solutions to problems. Marriage is important to this generation, who will redefine it, combining traditional values with equal partnership. This was a time of women's liberation, gay rights, ERA, and legal battles over abortion, all of which transformed our ideas about relationships.

Pluto in Scorpio

BIRTH DATES:
August 28, 1984–January 17, 1995

Pluto was in its ruling sign for a comparatively short period of time. In 1989, it was at its perihelion, or closest point to the sun and Earth. We have all felt the transforming power somewhere in our lives. This was a time of record achievements, destructive sexually transmitted diseases, nuclear power controversies, and explosive political issues. Pluto destroys in order to create new understanding—the phoenix rising from the ashes, which should be some consolation for those of you who felt Pluto's force before 1995. Sexual shockers were par for the course during these intense years, when black clothing, transvestites, body piercing, tattoos, and sexually explicit advertising pushed the boundaries of good taste.

Pluto in Sagittarius

BIRTH DATES:
January 17, 1995–January 27, 2008

During our current Pluto transit, we are being pushed to expand our horizons. For many of us, this will mean rolling down the information superhighway into the future. Another trend is to find deeper spiritual meaning in life. This is a time when spiritual emphasis will become pervasive, when religious convictions will exert more power in our political life as well.

Since Sagittarius is the sign that rules travel, there's a good possibility that Pluto, the planet of extremes, will make space travel a reality for some of us. Discovery of life on Mars, which traveled here on meteors, could transform our ideas about where we came from.

New dimensions in electronic publishing, concern with animal rights and the environment, and an increasing emphasis on extreme forms of religion are other signs of these times. Look for charismatic religious leaders to arise now. We'll also be developing far-reaching philosophies designed to elevate our lives with a new sense of purpose.

VENUS SIGNS 1901–2002

	Aries	Taurus	Gemini	Cancer	Leo	Virgo
1901	3/29–4/22	4/22–5/17	5/17–6/10	6/10–7/5	7/5–7/29	7/29–8/23
1902	5/7–6/3	6/3–6/30	6/30–7/25	7/25–8/19	8/19–9/13	9/13–10/7
1903	2/28–3/24	3/24–4/18	4/18–5/13	5/13–6/9	6/9–7/7	7/7–8/17
9/6–11/8
1904	3/13–5/7	5/7–6/1	6/1–6/25	6/25–7/19	7/19–8/13	8/13–9/6
1905	2/3–3/6
4/9–5/28	3/6–4/9
5/28–7/8	7/8–8/6	8/6–9/1	9/1–9/27	9/27–10/21
1906	3/1–4/7	4/7–5/2	5/2–5/26	5/26–6/20	6/20–7/16	7/16–8/11
1907	4/27–5/22	5/22–6/16	6/16–7/11	7/11–8/4	8/4–8/29	8/29–9/22
1908	2/14–3/10	3/10–4/5	4/5–5/5	5/5–9/8	9/8–10/8	10/8–11/3
1909	3/29–4/22	4/22–5/16	5/16–6/10	6/10–7/4	7/4–7/29	7/29–8/23
1910	5/7–6/3	6/4–6/29	6/30–7/24	7/25–8/18	8/19–9/12	9/13–10/6
1911	2/28–3/23	3/24–4/17	4/18–5/12	5/13–6/8	6/9–7/7	7/8–11/8
1912	4/13–5/6	5/7–5/31	6/1–6/24	6/24–7/18	7/19–8/12	8/13–9/5
1913	2/3–3/6
5/2–5/30	3/7–5/1
5/31–7/7	7/8–8/5	8/6–8/31	9/1–9/26	9/27–10/20
1914	3/14–4/6	4/7–5/1	5/2–5/25	5/26–6/19	6/20–7/15	7/16–8/10
1915	4/27–5/21	5/22–6/15	6/16–7/10	7/11–8/3	8/4–8/28	8/29–9/21
1916	2/14–3/9	3/10–4/5	4/6–5/5	5/6–9/8	9/9–10/7	10/8–11/2
1917	3/29–4/21	4/22–5/15	5/16–6/9	6/10–7/3	7/4–7/28	7/29–8/21
1918	5/7–6/2	6/3–6/28	6/29–7/24	7/25–8/18	8/19–9/11	9/12–10/5
1919	2/27–3/22	3/23–4/16	4/17–5/12	5/13–6/7	6/8–7/7	7/8–11/8
1920	4/12–5/6	5/7–5/30	5/31–6/23	6/24–7/18	7/19–8/11	8/12–9/4
1921	2/3–3/6
4/26–6/1	3/7–4/25
6/2–7/7	7/8–8/5	8/6–8/31	9/1–9/25	9/26–10/20
1922	3/13–4/6	4/7–4/30	5/1–5/25	5/26–6/19	6/20–7/14	7/15–8/9
1923	4/27–5/21	5/22–6/14	6/15–7/9	7/10–8/3	8/4–8/27	8/28–9/20
1924	2/13–3/8	3/9–4/4	4/5–5/5	5/6–9/8	9/9–10/7	10/8–11/12
1925	3/28–4/20	4/21–5/15	5/16–6/8	6/9–7/3	7/4–7/27	7/28–8/21

Libra	Scorpio	Sagittarius	Capricorn	Aquarius	Pisces
8/23–9/17	9/17–10/12	10/12–1/16	1/16–2/9 11/7–12/5	2/9–3/5 12/5–1/11	3/5–3/29
10/7–10/31	10/31–11/24	11/24–12/18	12/18–1/11	2/6–4/4	1/11–2/6 4/4–5/7
8/17–9/6 11/8–12/9	12/9–1/5			1/11–2/4	2/4–2/28
9/6–9/30	9/30–10/25	1/5–1/30 10/25–11/18	1/30–2/24 11/18–12/13	2/24–3/19 12/13–1/7	3/19–4/13
10/21–11/14	11/14–12/8	12/8–1/1/06			1/7–2/3
8/11–9/7	9/7–10/9 12/15–12/25	10/9–12/15 12/25–2/6	1/1–1/25	1/25–2/18	2/18–3/14
9/22–10/16	10/16–11/9	11/9–12/3	2/6–3/6 12/3–12/27	3/6–4/2 12/27–1/20	4/2–4/27
11/3–11/28	11/28–12/22	12/22–1/15			1/20–2/4
8/23–9/17	9/17–10/12	10/12–11/17	1/15–2/9 11/17–12/5	2/9–3/5 12/5–1/15	3/5–3/29
10/7–10/30	10/31–11/23	11/24–12/17	12/18–12/31	1/1–1/15 1/29–4/4	1/16–1/28 4/5–5/6
11/19–12/8	12/9–12/31		1/1–1/10	1/11–2/2	2/3–2/27
9/6–9/30	1/1–1/4 10/1–10/24	1/5–1/29 10/25–11/17	1/30–2/23 11/18–12/12	2/24–3/18 12/13–12/31	3/19–4/12
10/21–11/13	11/14–12/7	12/8–12/31		1/1–1/6	1/7–2/2
8/11–9/6	9/7–10/9 12/6–12/30	10/10–12/5 12/31	1/1–1/24	1/25–2/17	2/18–3/13
9/22–10/15	10/16–11/8	1/1–2/6 11/9–12/2	2/7–3/6 12/3–12/26	3/7–4/1 12/27–12/31	4/2–4/26
11/3–11/27	11/28–12/21	12/22–12/31		1/1–1/19	1/20–2/13
8/22–9/16	9/17–10/11	1/1–1/14 10/12–11/6	1/15–2/7 11/7–12/5	2/8–3/4 12/6–12/31	3/5–3/28
10/6–10/29	10/30–11/22	11/23–12/16	12/17–12/31	1/1–4/5	4/6–5/6
11/9–12/8	12/9–12/31		1/1–1/9	1/10–2/2	2/3–2/26
9/5–9/30	1/1–1/3 9/31–10/23	1/4–1/28 10/24–11/17	1/29–2/22 11/18–12/11	2/23–3/18 12/12–12/31	3/19–4/11
10/21–11/13	11/14–12/7	12/8–12/31		1/1–1/6	1/7–2/2
8/10–9/6	9/7–10/10 11/29–12/31	10/11–11/28	1/1–1/24	1/25–2/16	2/17–3/12
9/21–10/14	1/1 10/15–11/7	1/2–2/6 11/8–12/1	2/7–3/5 12/2–12/25	3/6–3/31 12/26–12/31	4/1–4/26
11/13–11/26	11/27–12/21	12/22–12/31		1/1–1/19	1/20–2/12
8/22–9/15	9/16–10/11	1/1–1/14 10/12–11/6	1/15–2/7 11/7–12/5	2/8–3/3 12/6–12/31	3/4–3/27

VENUS SIGNS 1901–2002

	Aries	Taurus	Gemini	Cancer	Leo	Virgo
1926	5/7–6/2	6/3–6/28	6/29–7/23	7/24–8/17	8/18–9/11	9/12–10/5
1927	2/27–3/22	3/23–4/16	4/17–5/11	5/12–6/7	6/8–7/7	7/8–11/9
1928	4/12–5/5	5/6–5/29	5/30–6/23	6/24–7/17	7/18–8/11	8/12–9/4
1929	2/3–3/7 4/20–6/2	3/8–4/19 6/3–7/7	7/8–8/4	8/5–8/30	8/31–9/25	9/26–10/19
1930	3/13–4/5	4/6–4/30	5/1–5/24	5/25–6/18	6/19–7/14	7/15–8/9
1931	4/26–5/20	5/21–6/13	6/14–7/8	7/9–8/2	8/3–8/26	8/27–9/19
1932	2/12–3/8	3/9–4/3	4/4–5/5 7/13–7/27	5/6–7/12 7/28–9/8	9/9–10/6	10/7–11/1
1933	3/27–4/19	4/20–5/28	5/29–6/8	6/9–7/2	7/3–7/26	7/27–8/20
1934	5/6–6/1	6/2–6/27	6/28–7/22	7/23–8/16	8/17–9/10	9/11–10/4
1935	2/26–3/21	3/22–4/15	4/16–5/10	5/11–6/6	6/7–7/6	7/7–11/8
1936	4/11–5/4	5/5–5/28	5/29–6/22	6/23–7/16	7/17–8/10	8/11–9/4
1937	2/2–3/8 4/14–6/3	3/9–4/13 6/4–7/6	7/7–8/3	8/4–8/29	8/30–9/24	9/25–10/18
1938	3/12–4/4	4/5–4/28	4/29–5/23	5/24–6/18	6/19–7/13	7/14–8/8
1939	4/25–5/19	5/20–6/13	6/14–7/8	7/9–8/1	8/2–8/25	8/26–9/19
1940	2/12–3/7	3/8–4/3	4/4–5/5 7/5–7/31	5/6–7/4 8/1–9/8	9/9–10/5	10/6–10/31
1941	3/27–4/19	4/20–5/13	5/14–6/6	6/7–7/1	7/2–7/26	7/27–8/20
1942	5/6–6/1	6/2–6/26	6/27–7/22	7/23–8/16	8/17–9/9	9/10–10/3
1943	2/25–3/20	3/21–4/14	4/15–5/10	5/11–6/6	6/7–7/6	7/7–11/8
1944	4/10–5/3	5/4–5/28	5/29–6/21	6/22–7/16	7/17–8/9	8/10–9/2
1945	2/2–3/10 4/7–6/3	3/11–4/6 6/4–7/6	7/7–8/3	8/4–8/29	8/30–9/23	9/24–10/18
1946	3/11–4/4	4/5–4/28	4/29–5/23	5/24–6/17	6/18–7/12	7/13–8/8
1947	4/25–5/19	5/20–6/12	6/13–7/7	7/8–8/1	8/2–8/25	8/26–9/18
1948	2/11–3/7	3/8–4/3	4/4–5/6 6/29–8/2	5/7–6/28 8/3–9/7	9/8–10/5	10/6–10/31
1949	3/26–4/19	4/20–5/13	5/14–6/6	6/7–6/30	7/1–7/25	7/26–8/19
1950	5/5–5/31	6/1–6/26	6/27–7/21	7/22–8/15	8/16–9/9	9/10–10/3
1951	2/25–3/21	3/22–4/15	4/16–5/10	5/11–6/6	6/7–7/7	7/8–11/9

Libra	Scorpio	Sagittarius	Capricorn	Aquarius	Pisces
10/6–10/29	10/30–11/22	11/23–12/16	12/17–12/31	1/1–4/5	4/6–5/6
11/10–12/8	12/9–12/31	1/1–1/7	1/8	1/9–2/1	2/2–2/26
9/5–9/28	1/1–1/3	1/4–1/28	1/29–2/22	2/23–3/17	3/18–4/11
	9/29–10/23	10/24–11/16	11/17–12/11	12/12–12/31	
10/20–11/12	11/13–12/6	12/7–12/30	12/31	1/1–1/5	1/6–2/2
8/10–9/6	9/7–10/11	10/12–11/21	1/1–1/23	1/24–2/16	2/17–3/12
	11/22–12/31				
9/20–10/13	1/1–1/3	1/4–2/6	2/7–3/4	3/5–3/31	4/1–4/25
	10/14–11/6	11/7–11/30	12/1–12/24	12/25–12/31	
11/2–11/25	11/26–12/20	12/21–12/31		1/1–1/18	1/19–2/11
8/21–9/14	9/15–10/10	1/1–1/13	1/14–2/6	2/7–3/2	3/3–3/26
		10/11–11/5	11/6–12/4	12/5–12/31	
10/5–10/28	10/29–11/21	11/22–12/15	12/16–12/31	1/1–4/5	4/6–5/5
11/9–12/7	12/8–12/31		1/1–1/7	1/8–1/31	2/1–2/25
9/5–9/27	1/1–1/2	1/3–1/27	1/28–2/21	2/22–3/16	3/17–4/10
	9/28–10/22	10/23–11/15	11/16–12/10	12/11–12/31	
10/19–11/11	11/12–12/5	12/6–12/29	12/30–12/31	1/1–1/5	1/6–2/1
8/9–9/6	9/7–10/13	10/14–11/14	1/1–1/22	1/23–2/15	2/16–3/11
	11/15–12/31				
9/20–10/13	1/1–1/3	1/4–2/5	2/6–3/4	3/5–3/30	3/31–4/24
	10/14–11/6	11/7–11/30	12/1–12/24	12/25–12/31	
11/1–11/25	11/26–12/19	12/20–12/31		1/1–1/18	1/19–2/11
8/21–9/14	9/15–10/9	1/1–1/12	1/13–2/5	2/6–3/1	3/2–3/26
		10/10–11/5	11/6–12/4	12/5–12/31	
10/4–10/27	10/28–11/20	11/21–12/14	12/15–12/31	1/1–4/4	4/6–5/5
11/9–12/7	12/8–12/31		1/1–1/7	1/8–1/31	2/1–2/24
9/3–9/27	1/1–1/2	1/3–1/27	1/28–2/20	2/21–3/16	3/17–4/9
	9/28–10/21	10/22–11/15	11/16–12/10	12/11–12/31	
10/19–11/11	11/12–12/5	12/6–12/29	12/30–12/31	1/1–1/4	1/5–2/1
8/9–9/6	9/7–10/15	10/16–11/7	1/1–1/21	1/22–2/14	2/15–3/10
	11/8–12/31				
9/19–10/12	1/1–1/4	1/5–2/5	2/6–3/4	3/5–3/29	3/30–4/24
	10/13–11/5	11/6–11/29	11/30–12/23	12/24–12/31	
11/1–11/25	11/26–12/19	12/20–12/31		1/1–1/17	1/18–2/10
8/20–9/14	9/15–10/9	1/1–1/12	1/13–2/5	2/6–3/1	3/2–3/25
		10/10–11/5	11/6–12/5	12/6–12/31	
10/4–10/27	10/28–11/20	11/21–12/13	12/14–12/31	1/1–4/5	4/6–5/4
11/10–12/7	12/8–12/31		1/1–1/7	1/8–1/31	2/1–2/24

VENUS SIGNS 1901–2002

	Aries	Taurus	Gemini	Cancer	Leo	Virgo
1952	4/10–5/4	5/5–5/28	5/29–6/21	6/22–7/16	7/17–8/9	8/10–9/3
1953	2/2–3/3 4/1–6/5	3/4–3/31 6/6–7/7	7/8–8/3	8/4–8/29	8/30–9/24	9/25–10/18
1954	3/12–4/4	4/5–4/28	4/29–5/23	5/24–6/17	6/18–7/13	7/14–8/8
1955	4/25–5/19	5/20–6/13	6/14–7/7	7/8–8/1	8/2–8/25	8/26–9/18
1956	2/12–3/7	3/8–4/4	4/5–5/7 6/24–8/4	5/8–6/23 8/5–9/8	9/9–10/5	10/6–10/31
1957	3/26–4/19	4/20–5/13	5/14–6/6	6/7–7/1	7/2–7/26	7/27–8/19
1958	5/6–5/31	6/1–6/26	6/27–7/22	7/23–8/15	8/16–9/9	9/10–10/3
1959	2/25–3/20	3/21–4/14	4/15–5/10	5/11–6/6	6/7–7/8 9/21–9/24	7/9–9/20 9/25–11/9
1960	4/10–5/3	5/4–5/28	5/29–6/21	6/22–7/15	7/16–8/9	8/10–9/2
1961	2/3–6/5	6/6–7/7	7/8–8/3	8/4–8/29	8/30–9/23	9/24–10/17
1962	3/11–4/3	4/4–4/28	4/29–5/22	5/23–6/17	6/18–7/12	7/13–8/8
1963	4/24–5/18	5/19–6/12	6/13–7/7	7/8–7/31	8/1–8/25	8/26–9/18
1964	2/11–3/7	3/8–4/4	4/5–5/9 6/18–8/5	5/10–6/17 8/6–9/8	9/9–10/5	10/6–10/31
1965	3/26–4/18	4/19–5/12	5/13–6/6	6/7–6/30	7/1–7/25	7/26–8/19
1966	5/6–6/31	6/1–6/26	6/27–7/21	7/22–8/15	8/16–9/8	9/9–10/2
1967	2/24–3/20	3/21–4/14	4/15–5/10	5/11–6/6	6/7–7/8 9/10–10/1	7/9–9/9 10/2–11/9
1968	4/9–5/3	5/4–5/27	5/28–6/20	6/21–7/15	7/16–8/8	8/9–9/2
1969	2/3–6/6	6/7–7/6	7/7–8/3	8/4–8/28	8/29–9/22	9/23–10/17
1970	3/11–4/3	4/4–4/27	4/28–5/22	5/23–6/16	6/17–7/12	7/13–8/8
1971	4/24–5/18	5/19–6/12	6/13–7/6	7/7–7/31	8/1–8/24	8/25–9/17
1972	2/11–3/7	3/8–4/3	4/4–5/10 6/12–8/6	5/11–6/11 8/7–9/8	9/9–10/5	10/6–10/30
1973	3/25–4/18	4/18–5/12	5/13–6/5	6/6–6/29	7/1–7/25	7/26–8/19
1974		5/5–5/31	6/1–6/25	6/26–7/21	7/22–8/14	8/15–9/8	9/9–10/2
1975	2/24–3/20	3/21–4/13	4/14–5/9	5/10–6/6	6/7–7/9 9/3–10/4	7/10–9/2 10/5–11/9

Libra	Scorpio	Sagittarius	Capricorn	Aquarius	Pisces
9/4–9/27	1/1–1/2	1/3–1/27	1/28–2/20	2/21–3/16	3/17–4/9
	9/28–10/21	10/22–11/15	11/16–12/10	12/11–12/31	
10/19–11/11	11/12–12/5	12/6–12/29	12/30–12/31	1/1–1/5	1/6–2/1
8/9–9/6	9/7–10/22	10/23–10/27	1/1–1/22	1/23–2/15	2/16–3/11
	10/28–12/31				
9/19–10/13	1/1–1/6	1/7–2/5	2/6–3/4	3/5–3/30	3/31–4/24
	10/14–11/5	11/6–11/30	12/1–12/24	12/25–12/31	
11/1–11/25	11/26–12/19	12/20–12/31		1/1–1/17	1/18–2/11
8/20–9/14	9/15–10/9	1/1–1/12	1/13–2/5	2/6–3/1	3/2–3/25
		10/10–11/5	11/6–12/6	12/7–12/31	
10/4–10/27	10/28–11/20	11/21–12/14	12/15–12/31	1/1–4/6	4/7–5/5
11/10–12/7	12/8–12/31		1/1–1/7	1/8–1/31	2/1–2/24
9/3–9/26	1/1–1/2	1/3–1/27	1/28–2/20	2/21–3/15	3/16–4/9
	9/27–10/21	10/22–11/15	11/16–12/10	12/11–12/31	
10/18–11/11	11/12–12/4	12/5–12/28	12/29–12/31	1/1–1/5	1/6–2/2
8/9–9/6	9/7–12/31		1/1–1/21	1/22–2/14	2/15–3/10
9/19–10/12	1/1–1/6	1/7–2/5	2/6–3/4	3/5–3/29	3/30–4/23
	10/13–11/5	11/6–11/29	11/30–12/23	12/24–12/31	
11/1–11/24	11/25–12/19	12/20–12/31		1/1–1/16	1/17–2/10
8/20–9/13	9/14–10/9	1/1–1/12	1/13–2/5	2/6–3/1	3/2–3/25
		10/10–11/5	11/6–12/7	12/8–12/31	
10/3–10/26	10/27–11/19	11/20–12/13	2/7–2/25	1/1–2/6	4/7–5/5
			12/14–12/31	2/26–4/6	
11/10–12/7	12/8–12/31		1/1–1/6	1/7–1/30	1/31–2/23
9/3–9/26	1/1	1/2–1/26	1/27–2/20	2/21–3/15	3/16–4/8
	9/27–10/21	10/22–11/14	11/15–12/9	12/10–12/31	
10/18–11/10	11/11–12/4	12/5–12/28	12/29–12/31	1/1–1/4	1/5–2/2
8/9–9/7	9/8–12/31		1/1–1/21	1/22–2/14	2/15–3/10
9/18–10/11	1/1–1/7	1/8–2/5	2/6–3/4	3/5–3/29	3/30–4/23
	10/12–11/5	11/6–11/29	11/30–12/23	12/24–12/31	
	11/25–12/18	12/19–12/31		1/1–1/16	1/17–2/10
10/31–11/24					
8/20–9/13	9/14–10/8	1/1–1/12	1/13–2/4	2/5–2/28	3/1–3/24
		10/9–11/5	11/6–12/7	12/8–12/31	
			1/30–2/28	1/1–1/29	
10/3–10/26	10/27–11/19	11/20–12/13	12/14–12/31	3/1–4/6	4/7–5/4
			1/1–1/6	1/7–1/30	1/31–2/23
11/10–12/7	12/8–12/31				

VENUS SIGNS 1901–2002

	Aries	Taurus	Gemini	Cancer	Leo	Virgo
1976	4/8–5/2	5/2–5/27	5/27–6/20	6/20–7/14	7/14–8/8	8/8–9/1
1977	2/2–6/6	6/6–7/6	7/6–8/2	8/2–8/28	8/28–9/22	9/22–10/17
1978	3/9–4/2	4/2–4/27	4/27–5/22	5/22–6/16	6/16–7/12	7/12–8/6
1979	4/23–5/18	5/18–6/11	6/11–7/6	7/6–7/30	7/30–8/24	8/24–9/17
1980	2/9–3/6	3/6–4/3	4/3–5/12 6/5–8/6	5/12–6/5 8/6–9/7	9/7–10/4	10/4–10/30
1981	3/24–4/17	4/17–5/11	5/11–6/5	6/5–6/29	6/29–7/24	7/24–8/18
1982	5/4–5/30	5/30–6/25	6/25–7/20	7/20–8/14	8/14–9/7	9/7–10/2
1983	2/22–3/19	3/19–4/13	4/13–5/9	5/9–6/6	6/6–7/10 8/27–10/5	7/10–8/27 10/5–11/9
1984	4/7–5/2	5/2–5/26	5/26–6/20	6/20–7/14	7/14–8/7	8/7–9/1
1985	2/2–6/6	6/7–7/6	7/6–8/2	8/2–8/28	8/28–9/22	9/22–10/16
1986	3/9–4/2	4/2–4/26	4/26–5/21	5/21–6/15	6/15–7/11	7/11–8/7
1987	4/22–5/17	5/17–6/11	6/11–7/5	7/5–7/30	7/30–8/23	8/23–9/16
1988	2/9–3/6	3/6–4/3	4/3–5/17 5/27–8/6	5/17–5/27 8/28–9/22	9/7–10/4 9/22–10/16	10/4–10/29
1989	3/23–4/16	4/16–5/11	5/11–6/4	6/4–6/29	6/29–7/24	7/24–8/18
1990	5/4–5/30	5/30–6/25	6/25–7/20	7/20–8/13	8/13–9/7	9/7–10/1
1991	2/22–3/18	3/18–4/13	4/13–5/9	5/9–6/6	6/6–7/11 8/21–10/6	7/11–8/21 10/6–11/9
1992	4/7–5/1	5/1–5/26	5/26–6/19	6/19–7/13	7/13–8/7	8/7–8/31
1993	2/2–6/6	6/6–7/6	7/6–8/1	8/1–8/27	8/27–9/21	9/21–10/16
1994	3/8–4/1	4/1–4/26	4/26–5/21	5/21–6/15	6/15–7/11	7/11–8/7
1995	4/22–5/16	5/16–6/10	6/10–7/5	7/5–7/29	7/29–8/23	8/23–9/16
1996	2/9–3/6	3/6–4/3	4/3–8/7	8/7–9/7	9/7–10/4	10/4–10/29
1997	3/23–4/16	4/16–5/10	5/10–6/4	6/4–6/28	6/28–7/23	7/23–8/17
1998	5/3–5/29	5/29–6/24	6/24–7/19	7/19–8/13	8/13–9/6	9/6–9/30
1999	2/21–3/18	3/18–4/12	4/12–5/8	5/8–6/5	6/5–7/12 8/15–10/7	7/12–8/15 10/7–11/9
2000	4/6–5/1	5/1–5/25	5/25–6/13	6/13–7/13	7/13–8/6	8/6–8/31
2001	2/2–6/6	6/6–7/5	7/5–8/1	8/1–8/26	8/26–9/20	9/20–10/15
2002	3/7–4/1	4/1–4/25	4/25–5/20	5/20–6/14	6/14–7/10	7/10–8/7

Libra	Scorpio	Sagittarius	Capricorn	Aquarius	Pisces
9/1–9/26	9/26–10/20	1/1–1/26	1/26–2/19	2/19–3/15	3/15–4/8
		10/20–11/14	11/14–12/8	12/9–1/4	
10/17–11/10	11/10–12/4	12/4–12/27	12/27–1/20/78		1/4–2/2
8/6–9/7	9/7–1/7			1/20–2/13	2/13–3/9
9/17–10/11	10/11–11/4	1/7–2/5	2/5–3/3	3/3–3/29	3/29–4/23
		11/4–11/28	11/28–12/22	12/22–1/16/80	
10/30–11/24	11/24–12/18	12/18–1/11/81			1/16–2/9
8/18–9/12	9/12–10/9	10/9–11/5	1/11–2/4	2/4–2/28	2/28–3/24
			11/5–12/8	12/8–1/23/82	
10/2–10/26	10/26–11/18	11/18–12/12	1/23–3/2	3/2–4/6	4/6–5/4
			12/12–1/5/83		
11/9–12/6	12/6–1/1/84			1/5–1/29	1/29–2/22
9/1–9/25	9/25–10/20	1/1–1/25	1/25–2/19	2/19–3/14	3/14–4/7
		10/20–11/13	11/13–12/9	12/10–1/4	
10/16–11/9	11/9–12/3	12/3–12/27	12/28–1/19		1/4–2/2
8/7–9/7	9/7–1/7			1/20–2/13	2/13–3/9
9/16–10/10	10/10–11/3	1/7–2/5	2/5–3/3	3/3–3/28	3/28–4/22
		11/3–11/28	11/28–12/22	12/22–1/15	
10/29–11/23	11/23–12/17	12/17–1/10			1/15–2/9
8/18–9/12	9/12–10/8	10/8–11/5	1/10–2/3	2/3–2/27	2/27–3/23
			11/5–12/10	12/10–1/16/90	
10/1–10/25	10/25–11/18	11/18–12/12	1/16–3/3	3/3–4/6	4/6–5/4
			12/12–1/5		
11/9–12/6	12/6–12/31	12/31–1/25/92		1/5–1/29	1/29–2/22
8/31–9/25	9/25–10/19	10/19–11/13	1/25–2/18	2/18–3/13	3/13–4/7
			11/13–12/8	12/8–1/3/93	
10/16–11/9	11/9–12/2	12/2–12/26	12/26–1/19		1/3–2/2
8/7–9/7	9/7–1/7			1/19–2/12	2/12–3/8
9/16–10/10	10/10–11/13	1/7–2/4	2/4–3/2	3/2–3/28	3/28–4/22
		11/3–11/27	11/27–12/21	12/21–1/15	
10/29–11/23	11/23–12/17	12/17–1/10/97			1/15–2/9
8/17–9/12	9/12–10/8	10/8–11/5	1/10–2/3	2/3–2/27	2/27–3/23
			11/5–12/12	12/12–1/9	
9/30–10/24	10/24–11/17	11/17–12/11	1/9–3/4	3/4–4/6	4/6–5/3
11/9–12/5	12/5–12/31	12/31–1/24		1/4–1/28	1/28–2/21
8/31–9/24	9/24–10/19	10/19–11/13	1/24–2/18	2/18–3/12	3/13–4/6
			11/13–12/8	12/8	
10/15–11/8	11/8–12/2	12/2–12/26	12/26/01–	12/8/00–	1/3–2/2
			1/19/02	1/3/01	
8/7–9/7	9/7–1/7/03		1/26/01–1/18	1/18–2/11	2/11–3/7

How to Use the Mars, Jupiter, and Saturn Tables

Find the year of your birth on the left side of each column. The dates when the planet entered each sign are listed on the right side of each column. (Signs are abbreviated to three letters.) Your birthday should fall on or between each date listed, and your planetary placement should correspond to the earlier sign of that period.

MARS SIGNS 1901–2002

Year	Month	Day	Sign	Year	Month	Day	Sign
1901	MAR	1	Leo	1905	JAN	13	Scp
	MAY	11	Vir		AUG	21	Sag
	JUL	13	Lib		OCT	8	Cap
	AUG	31	Scp		NOV	18	Aqu
	OCT	14	Sag		DEC	27	Pic
	NOV	24	Cap	1906	FEB	4	Ari
1902	JAN	1	Aqu		MAR	17	Tau
	FEB	8	Pic		APR	28	Gem
	MAR	19	Ari		JUN	11	Can
	APR	27	Tau		JUL	27	Leo
	JUN	7	Gem		SEP	12	Vir
	JUL	20	Can		OCT	30	Lib
	SEP	4	Leo		DEC	17	Scp
	OCT	23	Vir	1907	FEB	5	Sag
	DEC	20	Lib		APR	1	Cap
1903	APR	19	Vir		OCT	13	Aqu
	MAY	30	Lib		NOV	29	Pic
	AUG	6	Scp	1908	JAN	11	Ari
	SEP	22	Sag		FEB	23	Tau
	NOV	3	Cap		APR	7	Gem
	DEC	12	Aqu		MAY	22	Can
1904	JAN	19	Pic		JUL	8	Leo
	FEB	27	Ari		AUG	24	Vir
	APR	6	Tau		OCT	10	Lib
	MAY	18	Gem		NOV	25	Scp
	JUN	30	Can	1909	JAN	10	Sag
	AUG	15	Leo		FEB	24	Cap
	OCT	1	Vir		APR	9	Aqu
	NOV	20	Lib		MAY	25	Pic

	JUL	21	Ari		AUG	19	Can
	SEP	26	Pic		OCT	7	Leo
	NOV	20	Ari	1916	MAY	28	Vir
1910	JAN	23	Tau		JUL	23	Lib
	MAR	14	Gem		SEP	8	Scp
	MAY	1	Can		OCT	22	Sag
	JUN	19	Leo		DEC	1	Cap
	AUG	6	Vir	1917	JAN	9	Aqu
	SEP	22	Lib		FEB	16	Pic
	NOV	6	Scp		MAR	26	Ari
	DEC	20	Sag		MAY	4	Tau
1911	JAN	31	Cap		JUN	14	Gem
	MAR	14	Aqu		JUL	28	Can
	APR	23	Pic		SEP	12	Leo
	JUN	2	Ari		NOV	2	Vir
	JUL	15	Tau	1918	JAN	11	Lib
	SEP	5	Gem		FEB	25	Vir
	NOV	30	Tau		JUN	23	Lib
1912	JAN	30	Gem		AUG	17	Scp
	APR	5	Can		OCT	1	Sag
	MAY	28	Leo		NOV	11	Cap
	JUL	17	Vir		DEC	20	Aqu
	SEP	2	Lib	1919	JAN	27	Pic
	OCT	18	Scp		MAR	6	Ari
	NOV	30	Sag		APR	15	Tau
1913	JAN	10	Cap		MAY	26	Gem
	FEB	19	Aqu		JUL	8	Can
	MAR	30	Pic		AUG	23	Leo
	MAY	8	Ari		OCT	10	Vir
	JUN	17	Tau		NOV	30	Lib
	JUL	29	Gem	1920	JAN	31	Scp
	SEP	15	Can		APR	23	Lib
1914	MAY	1	Leo		JUL	10	Scp
	JUN	26	Vir		SEP	4	Sag
	AUG	14	Lib		OCT	18	Cap
	SEP	29	Scp		NOV	27	Aqu
	NOV	11	Sag	1921	JAN	5	Pic
	DEC	22	Cap		FEB	13	Ari
1915	JAN	30	Aqu		MAR	25	Tau
	MAR	9	Pic		MAY	6	Gem
	APR	16	Ari		JUN	18	Can
	MAY	26	Tau		AUG	3	Leo
	JUL	6	Gem		SEP	19	Vir

	NOV	6	Lib		APR	7	Pic
	DEC	26	Scp		MAY	16	Ari
1922	FEB	18	Sag		JUN	26	Tau
	SEP	13	Cap		AUG	9	Gem
	OCT	30	Aqu		OCT	3	Can
	DEC	11	Pic		DEC	20	Gem
1923	JAN	21	Ari	1929	MAR	10	Can
	MAR	4	Tau		MAY	13	Leo
	APR	16	Gem		JUL	4	Vir
	MAY	30	Can		AUG	21	Lib
	JUL	16	Leo		OCT	6	Scp
	SEP	1	Vir		NOV	18	Sag
	OCT	18	Lib		DEC	29	Cap
	DEC	4	Scp	1930	FEB	6	Aqu
1924	JAN	19	Sag		MAR	17	Pic
	MAR	6	Cap		APR	24	Ari
	APR	24	Aqu		JUN	3	Tau
	JUN	24	Pic		JUL	14	Gem
	AUG	24	Aqu		AUG	28	Can
	OCT	19	Pic		OCT	20	Leo
	DEC	19	Ari	1931	FEB	16	Can
1925	FEB	5	Tau		MAR	30	Leo
	MAR	24	Gem		JUN	10	Vir
	MAY	9	Can		AUG	1	Lib
	JUN	26	Leo		SEP	17	Scp
	AUG	12	Vir		OCT	30	Sag
	SEP	28	Lib		DEC	10	Cap
	NOV	13	Scp	1932	JAN	18	Aqu
	DEC	28	Sag		FEB	25	Pic
1926	FEB	9	Cap		APR	3	Ari
	MAR	23	Aqu		MAY	12	Tau
	MAY	3	Pic		JUN	22	Gem
	JUN	15	Ari		AUG	4	Can
	AUG	1	Tau		SEP	20	Leo
1927	FEB	22	Gem		NOV	13	Vir
	APR	17	Can	1933	JUL	6	Lib
	JUN	6	Leo		AUG	26	Scp
	JUL	25	Vir		OCT	9	Sag
	SEP	10	Lib		NOV	19	Cap
	OCT	26	Scp		DEC	28	Aqu
	DEC	8	Sag	1934	FEB	4	Pic
1928	JAN	19	Cap		MAR	14	Ari
	FEB	28	Aqu		APR	22	Tau

	JUN	2	Gem		AUG	19	Vir
	JUL	15	Can		OCT	5	Lib
	AUG	30	Leo		NOV	20	Scp
	OCT	18	Vir	1941	JAN	4	Sag
	DEC	11	Lib		FEB	17	Cap
1935	JUL	29	Scp		APR	2	Aqu
	SEP	16	Sag		MAY	16	Pic
	OCT	28	Cap		JUL	2	Ari
	DEC	7	Aqu	1942	JAN	11	Tau
1936	JAN	14	Pic		MAR	7	Gem
	FEB	22	Ari		APR	26	Can
	APR	1	Tau		JUN	14	Leo
	MAY	13	Gem		AUG	1	Vir
	JUN	25	Can		SEP	17	Lib
	AUG	10	Leo		NOV	1	Scp
	SEP	26	Vir		DEC	15	Sag
	NOV	14	Lib	1943	JAN	26	Cap
1937	JAN	5	Scp		MAR	8	Aqu
	MAR	13	Sag		APR	17	Pic
	MAY	14	Scp		MAY	27	Ari
	AUG	8	Sag		JUL	7	Tau
	SEP	30	Cap		AUG	23	Gem
	NOV	11	Aqu	1944	MAR	28	Can
	DEC	21	Pic		MAY	22	Leo
1938	JAN	30	Ari		JUL	12	Vir
	MAR	12	Tau		AUG	29	Lib
	APR	23	Gem		OCT	13	Scp
	JUN	7	Can		NOV	25	Sag
	JUL	22	Leo	1945	JAN	5	Cap
	SEP	7	Vir		FEB	14	Aqu
	OCT	25	Lib		MAR	25	Pic
	DEC	11	Scp		MAY	2	Ari
1939	JAN	29	Sag		JUN	11	Tau
	MAR	21	Cap		JUL	23	Gem
	MAY	25	Aqu		SEP	7	Can
	JUL	21	Cap		NOV	11	Leo
	SEP	24	Aqu		DEC	26	Can
	NOV	19	Pic	1946	APR	22	Leo
1940	JAN	4	Ari		JUN	20	Vir
	FEB	17	Tau		AUG	9	Lib
	APR	1	Gem		SEP	24	Scp
	MAY	17	Can		NOV	6	Sag
	JUL	3	Leo		DEC	17	Cap

1947	JAN	25	Aqu		MAR	20	Tau
	MAR	4	Pic		MAY	1	Gem
	APR	11	Ari		JUN	14	Can
	MAY	21	Tau		JUL	29	Leo
	JUL	1	Gem		SEP	14	Vir
	AUG	13	Can		NOV	1	Lib
	OCT	1	Leo		DEC	20	Scp
	DEC	1	Vir	1954	FEB	9	Sag
1948	FEB	12	Leo		APR	12	Cap
	MAY	18	Vir		JUL	3	Sag
	JUL	17	Lib		AUG	24	Cap
	SEP	3	Scp		OCT	21	Aqu
	OCT	17	Sag		DEC	4	Pic
	NOV	26	Cap	1955	JAN	15	Ari
1949	JAN	4	Aqu		FEB	26	Tau
	FEB	11	Pic		APR	10	Gem
	MAR	21	Ari		MAY	26	Can
	APR	30	Tau		JUL	11	Leo
	JUN	10	Gem		AUG	27	Vir
	JUL	23	Can		OCT	13	Lib
	SEP	7	Leo		NOV	29	Scp
	OCT	27	Vir	1956	JAN	14	Sag
	DEC	26	Lib		FEB	28	Cap
1950	MAR	28	Vir		APR	14	Aqu
	JUN	11	Lib		JUN	3	Pic
	AUG	10	Scp		DEC	6	Ari
	SEP	25	Sag	1957	JAN	28	Tau
	NOV	6	Cap		MAR	17	Gem
	DEC	15	Aqu		MAY	4	Can
1951	JAN	22	Pic		JUN	21	Leo
	MAR	1	Ari		AUG	8	Vir
	APR	10	Tau		SEP	24	Lib
	MAY	21	Gem		NOV	8	Scp
	JUL	3	Can		DEC	23	Sag
	AUG	18	Leo	1958	FEB	3	Cap
	OCT	5	Vir		MAR	17	Aqu
	NOV	24	Lib		APR	27	Pic
1952	JAN	20	Scp		JUN	7	Ari
	AUG	27	Sag		JUL	21	Tau
	OCT	12	Cap		SEP	21	Gem
	NOV	21	Aqu		OCT	29	Tau
	DEC	30	Pic	1959	FEB	10	Gem
1953	FEB	8	Ari		APR	10	Can

	JUN	1	Leo		NOV	14	Cap
	JUL	20	Vir		DEC	23	Aqu
	SEP	5	Lib	1966	JAN	30	Pic
	OCT	21	Scp		MAR	9	Ari
	DEC	3	Sag		APR	17	Tau
1960	JAN	14	Cap		MAY	28	Gem
	FEB	23	Aqu		JUL	11	Can
	APR	2	Pic		AUG	25	Leo
	MAY	11	Ari		OCT	12	Vir
	JUN	20	Tau		DEC	4	Lib
	AUG	2	Gem	1967	FEB	12	Scp
	SEP	21	Can		MAR	31	Lib
1961	FEB	5	Gem		JUL	19	Scp
	FEB	7	Can		SEP	10	Sag
	MAY	6	Leo		OCT	23	Cap
	JUN	28	Vir		DEC	1	Aqu
	AUG	17	Lib	1968	JAN	9	Pic
	OCT	1	Scp		FEB	17	Ari
	NOV	13	Sag		MAR	27	Tau
	DEC	24	Cap		MAY	8	Gem
1962	FEB	1	Aqu		JUN	21	Can
	MAR	12	Pic		AUG	5	Leo
	APR	19	Ari		SEP	21	Vir
	MAY	28	Tau		NOV	9	Lib
	JUL	9	Gem		DEC	29	Scp
	AUG	22	Can	1969	FEB	25	Sag
	OCT	11	Leo		SEP	21	Cap
1963	JUN	3	Vir		NOV	4	Aqu
	JUL	27	Lib		DEC	15	Pic
	SEP	12	Scp	1970	JAN	24	Ari
	OCT	25	Sag		MAR	7	Tau
	DEC	5	Cap		APR	18	Gem
1964	JAN	13	Aqu		JUN	2	Can
	FEB	20	Pic		JUL	18	Leo
	MAR	29	Ari		SEP	3	Vir
	MAY	7	Tau		OCT	20	Lib
	JUN	17	Gem		DEC	6	Scp
	JUL	30	Can	1971	JAN	23	Sag
	SEP	15	Leo		MAR	12	Cap
	NOV	6	Vir		MAY	3	Aqu
1965	JUN	29	Lib		NOV	6	Pic
	AUG	20	Scp		DEC	26	Ari
	OCT	4	Sag	1972	FEB	10	Tau

	MAR	27	Gem	1978	JAN	26	Can
	MAY	12	Can		APR	10	Leo
	JUN	28	Leo		JUN	14	Vir
	AUG	15	Vir		AUG	4	Lib
	SEP	30	Lib		SEP	19	Scp
	NOV	15	Scp		NOV	2	Sag
	DEC	30	Sag		DEC	12	Cap
1973	FEB	12	Cap	1979	JAN	20	Aqu
	MAR	26	Aqu		FEB	27	Pic
	MAY	8	Pic		APR	7	Ari
	JUN	20	Ari		MAY	16	Tau
	AUG	12	Tau		JUN	26	Gem
	OCT	29	Ari		AUG	8	Can
	DEC	24	Tau		SEP	24	Leo
1974	FEB	27	Gem		NOV	19	Vir
	APR	20	Can	1980	MAR	11	Leo
	JUN	9	Leo		MAY	4	Vir
	JUL	27	Vir		JUL	10	Lib
	SEP	12	Lib		AUG	29	Scp
	OCT	28	Scp		OCT	12	Sag
	DEC	10	Sag		NOV	22	Cap
1975	JAN	21	Cap		DEC	30	Aqu
	MAR	3	Aqu	1981	FEB	6	Pic
	APR	11	Pic		MAR	17	Ari
	MAY	21	Ari		APR	25	Tau
	JUL	1	Tau		JUN	5	Gem
	AUG	14	Gem		JUL	18	Can
	OCT	17	Can		SEP	2	Leo
	NOV	25	Gem		OCT	21	Vir
1976	MAR	18	Can		DEC	16	Lib
	MAY	16	Leo	1982	AUG	3	Scp
	JUL	6	Vir		SEP	20	Sag
	AUG	24	Lib		OCT	31	Cap
	OCT	8	Scp		DEC	10	Aqu
	NOV	20	Sag	1983	JAN	17	Pic
1977	JAN	1	Cap		FEB	25	Ari
	FEB	9	Aqu		APR	5	Tau
	MAR	20	Pic		MAY	16	Gem
	APR	27	Ari		JUN	29	Can
	JUN	6	Tau		AUG	13	Leo
	JUL	17	Gem		SEP	30	Vir
	SEP	1	Can		NOV	18	Lib
	OCT	26	Leo	1984	JAN	11	Scp

	AUG	17	Sag		JUL	12	Tau
	OCT	5	Cap		AUG	31	Gem
	NOV	15	Aqu		DEC	14	Tau
	DEC	25	Pic	1991	JAN	21	Gem
1985	FEB	2	Ari		APR	3	Can
	MAR	15	Tau		MAY	26	Leo
	APR	26	Gem		JUL	15	Vir
	JUN	9	Can		SEP	1	Lib
	JUL	25	Leo		OCT	16	Scp
	SEP	10	Vir		NOV	29	Sag
	OCT	27	Lib	1992	JAN	9	Cap
	DEC	14	Scp		FEB	18	Aqu
1986	FEB	2	Sag		MAR	28	Pic
	MAR	28	Cap		MAY	5	Ari
	OCT	9	Aqu		JUN	14	Tau
	NOV	26	Pic		JUL	26	Gem
1987	JAN	8	Ari		SEP	12	Can
	FEB	20	Tau	1993	APR	27	Leo
	APR	5	Gem		JUN	23	Vir
	MAY	21	Can		AUG	12	Lib
	JUL	6	Leo		SEP	27	Scp
	AUG	22	Vir		NOV	9	Sag
	OCT	8	Lib		DEC	20	Cap
	NOV	24	Scp	1994	JAN	28	Aqu
1988	JAN	8	Sag		MAR	7	Pic
	FEB	22	Cap		APR	14	Ari
	APR	6	Aqu		MAY	23	Tau
	MAY	22	Pic		JUL	3	Gem
	JUL	13	Ari		AUG	16	Can
	OCT	23	Pic		OCT	4	Leo
	NOV	1	Ari		DEC	12	Vir
1989	JAN	19	Tau	1995	JAN	22	Leo
	MAR	11	Gem		MAY	25	Vir
	APR	29	Can		JUL	21	Lib
	JUN	16	Leo		SEP	7	Scp
	AUG	3	Vir		OCT	20	Sag
	SEP	19	Lib		NOV	30	Cap
	NOV	4	Scp	1996	JAN	8	Aqu
	DEC	18	Sag		FEB	15	Pic
1990	JAN	29	Cap		MAR	24	Ari
	MAR	11	Aqu		MAY	2	Tau
	APR	20	Pic		JUN	12	Gem
	MAY	31	Ari		JUL	25	Can

	SEP	9	Leo		NOV	26	Aqu
	OCT	30	Vir	2000	JAN	4	Pic
1997	JAN	3	Lib		FEB	12	Ari
	MAR	8	Vir		MAR	23	Tau
	JUN	19	Lib		MAY	3	Gem
	AUG	14	Scp		JUN	16	Can
	SEP	28	Sag		AUG	1	Leo
	NOV	9	Cap		SEP	17	Vir
	DEC	18	Aqu		NOV	4	Lib
1998	JAN	25	Pic		DEC	23	Scp
	MAR	4	Ari	2001	FEB	14	Sag
	APR	13	Tau		SEP	8	Cap
	MAY	24	Gem		OCT	27	Aqu
	JUL	6	Can		DEC	8	Pic
	AUG	20	Leo	2002	JAN	18	Ari
	OCT	7	Vir		MAR	1	Tau
	NOV	27	Lib		APR	13	Gem
1999	JAN	26	Scp		MAY	28	Can
	MAY	5	Lib		JUL	13	Leo
	JUL	5	Scp		AUG	29	Vir
	SEP	2	Sag		OCT	15	Lib
	OCT	17	Cap		DEC	1	Scp

JUPITER SIGNS 1901–2002

1901	JAN	19	Cap	1911	DEC	10	Sag
1902	FEB	6	Aqu	1913	JAN	2	Cap
1903	FEB	20	Pic	1914	JAN	21	Aqu
1904	MAR	1	Ari	1915	FEB	4	Pic
	AUG	8	Tau	1916	FEB	12	Ari
	AUG	31	Ari		JUN	26	Tau
1905	MAR	7	Tau		OCT	26	Ari
	JUL	21	Gem	1917	FEB	12	Tau
	DEC	4	Tau		JUN	29	Gem
1906	MAR	9	Gem	1918	JUL	13	Can
	JUL	30	Can	1919	AUG	2	Leo
1907	AUG	18	Leo	1920	AUG	27	Vir
1908	SEP	12	Vir	1921	SEP	25	Lib
1909	OCT	11	Lib	1922	OCT	26	Scp
1910	NOV	11	Scp	1923	NOV	24	Sag

Year	Month	Day	Sign
1924	DEC	18	Cap
1926	JAN	6	Aqu
1927	JAN	18	Pic
	JUN	6	Ari
	SEP	11	Pic
1928	JAN	23	Ari
	JUN	4	Tau
1929	JUN	12	Gem
1930	JUN	26	Can
1931	JUL	17	Leo
1932	AUG	11	Vir
1933	SEP	10	Lib
1934	OCT	11	Scp
1935	NOV	9	Sag
1936	DEC	2	Cap
1937	DEC	20	Aqu
1938	MAY	14	Pic
	JUL	30	Aqu
	DEC	29	Pic
1939	MAY	11	Ari
	OCT	30	Pic
	DEC	20	Ari
1940	MAY	16	Tau
1941	MAY	26	Gem
1942	JUN	10	Can
1943	JUN	30	Leo
1944	JUL	26	Vir
1945	AUG	25	Lib
1946	SEP	25	Scp
1947	OCT	24	Sag
1948	NOV	15	Cap
1949	APR	12	Aqu
	JUN	27	Cap
	NOV	30	Aqu
1950	APR	15	Pic
	SEP	15	Aqu
	DEC	1	Pic
1951	APR	21	Ari
1952	APR	28	Tau
1953	MAY	9	Gem
1954	MAY	24	Can
1955	JUN	13	Leo
	NOV	17	Vir
1956	JAN	18	Leo
	JUL	7	Vir
	DEC	13	Lib
1957	FEB	19	Vir
	AUG	7	Lib
1958	JAN	13	Scp
	MAR	20	Lib
	SEP	7	Scp
1959	FEB	10	Sag
	APR	24	Scp
	OCT	5	Sag
1960	MAR	1	Cap
	JUN	10	Sag
	OCT	26	Cap
1961	MAR	15	Aqu
	AUG	12	Cap
	NOV	4	Aqu
1962	MAR	25	Pic
1963	APR	4	Ari
1964	APR	12	Tau
1965	APR	22	Gem
	SEP	21	Can
	NOV	17	Gem
1966	MAY	5	Can
	SEP	27	Leo
1967	JAN	16	Can
	MAY	23	Leo
	OCT	19	Vir
1968	FEB	27	Leo
	JUN	15	Vir
	NOV	15	Lib
1969	MAR	30	Vir
	JUL	15	Lib
	DEC	16	Scp
1970	APR	30	Lib
	AUG	15	Scp
1971	JAN	14	Sag
	JUN	5	Scp
	SEP	11	Sag

1972	FEB	6	Cap	1986	FEB	20	Pic
	JUL	24	Sag	1987	MAR	2	Ari
	SEP	25	Cap	1988	MAR	8	Tau
1973	FEB	23	Aqu		JUL	22	Gem
1974	MAR	8	Pic		NOV	30	Tau
1975	MAR	18	Ari	1989	MAR	11	Gem
1976	MAR	26	Tau		JUL	30	Can
	AUG	23	Gem	1990	AUG	18	Leo
	OCT	16	Tau	1991	SEP	12	Vir
1977	APR	3	Gem	1992	OCT	10	Lib
	AUG	20	Can	1993	NOV	10	Scp
	DEC	30	Gem	1994	DEC	9	Sag
1978	APR	12	Can	1996	JAN	3	Cap
	SEP	5	Leo	1997	JAN	21	Aqu
1979	FEB	28	Can	1998	FEB	4	Pic
	APR	20	Leo	1999	FEB	13	Ari
	SEP	29	Vir		JUN	28	Tau
1980	OCT	27	Lib		OCT	23	Ari
1981	NOV	27	Scp	2000	FEB	14	Tau
1982	DEC	26	Sag		JUN	30	Gem
1984	JAN	19	Cap	2001	JUL	14	Can
1985	FEB	6	Aqu				

SATURN SIGNS 1903–2002

1903	JAN	19	Aqu	1916	OCT	17	Leo
1905	APR	13	Pic		DEC	7	Can
	AUG	17	Aqu	1917	JUN	24	Leo
1906	JAN	8	Pic	1919	AUG	12	Vir
1908	MAR	19	Ari	1921	OCT	7	Lib
1910	MAY	17	Tau	1923	DEC	20	Scp
	DEC	14	Ari	1924	APR	6	Lib
1911	JAN	20	Tau		SEP	13	Scp
1912	JUL	7	Gem	1926	DEC	2	Sag
	NOV	30	Tau	1929	MAR	15	Cap
1913	MAR	26	Gem		MAY	5	Sag
1914	AUG	24	Can		NOV	30	Cap
	DEC	7	Gem	1932	FEB	24	Aqu
1915	MAY	11	Can		AUG	13	Cap

	NOV	20	Aqu		FEB	21	Gem
1935	FEB	14	Pic	1973	AUG	1	Can
1937	APR	25	Ari	1974	JAN	7	Gem
	OCT	18	Pic		APR	18	Can
1938	JAN	14	Ari	1975	SEP	17	Leo
1939	JUL	6	Tau	1976	JAN	14	Can
	SEP	22	Ari				
1940	MAR	20	Tau		JUN	5	Leo
1942	MAY	8	Gem	1977	NOV	17	Vir
1944	JUN	20	Can	1978	JAN	5	Leo
1946	AUG	2	Leo		JUL	26	Vir
1948	SEP	19	Vir	1980	SEP	21	Lib
1949	APR	3	Leo	1982	NOV	29	Scp
	MAY	29	Vir	1983	MAY	6	Lib
1950	NOV	20	Lib		AUG	24	Scp
1951	MAR	7	Vir	1985	NOV	17	Sag
	AUG	13	Lib	1988	FEB	13	Cap
1953	OCT	22	Scp		JUN	10	Sag
1956	JAN	12	Sag		NOV	12	Cap
	MAY	14	Scp	1991	FEB	6	Aqu
	OCT	10	Sag	1993	MAY	21	Pic
1959	JAN	5	Cap		JUN	30	Aqu
1962	JAN	3	Aqu	1994	JAN	28	Pic
1964	MAR	24	Pic	1996	APR	7	Ari
	SEP	16	Aqu	1998	JUN	9	Tau
	DEC	16	Pic		OCT	25	Ari
1967	MAR	3	Ari	1999	MAR	1	Tau
1969	APR	29	Tau	2000	AUG	10	Gem
1971	JUN	18	Gem		OCT	16	Tau
1972	JAN	10	Tau	2001	APR	21	Gem

CHAPTER 4

Crack the Astrology Code—Decipher Those Mysterious Glyphs on Your Chart

The first time you look at a horoscope, you'll realize that astrology has a code all its own, written in strange-looking characters which represent the planets and signs. These symbols, or *glyphs,* are used by astrologers worldwide and by computer astrology programs. So, if you want to progress in astrology enough to read a horoscope, there's no way around it . . . you've got to know the meaning of the glyphs.

Besides enabling you to read a horoscope chart, learning the astrology code can help you interpret the meaning of the signs and planets, because each glyph contains a minilesson in what its planet or sign represents. And since there are only twelve signs and ten planets (not counting a few asteroids and other space creatures some astrologers use), they're a lot easier to learn than, say, Chinese!

Here's a code cracker for the glyphs, beginning with the glyphs for the planets. To those who already know their glyphs, don't just skim over the chapter! There are hidden meanings to discover, so test your glyphese.

The Glyphs for the Planets

The glyphs for the planets are easy to learn. They're simple combinations of the most basic visual elements: the circle, the semicircle or arc, and the cross. However, each component of a glyph has a special meaning in relation to the others, which adds up to create the total meaning of the symbol.

The circle, which has no beginning or end, is one of the oldest symbols of spirit or spiritual forces. All of the early diagrams of the heavens—spiritual territory—are shown in circular form. The never-ending line of the circle is the perfect symbol for eternity. The semicircle or arc is an incomplete circle, symbolizing the receptive, finite soul, which contains spiritual potential in the curving line.

The vertical line of the cross symbolizes movement from heaven to earth. The horizontal line describes temporal movement, here and now, in time and space. Combined in a cross, the vertical and horizontal planes symbolize manifestation in the material world.

The Sun Glyph ☉

The sun is always shown by this powerful solar symbol, a circle with a point in the center. The center point is you, your spiritual center, and the symbol represents your infinite personality incarnating (the point) into the finite cycles of birth and death.

The sun has been represented by a circle or disk since ancient Egyptian times, when the solar disk represented the sun god, Ra. Some archaeologists believe the great stone circles found in England were centers of sun worship. This particular version of the symbol was brought into common use in the sixteenth century, after German occultist and scholar Cornelius Agrippa (1486–1535) wrote a book called *Die Occulta Philosophia,* which became accepted as the standard work in its field. Agrippa collected many medieval astrological and magical symbols in this book, which have been used by astrologers since then.

The Moon Glyph ☽

The moon glyph is the most recognizable symbol on a chart, a left-facing arc stylized into the crescent moon. As part of a circle, the arc symbolizes the potential fulfillment of the entire circle, the life force that is still incomplete. Therefore, it is the ideal representation of the reactive, receptive, emotional nature of the moon.

The Mercury Glyph ☿

Mercury contains all three elemental symbols, the crescent, the circle, and the cross in vertical order. This is the "Venus with a hat" glyph (compare with the symbol of Venus). With another stretch of the imagination, can't you see the winged cap of Mercury the messenger? Think of the upturned crescent as antennae that tune in and transmit messages from the sun, reminding you that Mercury is the way you communicate, the way your mind works. The upturned arc is receiving energy into the spirit or solar circle, which will later be translated into action on the material plane, symbolized by the cross. All the elements are equally sized because Mercury is neutral; it doesn't play favorites! This planet symbolizes objective, detached, unemotional thinking.

The Venus Glyph ♀

Here the relationship is between two components, the circle or spirit and the cross of matter. Spirit is elevated over matter, pulling it upward. Venus asks, "What is beautiful? What do you like best? What do you love to have done to you?" Consequently,

Venus determines both your ideal of beauty and what feels good sensually. It governs your own allure and power to attract, as well as what attracts and pleases you.

The Mars Glyph ♂

In this glyph, the cross of matter is stylized into an arrowhead pointed up and outward, propelled by the circle of spirit. With a little imagination, you can visualize it as the shield and spear of Mars, the ancient god of war. You can deduce that Mars embodies your spiritual energy projected into the outer world. It's your assertiveness, your initiative, your aggressive drive, what you like to do to others, your temper. If you know someone's Mars, you know whether they'll blow up when angry or do a slow burn. Your task is to use your outgoing Mars energy wisely and well.

The Jupiter Glyph ♃

Jupiter is the basic cross of matter, with a large stylized crescent perched on the left side of the horizontal, temporal plane. You might think of the crescent as an open hand, because one meaning of Jupiter is "luck," what's handed to you. You don't work for what you get from Jupiter; it comes to you, if you're open to it.

The Jupiter glyph might also remind you of a jumbo jet plane with a huge tail fin, about to take off. This is the planet of travel, mental and spiritual, of expanding your horizons via new ideas, new spiritual dimensions, and new places. Jupiter embodies the optimism and enthusiasm of the traveler about to embark on an exciting adventure.

The Saturn Glyph ♄

Flip Jupiter over and you've got Saturn. (This might not be immediately apparent, because Saturn is usually stylized into an "h" form like the one shown here.) The principle it expresses is the opposite of Jupiter's expansive tendencies. Saturn pulls you back to earth—the receptive arc is pushed down underneath the cross of matter. Before there are any rewards or expansion, the duties and obligations of the material world must be considered. Saturn says, "Stop, wait, finish your chores before you take off!"

Saturn's glyph also resembles the scythe of old "Father Time." Saturn was first known as Chronos, the Greek god of time, for time brings all matter to an end. When it was the most distant planet (before the discovery of Uranus), Saturn was believed to be the place where time stopped. After the soul departed from Earth, it journeyed back to the outer reaches of the universe and finally stopped at Saturn, or at "the end of time."

The Uranus Glyph ♅

The glyph for Uranus is often stylized to form a capital "H" after Sir William Herschel, who discovered the planet. But the more esoteric version curves the two pillars of the H into crescent antennae, or "ears," like satellite disks receiving signals from space. These are perched on the horizontal material line of the cross (matter) and pushed from below by the circle of the spirit. To many sci-fi fans, Uranus looks like an orbiting satellite.

Uranus channels the highest energy of all, the white electrical light of the universal spiritual force which holds the cosmos together. This pure electrical energy is gathered from all over the universe. Because Uranian energy doesn't follow any ordinary celestial drumbeat, it can't be controlled or predicted (which is also true of those who are strongly influenced by this eccentric planet). In the symbol, this energy is manifested through the balance of polarities (the two opposite arms of the glyph) like the two polarized wires of a light bulb.

The Neptune Glyph ♆

Neptune's glyph is usually stylized to look like a trident, the weapon of the Roman god Neptune. However, on a more esoteric level, it shows the large, upturned crescent of the soul pierced through by the cross of matter. Neptune nails down, or materializes, soul energy, bringing impulses from the soul level into manifestation. That is why Neptune is associated with imagination or "imagining in," making an image of the soul. Neptune works through feeling, sensitivity, and a mystical capacity to bring the divine into the earthly realm.

The Pluto Glyph ♀

Pluto is written two ways. One is a composite of the letters PL, the first two letters of the word "Pluto" and coincidentally the initials of Percival Lowell, one of the planet's discoverers. The other, more esoteric symbol is a small circle above a large open crescent which surmounts the cross of matter. This depicts Pluto's power to regenerate—imagine a new little spirit emerging from the sheltering cup of the soul. Pluto rules the forces of life and death—after this planet has passed a sensitive point in your chart, you are transformed, reborn in some way.

Sci-fi fans might visualize this glyph as a small satellite (the circle) being launched. It was shortly after Pluto's discovery that we learned how to harness the nuclear forces that made space exploration possible. Pluto rules the transformative power of atomic energy, which totally changed our lives and from which there is no turning back.

The Glyphs for the Signs

On an astrological chart, the glyph for the sign will appear after that of the planet. For example, when you see the moon glyph followed first by a number and then by another glyph representing the sign, this means that the moon was passing over a certain degree of that astrological sign at the time of the chart. On the dividing lines between the segments or "houses" on your chart, you'll find the symbol for the sign that rules the house.

Because sun sign symbols do not contain the same basic geometric components of the planetary glyphs, we must look elsewhere for clues to their meanings. Many have been passed down from ancient Egyptian and Chaldean civilizations with few modifications. Others have been adapted over the centuries. In deciphering many of the glyphs, you'll often find that the symbols reveal a dual nature of the sign, which is not always apparent in the usual sun sign descriptions. For instance, the Gemini glyph is similar to the Roman numeral for two, and reveals this sign's longing to discover a twin soul. The Cancer glyph may be interpreted as resembling either the nurturing breasts or the self-protective claws of the crab, both symbols associated with the contrasting qualities of this sign. Libra's glyph embodies the duality of the spirit balanced with material reality. The Sagittarius glyph shows that the aspirant must also carry along the earthly animal nature in his quest. The Capricorn sea goat is another symbol with dual emphasis. The goat climbs high, yet is always pulled back by the deep waters of the unconscious. Aquarius embodies the double waves of mental detachment, balanced by the desire for connection with others in a friendly way. And finally, the two fishes of Pisces, which are forever tied together, show the duality of the soul and the spirit that must be reconciled.

The Aries Glyph ♈

Since the symbol for Aries is the ram, this glyph is obviously associated with a ram's horns, which characterize one aspect of the Aries personality—an aggressive, me-first, leaping-headfirst attitude. But the symbol can be interpreted in other ways as well. Some astrologers liken it to a fountain of energy, which Aries people also embody. The first sign of the zodiac bursts on the scene eagerly, ready to go. Another analogy is to the eyebrows and nose of the human head, which Aries rules, and the thinking power that is initiated in the brain.

One theory of this symbol links it to the Egyptian god Amun, represented by a ram in ancient times. As Amun-Ra, this god was believed to embody the creator of the universe, the leader of all the other gods. This relates easily to the position of Aries as the leader (or first sign) of the zodiac, which begins at the spring equinox, a time of the year when nature is renewed.

The Taurus Glyph ♉

This is another easy glyph to draw and identify. It takes little imagination to decipher the bull's head with long curving horns. Like the bull, the archetypal Taurus is slow to anger, but ferocious when provoked, as well as stubborn, steady, and sensual. Another association is the larynx (and thyroid) of the throat area (ruled by Taurus) and the eustachian tubes running up to the ears, which coincide with the relationship of Taurus to the voice, song, and music. Many famous singers, musicians, and composers have prominent Taurus influences.

Many ancient religions involved a bull as the central figure in fertility rites or initiations, usually symbolizing the victory of man over his animal nature. Another possible origin is in the sacred bull of Egypt, who embodied the incarnate form of Osiris, god of death and resurrection. In early Christian imagery, the Taurean bull represented St. Luke.

The Gemini Glyph ♊

The standard glyph immediately calls to mind the Roman numeral II and the "twins" symbol for Gemini. In almost all drawings and images used for this sign, the relationship between two persons is emphasized. Usually one twin will be touching the other, which signifies communication, human contact, and the desire to share.

The top line of the Gemini glyph indicates mental communication, while the bottom line indicates shared physical space.

The most famous Gemini legend is that of the twin sons, Castor and Pollux, one of whom had a mortal father, while the other was the son of Zeus, king of the gods. When it came time for the mortal twin to die, his grief-stricken brother pleaded with Zeus, who agreed to let them spend half the year on earth in mortal form and half in immortal life, with the gods on Mt. Olympus. This reflects a basic duality of humankind, which possesses an immortal soul, yet is also subject to the limits of mortality.

The Cancer Glyph ♋

Two convenient images relate to the Cancer glyph. It is easiest to decode the curving claws of the Cancer symbol, the crab. Like the crab, Cancer's element is water. This sensitive sign also has a hard protective shell to protect its tender interior. The crab must be wily to escape predators, scampering sideways and hiding under rocks. The crab also responds to the cycles of the moon, as do all shellfish. The other image is that of two female breasts, which Cancer rules, showing that this is a sign that nurtures and protects others as well as itself.

In ancient Egypt, Cancer was also represented by

the scarab beetle, a symbol of regeneration and eternal life.

The Leo Glyph ♌

Notice that the Leo glyph seems to be an extension of Cancer's glyph, with a significant difference. In the Cancer glyph, the lines curve inward protectively, while the Leo glyph expresses energy outwardly and there is no duality in the symbol (or in Leo).

Lions have belonged to the sign of Leo since earliest times, and it is not difficult to imagine the king of beasts with his sweeping mane and curling tail from this glyph. The upward sweep of the glyph easily describes the positive energy of Leos: the flourishing tail, their flamboyant qualities. Another analogy, which is a stretch of the imagination, is that of a heart leaping up with joy and enthusiasm, very typical of Leo, which also rules the heart. In early Christian imagery, the Leo lion represented St. Mark.

The Virgo Glyph ♍

You can read much into this mysterious glyph. For instance, it could represent the initials of "Mary Virgin," or a young woman holding a stalk of wheat, or stylized female genitalia, all common interpretations. The "M" shape might also remind you that Virgo is ruled by Mercury. The cross beneath the symbol reveals the grounded, practical nature of this earth sign.

The earliest zodiacs link Virgo with the Egyptian goddess Isis, who gave birth to the god Horus after her husband Osiris had been killed, in the archetype of a miraculous conception. There are many ancient statues of Isis nursing her baby son, which are reminiscent of medieval Virgin and Child motifs. This sign has also been associated with the image of the Holy

Grail, when the Virgo symbol was substituted with a chalice.

The Libra Glyph ♎

It is not difficult to read the standard image for Libra, the scales, into this glyph. There is another meaning, however, that is equally relevant: the setting sun as it descends over the horizon. Libra's natural position on the zodiac wheel is the descendant or sunset position (as Aries's natural position is the ascendant, or rising sign). Both images relate to Libra's personality. Libra is always weighing pros and cons for a balanced decision. In the sunset image, the sun (male) hovers over the horizontal Earth (female) before setting. Libra is the space between these lines, harmonizing yin and yang, spiritual and material, male and female, ideal and real worlds. The glyph has also been linked to the kidneys, which are ruled by Libra.

The Scorpio Glyph ♏

With its barbed tail, this glyph is easy to identify with the sign of the Scorpion. It also represents the male sexual parts, over which the sign rules. However, some earlier Egyptian symbols for Scorpio represent it as an erect serpent. You can also draw the conclusion that Mars was once its ruler by the arrowhead.

Another image for Scorpio, which is not identifiable in this glyph, is the eagle. Scorpios can go to extremes, either soaring like the eagle or self-destructing like the scorpion. In early Christian imagery, which often used zodiacal symbols, the Scorpio eagle was chosen to symbolize the intense apostle St. John the Evangelist.

The Sagittarius Glyph ♐

This glyph is one of the easiest to spot and draw—an upward pointing arrow lifting up a cross. The arrow is pointing skyward, while the cross represents the four elements of the material world, which the arrow must convey. Elevating materiality into spirituality is an important Sagittarius quality, which explains why this sign is associated with higher learning, religion, philosophy, and travel—the aspiring professions. Sagittarians can also send barbed arrows of frankness in their pursuit of truth. (This is also the sign of the super-salesman.)

Sagittarius is symbolically represented by the centaur, a mythological creature who is half man, half horse, aiming his arrow toward the skies. Though Sagittarius is motivated by spiritual aspiration, it also must balance the powerful appetites of the animal nature. The centaur Chiron, a figure in Greek mythology, became a wise teacher who, after many adventures and world travels, was killed by a poisoned arrow.

The Capricorn Glyph ♑

One of the most difficult symbols to draw, this glyph may take some practice. It is a representation of the sea goat: a mythical animal that is a goat with a curving fish's tail. The goat part of Capricorn wants to leave the waters of the emotions and climb to the elevated areas of life. But the fish tail is the unconscious, the deep chaotic psychic level that draws the goat back. Capricorn is often trying to escape the deep, feeling part of life by submerging himself in work, steadily ascending to the top. To some people, the glyph represents a seated figure with a bent knee, a reminder that Capricorn governs the knee area of the body.

An interesting aspect of this glyph is the contrast of the sharp pointed horns of the symbol, which represent the penetrating, shrewd, conscious side of Capricorn, with the swishing tail, which represents its serpentine, unconscious, emotional force. One Capricorn legend, which dates from Roman times, tells of the earthy fertility god, Pan, who tried to save himself from uncontrollable sexual desires by jumping into the Nile. His upper body then turned into a goat, while the lower part became a fish. Later, Jupiter gave him a safe haven in the skies, as a constellation.

The Aquarius Glyph ≈

This ancient water symbol can be traced back to an Egyptian hieroglyph representing streams of life force. Symbolized by the water bearer, Aquarius is distributor of the waters of life—the magic liquid of regeneration. The two waves can also be linked to the positive and negative charges of the electrical energy that Aquarius rules, a sort of universal wavelength. Aquarius is tuned in intuitively to higher forces via this electrical force. The duality of the glyph could also refer to the dual nature of Aquarius, a sign that runs hot and cold, is friendly but also detached in the mental world of air signs.

In Greek legends, Aquarius is represented by Ganymede, who was carried to heaven by an eagle in order to become the cup bearer of Zeus and to supervise the annual flooding of the Nile. The sign later became associated with aviation and notions of flight.

The Pisces Glyph)(

Here is an abstraction of the familiar image of Pisces, two fishes swimming in opposite directions, yet bound together by a cord. The fishes represent the spirit, which yearns for the freedom of heaven, and the soul, which remains attached to the desires of the temporal world. During life on Earth, the spirit and the soul are bound together. When they complement each other, instead of pulling in opposite directions they facilitate the Pisces creativity. The ancient version of this glyph, taken from the Egyptians, had no connecting line, which was added in the fourteenth century.

In another interpretation, it is said that the left fish

indicates the direction of involution or the beginning of a cycle, while the right fish signifies the direction of evolution, the way to completion of a cycle. It's an appropriate grand finale for Pisces, the last sign of the zodiac.

CHAPTER 5

How Your Rising Sign Personalizes Your Horoscope

Have you ever wondered what makes your horoscope unique, how your chart could be different from that of anyone else born on your birthday? Yes, other babies who may have been born later or earlier on the same day, in the same hospital, as you were, will be sure to have most planets in the same signs as you do. Most of your high school class, in fact, will have several planets in the same signs as your planets, especially the slow-moving planets (Uranus, Neptune, Pluto) and very possibly Jupiter and Saturn, which usually spend a year or more in each sign.

What makes a horoscope truly "yours" is the rising sign (or ascendant), the sign that was coming up over the eastern horizon at the moment you were born. This sign establishes the exact horoscope of your birth time. In astrology, this is called the *rising sign,* often referred to as the ascendant. As the earth moves, a different sign rises every two hours.

If you have read the chapter in this book on houses, you'll know that the houses are twelve stationary divisions of the horoscope, which represent areas of life. The sign which is moving over the house describes that area of life. The rising sign marks the border of the first house, which represents your first presentation to the world, your physical body, and how you come across to others. It has been called your "shop window," the first impression you give to others. After the rising sign is determined, then each "house" will be influenced by the signs which follow it.

Once the rising sign is established, it becomes possible to analyze a chart accurately because the astrologer knows in which area of life (house) the planets will operate. For instance, if Mars is in Gemini and your rising sign is Taurus, then Mars will most likely be active in the second or financial house of your chart. If you were born later in the day and your rising sign is Virgo, then Mars will be positioned at the top of your chart, energizing your tenth house or career. That is why many astrologers insist on knowing the exact time of a client's birth, before they analyze a chart. The more exact your birthtime, the more accurately an astrologer can position the planets in your chart. This is important, because if you were born when the midportion of a sign was rotating over the horizon and a key planet—let's say Saturn—was in the early degrees of that sign, then it would already be over the horizon, located in the twelfth house, rather than the first. So the interpretation of your horoscope would be quite different: you would not have the serious Saturn influence in the way you come across to others, which would be the case if you were born an hour earlier. If a planet is near the ascendant, sometimes even a few minutes can make a big difference.

Your rising sign has an important relationship with your sun sign. Some will complement the sun sign; others hide it under a totally different mask, as if playing an entirely different role, so it is often difficult to guess the person's sun sign from outer appearances. For example, a Leo with a conservative Capricorn ascendant would come across as much less flamboyant than a Leo with a fiery Aries or Sagittarius ascendant. The exception is when the sun sign is reinforced by other planets; then, with other planets on its side, the sun may assert its personality much more strongly, overcoming the image of a contradictory rising sign. For example, a Leo with Venus and Jupiter also in

Leo might counteract the conservative image of the Capricorn ascendant, in the above example. However, in most cases, the ascendant is the ingredient most strongly reflected in the first impression you make.

Rising signs change every two hours with the Earth's rotation. Those born early in the morning when the sun was on the horizon will be most likely to project the image of their sun sign. These people are often called a "double Aries" or a "double Virgo," because the same sun sign and ascendant reinforce each other.

Look up your rising sign on the chart at the end of this chapter. Since rising signs change every two hours, it is important to know your birth time as close to the minute as possible. Even a few minutes' difference could change the rising sign and therefore the setup of your chart. If you are unsure about the exact time, but know within a few hours, check the following descriptions to see which is most like the personality you project.

Aries Rising—Fiery Emotions

You are the most aggressive version of your sun sign, with boundless energy which can be used productively, if it's channeled in the right direction. Watch a tendency to overreact emotionally and blow your top. You come across as openly competitive, a positive asset in business or sports. Be on guard against impatience, which could lead to head injuries. Your walk and bearing could have the telltale head-forward Aries posture. You may wear more bright colors, especially red, than others of your sign. You may also have a tendency to drive your car faster.

Taurus Rising—The Earth Mother

You'll exude a protective nurturing quality, even if you're male, which draws those in need of TLC and support. You're slow-moving, with a beautiful (or distinctive) speaking or singing voice that can be especially soothing or melodious. You probably surround yourself with comfort, good food, luxurious surroundings and sensual pleasures, and prefer welcoming others into your home to gadding about. You may have a talent for business, especially in trading, appraising, and real estate. This ascendant gives a well-padded or curvaceous physique, which gains weight easily. Women with this ascendant are naturally sexy in a bodacious way.

Gemini Rising—Expressive Talents

You're naturally sociable, with lighter, more ethereal mannerisms than others of your sign, especially if you're female. You love to communicate with people and express your ideas and feelings easily. You may have writing or public speaking talent. Like Drew Barrymore, you may thrive on a constantly changing scenario with a varied cast of characters, though you may be far more sympathetic and caring than you project. You will probably travel widely, changing partners and jobs several times (or juggling two at once). Physically, you should cultivate a calm, tranquil atmosphere, because your nerves are quite sensitive.

Cancer Rising—Sensitive Antennae

Like billionaire Bill Gates, you are naturally acquisitive, possessive, private, a moneymaker. You easily pick up others' needs and feelings, a great gift in business, the arts, and personal relationships, but guard against overreacting or taking things too personally, especially during full moon periods. Find creative outlets for your natural nurturing gifts, such as helping the less fortunate, particularly children. Your insights would be useful in psychology, your desire to feed and

...e for others in the restaurant, hotel, or child care industry. You may be especially fond of wearing romantic old clothes, collecting antiques, and of course, good food. Since your body may retain fluids, pay attention to your diet. To relax, escape to places near water.

Leo Rising—The Scene Player

You may come across as more poised than you really feel; however, you play it to the hilt, projecting a proud royal presence. This ascendant gives you a natural flair for drama, like Marilyn Monroe. You'll also project a much more outgoing, optimistic, sunny personality than others of your sign. You take care to please your public by always projecting your best star quality, probably tossing a luxuriant mane of hair or, if you're female, dazzling with a spectacular jewelry collection. Since you may have a strong parental nature, you could well be the regal family matriarch or patriarch.

Virgo Rising—Cool and Calculating

Virgo rising masks your inner nature with a practical, analytical outer image. You seem neat, orderly, more particular than others of your sign. Others in your life may feel they must live up to your high standards. Though at times you may be openly critical, this masks a well-meaning desire to have only the best for loved ones. Your sharp eye for details could be used in the financial world, or your literary skills could draw you to teaching or publishing. The healing arts, health care, service-oriented professions attract many with this Virgo emphasis in their chart. Like Madonna, you're likely to take good care of yourself, with great attention to health, diet, and exercise. Physically, you may have a very sensitive digestive system.

Libra Rising—The Charmer

Libra rising makes you appear as a charmer, more of a social, public person than others of your sign. Your private life will extend beyond your home and family to include an active social life. You may tend to avoid confrontations in relationships, preferring to smooth the way or negotiate diplomatically, rather than give in to an emotional reaction. Because you are interested in all aspects of a situation, you may be slow to reach decisions. Physically, you'll have good proportions and pleasing symmetry. You're likely to have pleasing, if not beautiful, facial features. You move gracefully, and you have a winning smile and good taste in your clothes and home decor. Legal, diplomatic, or public relations professions could draw your interest. Men with Libra rising, like Bill Clinton and John F. Kennedy, have charming smiles and easy social manner that charms the ladies.

Scorpio Rising—Magnetic Power

Even when you're in the public eye, like Jacqueline Kennedy Onassis, you never lose your intriguing air of mystery and sense of underlying power. You can be a master manipulator, always in control and moving comfortably in the world of power. Your physical impression comes across as intense, and many of you have remarkable eyes, with a direct, penetrating gaze. But you'll never reveal your private agenda, and you tend to keep your true feelings under wraps (watch a tendency toward paranoia). You may have an interesting romantic history with secret love affairs. Many of you heighten your air of mystery by wearing black. You're happiest near water and should provide yourself with a seaside retreat.

Sagittarius Rising—The Wanderer

You travel with this ascendant. You may also be a more outdoor, sportive type, with an athletic, casual, outgoing air. Your moods are camouflaged with cheerful optimism or a philosophical attitude. Though you don't hesitate to speak your mind, you can also laugh at your troubles or crack a joke more easily than others of your sign, like Candice Bergen, who is best known for her comedy role as the outspoken "Murphy Brown." This ascendant can also draw you to the field of higher education or to spiritual life. You'll seem to have less attachment to things and people and may travel widely. Your strong, fast legs are a physical bonus.

Capricorn Rising—Serious Business

This rising sign makes you come across as serious, goal-oriented, disciplined, and careful with cash. You are not one of the zodiac's big spenders, though you might splurge occasionally on items with good investment value. You're the traditional, conservative type in dress and environment, and you might come across as quite formal and businesslike. You'll function well in a structured or corporate environment where you can climb to the top. (You are always aware of who's the boss.) In your personal life, you could be a loner or a single parent who is "father and mother" to your children. Like Paul Newman, you're likely to prefer a quiet private life to living in the spotlight.

Aquarius Rising—One of a Kind

You come across as less concerned about what others think and could even be a bit eccentric. Your appearance is sure to be unique and memorable. You're more at ease with groups of people than others in your sign, and may be attracted to public life. Your appearance may be unique, either unconventional or unimportant to you. Those with the sun in a water sign (Cancer, Scorpio, Pisces) may exercise your nurturing qualities with a large group, an extended family, or a day care or community center. Audrey Hepburn and Princess Diana, who had this rising sign, were known for their unique charisma and work on behalf of worthy causes.

Pisces Rising—Romantic Roles

Your creative, nurturing talents are heightened and so is your ability to project emotional drama. And your dreamy eyes and poetic air bring out the protective instinct in others. You could be attracted to the arts, especially theater, dance, film, or photography, or to psychology or spiritual or charity work. You are happiest when you are using your creative ability to help others, as Robert Redford has done. Since you are vulnerable to mood swings, it is especially important for you to find interesting, creative work where you can express your talents and boost your self-esteem. Accentuate the positive and be wary of escapist tendencies, particularly involving alcohol or drugs, to which you are supersensitive.

RISING SIGNS—A.M. BIRTHS

	1 AM	2 AM	3 AM	4 AM	5 AM	6 AM	7 AM	8 AM	9 AM	10 AM	11 AM	12 NOON
Jan 1	Lib	Sc	Sc	Sc	Sag	Sag	Cap	Cap	Aq	Aq	Pis	Ar
Jan 9	Lib	Sc	Sc	Sag	Sag	Sag	Cap	Cap	Aq	Pis	Ar	Tau
Jan 17	Sc	Sc	Sc	Sag	Sag	Cap	Cap	Aq	Aq	Pis	Ar	Tau
Jan 25	Sc	Sc	Sag	Sag	Sag	Cap	Cap	Aq	Pis	Ar	Tau	Tau
Feb 2	Sc	Sc	Sag	Sag	Cap	Cap	Aq	Pis	Pis	Ar	Tau	Gem
Feb 10	Sc	Sag	Sag	Sag	Cap	Cap	Aq	Pis	Ar	Tau	Tau	Gem
Feb 18	Sc	Sag	Sag	Cap	Cap	Aq	Pis	Pis	Ar	Tau	Gem	Gem
Feb 26	Sag	Sag	Sag	Cap	Aq	Aq	Pis	Ar	Tau	Tau	Gem	Gem
Mar 6	Sag	Sag	Cap	Cap	Aq	Pis	Pis	Ar	Tau	Gem	Gem	Can
Mar 14	Sag	Cap	Cap	Aq	Aq	Pis	Ar	Tau	Tau	Gem	Gem	Can
Mar 22	Sag	Cap	Cap	Aq	Pis	Ar	Ar	Tau	Gem	Gem	Gem	Can
Mar 30	Cap	Cap	Aq	Pis	Pis	Ar	Tau	Tau	Gem	Can	Can	Can
Apr 7	Cap	Cap	Aq	Pis	Ar	Ar	Tau	Gem	Gem	Can	Can	Leo
Apr 14	Cap	Aq	Aq	Pis	Ar	Tau	Tau	Gem	Gem	Can	Can	Leo
Apr 22	Cap	Aq	Pis	Ar	Ar	Tau	Gem	Gem	Gem	Can	Leo	Leo
Apr 30	Aq	Aq	Pis	Ar	Tau	Tau	Gem	Can	Can	Can	Leo	Leo
May 8	Aq	Pis	Ar	Ar	Tau	Gem	Gem	Can	Can	Leo	Leo	Leo
May 16	Aq	Pis	Ar	Tau	Gem	Gem	Can	Can	Can	Leo	Leo	Vir
May 24	Pis	Ar	Ar	Tau	Gem	Gem	Can	Can	Leo	Leo	Leo	Vir
June 1	Pis	Ar	Tau	Gem	Gem	Can	Can	Can	Leo	Leo	Vir	Vir
June 9	Ar	Ar	Tau	Gem	Gem	Can	Can	Leo	Leo	Leo	Vir	Vir
June 17	Ar	Tau	Gem	Gem	Can	Can	Can	Leo	Leo	Vir	Vir	Vir
June 25	Tau	Tau	Gem	Gem	Can	Can	Leo	Leo	Leo	Vir	Vir	Lib
July 3	Tau	Gem	Gem	Can	Can	Can	Leo	Leo	Vir	Vir	Vir	Lib
July 11	Tau	Gem	Gem	Can	Can	Leo	Leo	Leo	Vir	Vir	Lib	Lib
July 18	Gem	Gem	Can	Can	Can	Leo	Leo	Vir	Vir	Vir	Lib	Lib
July 26	Gem	Gem	Can	Can	Leo	Leo	Vir	Vir	Vir	Lib	Lib	Lib
Aug 3	Gem	Can	Can	Can	Leo	Leo	Vir	Vir	Vir	Lib	Lib	Sc
Aug 11	Gem	Can	Can	Leo	Leo	Leo	Vir	Vir	Lib	Lib	Lib	Sc
Aug 18	Can	Can	Can	Leo	Leo	Vir	Vir	Vir	Lib	Lib	Sc	Sc
Aug 27	Can	Can	Leo	Leo	Leo	Vir	Vir	Lib	Lib	Lib	Sc	Sc
Sept 4	Can	Can	Leo	Leo	Leo	Vir	Vir	Vir	Lib	Lib	Sc	Sc
Sept 12	Can	Leo	Leo	Leo	Vir	Vir	Lib	Lib	Lib	Sc	Sc	Sag
Sept 20	Leo	Leo	Leo	Vir	Vir	Vir	Lib	Lib	Sc	Sc	Sc	Sag
Sept 28	Leo	Leo	Leo	Vir	Vir	Lib	Lib	Lib	Sc	Sc	Sag	Sag
Oct 6	Leo	Leo	Vir	Vir	Vir	Lib	Lib	Sc	Sc	Sc	Sag	Sag
Oct 14	Leo	Vir	Vir	Vir	Lib	Lib	Lib	Sc	Sc	Sag	Sag	Cap
Oct 22	Leo	Vir	Vir	Lib	Lib	Lib	Sc	Sc	Sc	Sag	Sag	Cap
Oct 30	Vir	Vir	Vir	Lib	Lib	Sc	Sc	Sc	Sag	Sag	Cap	Cap
Nov 7	Vir	Vir	Lib	Lib	Lib	Sc	Sc	Sc	Sag	Sag	Cap	Cap
Nov 15	Vir	Vir	Lib	Lib	Sc	Sc	Sc	Sag	Sag	Cap	Cap	Aq
Nov 23	Vir	Lib	Lib	Lib	Sc	Sc	Sag	Sag	Sag	Cap	Cap	Aq
Dec 1	Vir	Lib	Lib	Sc	Sc	Sc	Sag	Sag	Cap	Cap	Aq	Aq
Dec 9	Lib	Lib	Lib	Sc	Sc	Sag	Sag	Sag	Cap	Cap	Aq	Pis
Dec 18	Lib	Lib	Sc	Sc	Sc	Sag	Sag	Cap	Cap	Aq	Aq	Pis
Dec 28	Lib	Lib	Sc	Sc	Sag	Sag	Sag	Cap	Aq	Aq	Pis	Ar

RISING SIGNS—P.M. BIRTHS

	1 PM	2 PM	3 PM	4 PM	5 PM	6 PM	7 PM	8 PM	9 PM	10 PM	11 PM	12 MID-NIGHT
Jan 1	Tau	Gem	Gem	Can	Can	Can	Leo	Leo	Vir	Vir	Vir	Lib
Jan 9	Tau	Gem	Gem	Can	Can	Leo	Leo	Leo	Vir	Vir	Vir	Lib
Jan 17	Gem	Gem	Can	Can	Can	Leo	Leo	Vir	Vir	Vir	Lib	Lib
Jan 25	Gem	Gem	Can	Can	Leo	Leo	Leo	Vir	Vir	Lib	Lib	Lib
Feb 2	Gem	Can	Can	Can	Leo	Leo	Vir	Vir	Vir	Lib	Lib	Sc
Feb 10	Gem	Can	Can	Leo	Leo	Leo	Vir	Vir	Lib	Lib	Lib	Sc
Feb 18	Can	Can	Can	Leo	Leo	Vir	Vir	Vir	Lib	Lib	Sc	Sc
Feb 26	Can	Can	Leo	Leo	Leo	Vir	Vir	Lib	Lib	Lib	Sc	Sc
Mar 6	Can	Can	Leo	Leo	Vir	Vir	Vir	Lib	Lib	Sc	Sc	Sc
Mar 14	Can	Leo	Leo	Vir	Vir	Vir	Lib	Lib	Lib	Sc	Sc	Sag
Mar 22	Leo	Leo	Leo	Vir	Vir	Lib	Lib	Lib	Sc	Sc	Sc	Sag
Mar 30	Leo	Leo	Vir	Vir	Vir	Lib	Lib	Sc	Sc	Sc	Sag	Sag
Apr 7	Leo	Leo	Vir	Vir	Lib	Lib	Lib	Sc	Sc	Sc	Sag	Sag
Apr 14	Leo	Vir	Vir	Vir	Lib	Lib	Sc	Sc	Sc	Sag	Sag	Cap
Apr 22	Leo	Vir	Vir	Lib	Lib	Lib	Sc	Sc	Sc	Sag	Sag	Cap
Apr 30	Vir	Vir	Vir	Lib	Lib	Sc	Sc	Sc	Sag	Sag	Cap	Cap
May 8	Vir	Vir	Lib	Lib	Lib	Sc	Sc	Sag	Sag	Sag	Cap	Cap
May 16	Vir	Vir	Lib	Lib	Sc	Sc	Sc	Sag	Sag	Cap	Cap	Aq
May 24	Vir	Lib	Lib	Lib	Sc	Sc	Sag	Sag	Sag	Cap	Cap	Aq
June 1	Vir	Lib	Lib	Sc	Sc	Sc	Sag	Sag	Cap	Cap	Aq	Aq
June 9	Lib	Lib	Lib	Sc	Sc	Sag	Sag	Sag	Cap	Cap	Aq	Pis
June 17	Lib	Lib	Sc	Sc	Sc	Sag	Sag	Cap	Cap	Aq	Aq	Pis
June 25	Lib	Lib	Sc	Sc	Sag	Sag	Sag	Cap	Cap	Aq	Pis	Ar
July 3	Lib	Sc	Sc	Sc	Sag	Sag	Cap	Cap	Aq	Aq	Pis	Ar
July 11	Lib	Sc	Sc	Sag	Sag	Sag	Cap	Cap	Aq	Pis	Pis	Ar
July 18	Sc	Sc	Sc	Sag	Sag	Cap	Cap	Aq	Aq	Pis	Ar	Tau
July 26	Sc	Sc	Sag	Sag	Sag	Cap	Cap	Aq	Pis	Ar	Tau	Tau
Aug 3	Sc	Sc	Sag	Sag	Cap	Cap	Aq	Aq	Pis	Ar	Tau	Gem
Aug 11	Sc	Sag	Sag	Sag	Cap	Cap	Aq	Pis	Ar	Tau	Tau	Gem
Aug 18	Sc	Sag	Sag	Cap	Cap	Aq	Pis	Pis	Ar	Tau	Gem	Gem
Aug 27	Sag	Sag	Sag	Cap	Cap	Aq	Pis	Ar	Tau	Tau	Gem	Gem
Sept 4	Sag	Sag	Cap	Cap	Aq	Pis	Pis	Ar	Tau	Tau	Gem	Gem Can
Sept 12	Sag	Sag	Cap	Aq	Aq	Pis	Ar	Tau	Tau	Gem	Gem	Can
Sept 20	Sag	Cap	Cap	Aq	Pis	Pis	Ar	Tau	Gem	Gem	Can	Can
Sept 28	Cap	Cap	Aq	Aq	Pis	Ar	Tau	Tau	Gem	Gem	Can	Can
Oct 6	Cap	Cap	Aq	Pis	Ar	Ar	Tau	Gem	Gem	Can	Can	Leo
Oct 14	Cap	Aq	Aq	Pis	Ar	Tau	Tau	Gem	Gem	Can	Can	Leo
Oct 22	Cap	Aq	Pis	Ar	Ar	Tau	Gem	Gem	Can	Can	Leo	Leo
Oct 30	Aq	Aq	Pis	Ar	Tau	Tau	Gem	Can	Can	Can	Leo	Leo
Nov 7	Aq	Aq	Pis	Ar	Tau	Tau	Gem	Can	Can	Leo	Leo	Leo
Nov 15	Aq	Pis	Ar	Tau	Gem	Gem	Can	Can	Can	Leo	Leo	Vir
Nov 23	Pis	Ar	Ar	Tau	Gem	Gem	Can	Can	Leo	Leo	Leo	Vir
Dec 1	Pis	Ar	Tau	Gem	Gem	Can	Can	Can	Leo	Leo	Vir	Vir
Dec 9	Ar	Tau	Tau	Gem	Gem	Can	Can	Leo	Leo	Leo	Vir	Vir
Dec 18	Ar	Tau	Gem	Gem	Can	Can	Can	Leo	Leo	Vir	Vir	Vir
Dec 28	Tau	Tau	Gem	Gem	Can	Can	Leo	Leo	Vir	Vir	Vir	Lib

CHAPTER 6

The Moon—Our Light Within

In some astrology-conscious lands, the moon is given as much importance in a horoscope as the sun. Astrologers often refer to these two bodies as the "lights," an apt term, since they shed the most light upon our personality in a horoscope reading. This also is a more technically appropriate description, since the sun and moon are not really planets, but a star and a satellite.

The most fascinating aspect of the moon is its connection with our emotional state. Our moods seem to wax and wane with the moon. Even the state of shellfish, animals, and planets is affected by the moon phase. Imagine what would happen if the moon were somehow caused to change its orbit, perhaps by a bombarding asteroid. What would happen to the tides, to ocean and plant life, which respond to the moon, or to our own bodies, which are mostly water? Life on earth would be impossible!

As the closest celestial body, the moon represents your receptive, reflective, female, nurturing self. And it reflects who you were nurtured by—the "mother" or mother figure in your chart. In a man's chart, the moon position also describes his receptive, emotional, "yin" side, as well as the woman in his life who will have the deepest effect, usually his mother. (Venus reveals the kind of woman who attracts him physically.)

The sign the moon was passing through at birth reveals much about your inner life, your needs and secrets, as well as those of people you'd like to know better. You can learn what appeals to a person subconsciously by knowing their moon sign, which reflects their instinctive, emotional nature.

It's well worth having an accurate chart cast to determine your moon sign. Since accurate moon tables are too extensive for this book, check through these descriptions to find the moon sign that feels most familiar.

The moon is more at home in some signs than others. It rules maternal Cancer and is exalted in Taurus—both comforting, home-loving signs where the natural emotional energies of the moon are easily and productively expressed. But when the moon is in the opposite signs—Capricorn or Scorpio—it leaves the comfortable nest and deals with emotional issues of power and achievement in the outside world. Those of you with the moon in these signs are more likely to find your emotional role more challenging in life.

Moon in Aries

You are an idealistic, impetuous person who falls in and out of love easily. This placement makes you both independent and ardent. You love a challenge, but could cool once your quarry is captured. You should cultivate patience and tolerance—or you might tend to gravitate toward those who treat you rough, just for the sake of challenge and excitement.

Moon in Taurus

You are a sentimental soul who is very fond of the good life and gravitates toward solid, secure relationships. You like displays of affection and creature comforts—all the tangible trappings of a cozy, safe, calm atmosphere. You are sensual and steady emotionally, but very stubborn and determined. You can't be pushed and tend to dislike changes. You should make an effort to broaden your horizons and to take a risk sometimes.

Moon in Gemini

You crave mental stimulation and variety in life, which you usually get through either an ever-varied social life, the excitement of flirtation, and/or multiple professional involvements. You may marry more than once and have a rather chaotic emotional life due to your difficulty with commitment and settling down. Be sure to find a partner who is as outgoing as you are. You will have to learn at some point to focus your energies because you tend to be somewhat fragmented—to do two things at once, to have two homes or even two lovers. If you can find a creative way to express your many-faceted nature, you'll be ahead of the game.

Moon in Cancer

This is the most powerful lunar position, which is sure to make a deep imprint on your character. Your needs are very much associated with your reaction to the needs of others. You are very sensitive and self-protective, though some of you may mask this with a hard shell. This placement also gives you an excellent memory, keen intuition, and an uncanny ability to perceive the needs of others. All of the lunar phases will affect you, especially full moons and eclipses, so you would do well to mark them on your calendar. Because you're happiest at home, you may work at home or turn your office into a second home, where you can nurture and comfort people. (You may tend to "mother the world.") With natural psychic, intuitive ability, you might be drawn to occult work in some way. Or you may get professionally involved with providing food and shelter to others.

Moon in Leo

This warm, passionate moon takes everything to heart. You are attracted to all that is noble, generous, and aristocratic in life (and may be a bit of a snob). You have an innate ability to take command emotionally, but you do need strong support, loyalty, and loud applause from those you love. You are possessive of your loved ones and your turf and will roar if anyone threatens to take over your territory.

Moon in Virgo

You are rather cool until you decide if others measure up. But once someone or something meets your ideal standards, you hold up your end of the arrangement perfectly. You may, in fact, drive yourself too hard to attain some notion of perfection. Try to be a bit easier on yourself and others. Don't always act the censor! You love to be the teacher and are drawn to situations where you can change others for the better, but sometimes you must learn to accept others for what they are—enjoy what you have!

Moon in Libra

A partnership-oriented moon—you may find it difficult to be alone or to do things alone. After you have learned emotional balance by leaning on yourself first, you can have excellent relationships. It is best for you to avoid extremes, however, which set your scales swinging and can make your love life precarious. You thrive in a rather conservative, traditional, romantic relationship, where you receive attention and flattery—but not possessiveness—from your partner. You'll be your most charming in an elegant, harmonious atmosphere.

Moon in Scorpio

This is a moon that enjoys and responds to intense, passionate feelings. You may go to extremes and have a very dramatic emotional life, full of ardor, suspicion, jealousy, and obsession. It would be much healthier to channel your need for power and control into meaningful work. This is a good position for anyone in the fields of medicine, police work, research, the occult, psychoanalysis, or intuitive work, because life-and-death situations don't faze you. However, you do take personal disappointments very hard.

Moon in Sagittarius

You take life's ups and downs with good humor and the proverbial grain of salt. You'll love 'em and leave 'em, taking off on a great adventure at a moment's notice. "Born free" could be your slogan. Attracted by the exotic, you have wanderlust mentally and physically. You may be too much in search of new mental and spiritual stimulation to ever settle down.

Moon in Capricorn

Are you ever accused of being too cool and calculating? You have an earthy side, but you take prestige and position very seriously. Your strong drive to succeed extends to your romantic life, where you will be devoted to improving your lifestyle, rising to the top. A structured situation where you can advance methodically makes you feel wonderfully secure. You may be attracted to someone older or very much younger or from a different social world. It may be difficult to look at the lighter side of emotional relationships; however, the "up" side of this moon in the sign of its detriment is that you tend to be very dutiful and responsible to those you care for.

Moon in Aquarius

You are a people collector with many friends of all backgrounds. You are happiest surrounded by people and may feel uneasy when left alone. Though you usually stay friends with lovers, intense emotions and demanding one-on-one relationships turn you off. You don't like anything to be too rigid or scheduled. Though tolerant and understanding, you can be emotionally unpredictable and may opt for an unconventional love life. With plenty of space, you will be able to sustain relationships with liberal, freedom-loving types.

Moon in Pisces

You are very responsive and empathetic to others, especially if they have problems or are the underdog. (Be on guard against attracting too many people with sob stories.) You'll be happiest if you can express your creative imagination in the arts or in the spiritual or healing professions. Because you may tend to escape in fantasies or overreact to the moods of others, you need an emotional anchor to help you keep a firm foothold in reality. Steer clear of too much escapism (especially in alcohol) or reclusiveness. Places near water soothe your moods. Working in a field that gives you emotional variety will also help you to be productive.

What Eclipses Do to Your Moods

In case we've been taking the moon for granted, the eclipse seasons, which occur about every six months, remind us how important the moon is for our survival. Perhaps that is why eclipses have always had an ominous reputation. Folklore all over the world blames eclipses for catastrophes such as birth defects, crop failures, and hurricanes. Villagers on the peninsula of Baja California paint their fruit trees red and wear red ribbons and underwear to deflect "evil rays." During the total eclipse of July 1991, everyone retreated safely indoors to follow the eclipse on television. In other native societies, people play drums and make loud noises to frighten off heavenly monsters believed to destroy the light of the sun and moon. Only the romantic Tahitians seem to have positive feelings about an eclipse. In this sensual tropical paradise, legend declares that the "lights" go out when the sun and moon make love and procreate the stars.

Ancient Chaldean astrologer-priests were the first to time eclipses accurately. They discovered that 6,585 days after an eclipse, another eclipse would happen. By counting ahead after all the eclipses in a given year, they could predict eclipses eighteen years into the future. This technique was practiced by navigators through the centuries, including Christopher Columbus, who used his knowledge of an upcoming lunar eclipse to extort food from the frightened inhabitants of Jamaica in 1504. In ancient Mexico, Mayan astronomer-priests also discovered that eclipses occur at regular intervals and recorded them with a hieroglyph of a serpent swallowing the sun.

What Causes an Eclipse?

A solar eclipse is the passage of the new moon directly across the face of the sun. It is a very exciting and awesome event, which causes the sky to darken suddenly. Though the effect lasts only a few minutes, it is enough to strike panic in the uninformed viewer.

A lunar eclipse happens when the full moon passes through the shadow of the Earth on the opposite side from the sun; as a result, the Earth blocks out the sun's light from reaching the moon. The moon must be in level alignment with the sun and Earth for a lunar eclipse to occur.

Conditions are ripe for an eclipse twice a year, when a full or a new moon is most likely to cross the path of the sun at two points known as the *nodes*.

What to Know About Nodes

To understand the nodes, visualize two rings, one inside the other. As you move the rings, you'll notice that the two circles intersect at opposite points. Now imagine one ring as the moon's orbit and the other as the sun's (as seen from Earth). The crossing points are called the moon's "nodes."

For an eclipse to happen, two conditions must be met. First, the path of the orbiting moon must be close enough to a node. Second, this must happen at a time when there is either a new or a full moon. (Not every new or full moon happens close enough to the nodes to create an eclipse.) The axis of the nodes is continually moving backward through the zodiac at the rate of about one and a half degrees per month; therefore, eclipses will eventually occur in every sign of the zodiac.

How Often Do Eclipses Occur?

Whenever the sun draws close to one of the nodes, any new or full moon happening near that time will create an eclipse. This "eclipse season" happens twice a year, approximately six months apart. There are at least four eclipses each year, and there can be as many as seven. In 2002, there will be five eclipses:

- Full Moon in Sagittarius (lunar eclipse)—May 26
- New Moon in Gemini (solar eclipse)—June 10
- Full Moon in Capricorn (lunar eclipse)—June 24

- Full Moon in Taurus (lunar eclipse)—November 19
- New Moon in Sagittarius (solar eclipse)—December 4

Eclipses Have Family Ties

One of the most interesting things about eclipses is that they have "families." Each eclipse is a member of a string of related eclipses that pop up regularly. As mentioned before, the ancient Chaldeans, who were the first great sky-watchers, discovered that eclipses recur in patterns, repeating themselves after approximately eighteen years plus nine to eleven days, in a cycle lasting a total of approximately 1,300 years. Much later, in the eleventh century A.D., these patterns became known as the "Saros Series." (In ancient Greek, "saros" means repetition.)

Because each Saros Series begins at a moment in time, the initial eclipse has a horoscope, and therefore a "personality" which goes through stages of development as the series of eclipses progresses over its 1,300-year lifetime. So as a Saros Series moves through your chart, it will produce an eclipse with a similar "personality" every eighteen years. In the interim, you'll experience eclipses belonging to other Saros Series, which will exhibit their own special family characteristics. Therefore, there can be no one generic interpretation for eclipses, since each affects your horoscope in a different way, according to the personality of its particular Saros Series.

What Is the Purpose of an Eclipse in My Life?

Eclipses can bring on milestone events in your life, if they aspect a key point in your horoscope. In general, they shake up the status quo, bringing hidden areas out into the open. During this time, problems you've been avoiding or have brushed aside can surface to demand your attention. A good coping strategy is to accept whatever comes up as a challenge. It could make a big difference in your life. And don't forget the power of your sense of humor. If you can laugh at something, you'll never be afraid of it.

Second-guessing the eclipses is easy if you have a copy of your horoscope calculated by a computer. (If you do not have a computer or an astrology program, there are several sites on the Internet which will calculate your chart free. See the listings in the resource chapter of this book.) This enables you to pinpoint the area of your life which will be affected. However, you can make an educated guess, by setting up a rough diagram on your own. If you'd like to find out which area of your life this year's eclipses are most likely to affect, follow these easy steps. First, you must know the time of day you were born and look up your rising sign listed in the tables in this book. Then set up an estimated horoscope by drawing a circle, then dividing it into four parts by making a cross directly through the center. Continue to divide each of the parts into thirds, as if you were dividing a cake, until you have twelve slices. Write your rising sign on the middle left-hand slice, which would be the 9 o'clock point, if you were looking at your watch. Then continue listing the signs counterclockwise, until you have listed all twelve signs of the zodiac on the "slices" of the chart.

You should now have a basic diagram of your horoscope chart (minus the planets, of course). Starting with your rising sign "slice," number each portion consecutively, working counterclockwise. Since this year's eclipses will fall in Gemini, Sagittarius, Taurus, and Capricorn, find the number of these slices or "houses" on the chart and read the following descriptions for the kinds of issues that are likely to be emphasized.

If an eclipse falls in your FIRST HOUSE—
Events cause you to examine the ways you are acting independently, pushing you to become more visible and to assert yourself. This is a time when you feel compelled to make your own decisions and do your own thing. There is an emphasis on how you are coming across to others. You may want to change your physical appearance, body image, or style of dress in some way. Under affliction, there might be illness or physical harm.

If an eclipse falls in your SECOND HOUSE—
This is the place where you consider all matters of security. You consolidate your resources, earn money, acquire property, and decide what you value and what you want to own. On a deeper level, this house reveals your sense of self-worth, the inner values that draw wealth in various forms.

If an eclipse falls in your THIRD HOUSE—
Here you communicate, reach out to others, express your ideas, and explore different courses of action. You may feel especially restless, and have confrontations with neighbors or siblings. In your search for more knowledge, you may decide to improve your skills, get more education, or sign up for a course that interests you, which could ultimately alter your lifestyle. Local transportation, especially your car, might be affected by an eclipse here.

If an eclipse falls in your FOURTH HOUSE—
Here is where you put down roots and establish your home base. You'll consider what home really means to you. Issues involving parents, the physical setup or location of your home, or your immediate family demand your attention. You may be especially concerned with parenting or relationships with your own mother. You may consider moving your home to a new location or leaving home, untying family ties.

If an eclipse falls in your FIFTH HOUSE—
Here is where you express yourself, either through your personal talents or through procreating children. You are interested in making your special talents visible. This is also the house of love affairs and the romantic aspect of life, where you flirt, have fun, and enjoy the excitement of love. Hobbies and crafts, the ways you explore the playful child within, fall in this area.

If an eclipse falls in your SIXTH HOUSE—
This is your care and maintenance department, where you take care of your health, organize your life, and set up a daily routine. It is also the place where you perfect your skills and add polish to your life. The chores you do every day, the skills you learn, and the techniques you use fall here. If something doesn't "work" in your life, an eclipse is sure to bring this to light. If you've been neglecting your health, diet, and fitness, you'll probably pay the consequences during an eclipse. Or you may be faced with work that requires much routine organization and steady effort, rather than creative ability. Or you may be required to perform services for others. (In ancient astrology, this was the place of slavery!)

If an eclipse falls in your SEVENTH HOUSE—
This is the area of committed relationships, of those which involve legal agreements, of working in a close relationship with another. Here you'll be dealing with how you relate and what you'll be willing to give up for the sake of a marriage or partnership. Eclipses here can put extra pressure on a relationship and, if it's not working, precipitate a breakup. Lawsuits and open enemies also reside here.

If an eclipse falls in your EIGHTH HOUSE—
This area is concerned with power and control. Consider what you are willing to give up in order that

something might happen. Power struggles, intense relationships, and a desire to penetrate a deeper mystery belong here. Debts, loans, financial matters that involve another party, and wheeling and dealing also come into focus. So does sex, where you surrender your individual power to create a new life together. Matters involving birth and death are also involved here.

If an eclipse falls in your NINTH HOUSE—

Here is where you look at the Big Picture: how everything relates to form a pattern. You'll seek information that helps you find meaning in life: higher education, religion, travel, and global issues. Eclipses here can push you to get out of your rut, explore something you've never done before, and expand your horizons.

If an eclipse falls in your TENTH HOUSE—

This is the high-profile point in your chart. Here is where you consider how society looks at you, and what your position is in the outside world. You'll be concerned about whether you receive proper credit for your work and if you're recognized by higher-ups. Promotions, raises, and other forms of recognition can be given or denied. Your standing in your career or community can be challenged, or you'll get publicly acknowledged for achieving a goal. An eclipse here can make you famous . . . or burst your balloon if you've been too ambitious or neglecting other areas of your life.

If an eclipse falls in your ELEVENTH HOUSE—

Your relationship with groups of people comes under scrutiny during an eclipse—whom you are identified with, whom you socialize with, and how well you are accepted by other members of your team. Activities of clubs, political parties, networking, and social interactions become important. You'll be concerned about what other people think: "Do they like me?" "Will I make the team, or win the election?"

If an eclipse falls in your TWELFTH HOUSE—
This is the time when the focus turns to your inner life. An especially favorable eclipse here might bring you great insight and inspiration. Or events may happen which cause you to retreat from public life. Here is where we go to be alone, or to do spiritual or reparative work in retreats, hospitals, religious institutions, or psychotherapy. Here is where you deliver selfless service, through charitable acts. Good aspects from an eclipse could promote an ability to go with the flow, to rise above the competition and find an inner, almost mystical strength that enables you to connect with the deepest needs of others.

What Is the Best Thing to Do During an Eclipse?

When the natural rhythms of the sun and moon are disturbed, it's best to postpone important activities. Be sure to mark eclipse days on your calendar, especially if the eclipse falls in your birth sign. This year, Gemini, Sagittarius, Taurus, and Capricorn should take special note of the conscious and unconscious feelings that arise or are suppressed. With lunar eclipses, some possibilities could be a break from attachments, or the healing of an illness or substance abuse which had been triggered by the subconscious. The temporary event could be a healing time, when you gain perspective. During solar eclipses, when you could be in a highly subjective state, pay attention to the hidden subconscious patterns that surface, the emotional truth that is revealed in your feelings at this time.

The effect of the eclipse can reverberate for some time, often months after the event. But it is especially important to stay cool and make no major moves during the period known as the shadow of the eclipse, which begins about a week before as the energy begins to crescendo and lasts until at least three days after the eclipse, when the emotional atmosphere simmers down. After three days, the daily rhythms should be back to normal and you can proceed with business as usual.

The most positive way to view eclipses is as very special times, when we can receive great insight through a changed perspective. By blocking out the emotional pressure of the full moon, a lunar eclipse could be a time of reason, rather than confusion, a time when we can take a break from our problems. A solar eclipse, when the new moon blocks out the sun (or ego), could be a time when the moon's most positive qualities are expressed, bringing us a feeling of oneness, nurturing, and compassion.

CHAPTER 7

Astro-Mating—An Element-ary Guide to Love

How many people turn to astrology for the light it can shed on their love life! Probably the question astrologers hear most is: What sign is best for me in love? Or: I'm a Taurus and my lover is a Gemini—what are our prospects? Each sun sign does have certain predictable characteristics in love, and by comparing the sun signs, you can reach a better understanding of the dynamics of the relationship. However, it is very easy to oversimplify. Just because someone's sun sign is said to be "incompatible" is no reason why the relationship can't work out. A true in-depth comparison involves far more than just the sun sign. An astrologer considers the interrelationships of all the planets and houses (where they fall in your respective horoscopes). There are several bonds between planets that can offset any difficulties between sun signs. It's worthwhile to analyze them to learn more about your relationship. You can do this by making a very simple chart which compares the moon, Mars, and Venus, as well as the sun signs of the partners in a relationship. You can find the signs for Mars and Venus in the tables in this book. Unfortunately the moon tables are too long for a book of this size—so it might be worth your while to consult an astrological ephemeris (a book of planetary tables) in your local library or to have a computer chart cast to find out the moon placement.

Simply look up the signs of Mars and Venus (and

the Moon, if possible) for each person and list them, with the sun sign, next to each other, then add the *element* of each sign. The Earth signs are Taurus, Virgo, Capricorn. The Air signs are Gemini, Libra, Aquarius. The Fire signs are Aries, Leo, Sagittarius. And the Water signs are Cancer, Scorpio, Pisces.

Example:

ROMEO'S PLANETS:
SUN	MOON	MARS	VENUS
Aries/Fire	Leo/Fire	Scorpio/Water	Taurus/Earth

JULIET'S PLANETS:
SUN	MOON	MARS	VENUS
Pisces/Water	Leo/Fire	Aries/Fire	Aquarius/Air

As a rule of thumb, signs of the *same element* or *complementary elements* (fire with air and earth with water) get along best. So, after comparing this couple's planets, you can see that this particular Romeo and Juliet could have some challenges ahead.

The Lunar Link—Here's the Person You *Need*

The planet in your chart which governs your emotions is the moon. (Note: the moon is not technically a planet, but is usually referred to as one by astrologers.) So you would naturally take this into consideration when evaluating a potential romantic partnership. If a person's moon is in a good relationship to your sun, moon, Venus, or Mars, preferably in the same sign or element, you should relate well on some emotional level. Your needs will be compatible: you'll understand each other's feelings without much effort. If the moon is in a compatible element, such as earth with water or fire with air, you may have a few adjustments, but you will be able to make them easily. With a water-fire or earth-air combination, you'll have to make a considerable effort to understand where the other is coming from emotionally.

It's worth having a computer chart done, just to find the position of your moon. (Since the moon changes signs every two days, the tables are too long to print in this book.)

The Venus Attraction—Here's the One You *Want*

Venus is what you respond to, so if you and your partner have a good Venus aspect, you should have much in common. You'll enjoy doing things together. The same type of lovemaking will turn you both on. You'll have no trouble pleasing each other.

Look up both partners' Venus placements in the charts on page 69. Your lover's Venus in the same sign or a sign of the *same element* as your own Venus, Mars, moon, or sun is best. Second best is a sign of a compatible element (earth with water, air with fire). Venus in water with air, or earth with fire means that you may have to make a special effort to understand what appeals to each other. And you'll have to give each other plenty of space to enjoy activities that don't particularly appeal to you. By the way, this chart can work not only for lovers, but for any relationship where compatibility of tastes is important to you.

The Mars Connection—This One Lights Your Fire!

Mars positions reveal your sexual energy . . . how often you like to make love, for instance. It also shows your temper . . . do you explode or do a slow burn? Here you'll find out if your partner is direct, aggressive, and hot-blooded or more likely to take the cool, mental approach. Mutually supportive partners have their Mars working together in the same or complementary elements. But *any* contacts between Mars and Venus in two charts can strike sexy sparks. Even the difficult aspects, such as your partner's Mars three or six signs away from your sun, Mars, or Venus, can be sexually stimulating. Who doesn't get turned on by a challenge from time to time? On the other hand, the easy-flowing Mars relationships can drift into soporific dullness.

The Solar Bond

The sun is the focus of our personality and therefore the most powerful component involved. Each pair of sun signs has special lessons to teach and learn from each other. There is a negative side to the most ideal couple and a positive side to the unlikeliest match. Each has an up- and a downside. You'll find a comparison of your sun sign with every other one in the "pairs" section of the individual sun sign chapters in this book. If the forecast for you and your beloved (or business associate) seems like an uphill struggle, take heart! Such legendary lovers as Juan and Eva Peron, Ronald and Nancy Reagan, Harry and Bess Truman, Julius Caesar and Cleopatra, Billy and Ruth Graham, and George and Martha Washington are among the many who have made successful partnerships between supposedly incompatible sun signs.

Try astro-mating these hot celebrity couples for practice. Look up their planets in the "planet" tables in this book and discover the secret of their cosmic attraction. (Some may not be an "item" by the time this is published. Maybe you can figure out what went wrong!)

ARIES Matthew Broderick (3/21/62) and ARIES Sarah Jessica Parker (3/24/65)
PISCES Tea Leoni (2/25/66) and LEO David Duchovny (8/7/61)

ARIES Warren Beatty (3/30/37) and GEMINI Annette Bening (5/29/58)
ARIES Al Gore (3/31/48) and LEO Tipper Gore (8/19/48)
ARIES Alec Baldwin (4/3/58) and SAGITTARIUS Kim Basinger (12/8/53)
TAURUS Barbra Streisand (4/24/42) and CANCER James Brolin (7/18/40)
TAURUS Uma Thurman (4/29/70) and SCORPIO Ethan Hawke (11/6/70)
TAURUS Carmen Electra (4/20/72) and TAURUS Dennis Rodman (5/13/61)
GEMINI Liz Hurley (6/10/65) and VIRGO Hugh Grant (9/9/60)
GEMINI Angelina Jolie (6/4/75) and LEO Billy Bob Thornton (8/4/55)
GEMINI Nicole Kidman (6/21/67) and CANCER Tom Cruise (7/3/62)
LEO Jennifer Lopez (7/24/70) and SCORPIO Sean "Puffy" Combs (11/4/69)
LEO Arnold Schwarzenegger (7/30/47) and SCORPIO Maria Shriver (11/6/55)
LEO Whitney Houston (8/9/53) and AQUARIUS Bobby Brown (2/5/69)
LEO Melanie Griffith (8/9/57) and LEO Antonio Banderas (8/10/60)
LIBRA Michael Douglas (9/25/44) and LIBRA Catherine Zeta-Jones (9/25/69)
TAURUS Jessica Lange (4/20/49) and SCORPIO Sam Shepard (11/5/43)
SCORPIO Hillary Clinton (10/26/47) and LEO Bill Clinton (8/19/46)
PISCES Kurt Russell (3/17/51) and SCORPIO Goldie Hawn (11/21/45)
SCORPIO Prince Charles (11/14/48) and CANCER Camilla Parker Bowles (7/17/47)
SAGITTARIUS Brad Pitt (12/18/63) and AQUARIUS Jennifer Aniston (2/11/69)
CAPRICORN Diane Sawyer (12/22/45) and SCORPIO Mike Nichols (11/6/46)

AQUARIUS Oprah Winfrey (1/29/54) and PISCES Stedman Graham (3/6/51)

Now it's time to do a bit of astro-mating of your own! Do you have what it takes to seduce these celebrity hunks? Check your sun, moon, Mars, and Venus with theirs!

Prince William (6/21/82)

SUN: Cancer (water)
MOON: Cancer (water)
MARS: Libra (air)
VENUS: Taurus (earth)

Russell Crowe (4/7/64)

SUN: Aries (fire)
MOON: Aquarius (air)
MARS: Aries (fire)
VENUS: Gemini (earth)

Jude Law (12/29/72)

SUN: Capricorn (earth)
MOON: Scorpio (water)
MARS: Scorpio (water)
VENUS: Sagittarius (fire)

Leonardo DiCaprio (11/11/74)

SUN: Scorpio (water)
MOON: Libra (air)
MARS: Scorpio (water)
VENUS: Scorpio (water)

Matt Damon (10/8/70)

SUN: Libra (air)
MOON: Gemini (air)
MARS: Aquarius (air)
VENUS: Libra (air)

George Clooney (5/6/61)

SUN: Taurus (earth)
MOON: Capricorn (earth)
MARS: Leo (fire)
VENUS: Aries (fire)

Richard Gere (8/31/49)

SUN: Virgo (earth)
MOON: Sagittarius (fire)
MARS: Cancer (water)
VENUS: Libra (air)

Hugh Grant (9/9/60)

SUN: Virgo (earth)
MOON: Taurus (earth)
MARS: Gemini (air)
VENUS: Libra (air)

Kevin Costner (1/18/55)

SUN: Capricorn (earth)
MOON: Sagittarius (fire)
MARS: Aries (fire)
VENUS: Sagittarius (fire)

Mel Gibson (1/3/56)

SUN: Capricorn (earth)
MOON: Virgo (earth)
MARS: Scorpio (water)
VENUS: Aquarius (air)

Fabio (3/15/61)

SUN: Pisces (water)
MOON: Pisces (water)
MARS: Cancer (water)
VENUS: Aries (fire)

Brad Pitt (12/18/63)

SUN: Sagittarius (fire)
MOON: Capricorn (earth)
MARS: Capricorn (earth)
VENUS: Capricorn (earth)

Johnny Depp (6/9/63)

SUN: Gemini (air)
MOON: Capricorn (earth)
MARS: Virgo (earth)
VENUS: Taurus (earth)

Keanu Reeves (9/2/64)

SUN: Virgo (earth)
MOON: Leo (fire)
MARS: Cancer (water)
VENUS: Cancer (water)

Joaquin Phoenix (10/28/74)

SUN: Scorpio (water)
MOON: Aries (fire)
MARS: Scorpio (water)
VENUS: Scorpio (water)

CHAPTER 8

Ask the Expert—Should You Have a Personal Reading?

Though you can learn much about yourself and others from studying astrology yourself, there comes a time when you might want the objective opinion of a professional astrologer. Done by a qualified astrologer, the personal reading can be an empowering experience if you want to reach your full potential, size up a lover or business situation, or find out what the future has in store. There are so many options for readings today, however, that sorting through them can be a daunting task. Besides face-to-face consultations, there are readings by mail, phone, tape, and Internet. There are astrologers who are specialists in certain areas, such as finance or medical astrology. And unfortunately, there are many questionable practitioners who range from streetwise gypsy fortunetellers to unscrupulous scam artists. The following basic guidelines can help you sort out your options to find the reading that's right for you.

The One-on-One Reading

Nothing compares to a one-on-one consultation with a professional astrologer who has analyzed thousands of charts and can pinpoint the potential in yours. During your reading, you can get your specific questions answered. For instance, how to get along better with your mate or coworker. There are many astrologers who now combine their skills with training in psychology and are well suited to help you examine your alternatives.

To give you an accurate reading, an astrologer needs certain information from you, such as the date, time, and place where you were born. (A horoscope can be cast about anyone or anything that has a specific time and place.) Most astrologers will then enter this information into a computer, which will calculate a chart in seconds. From the resulting chart, the astrologer will do an interpretation.

If you don't know your exact birth time, you can usually locate it at the Bureau of Vital Statistics at the city hall or county seat of the state where you were born. If you still have no success in getting your time of birth, some astrologers can estimate an approximate birth time by using past events in your life to determine the chart. This technique is called *rectification*.

How to Find a Good Astrologer

Your first priority should be to choose a qualified astrologer. Rather than relying on word of mouth or grandiose advertising claims, choose your astrologer with the same care as any trusted adviser such as a doctor, lawyer, or banker. Unfortunately, anyone can claim to be an astrologer—to date, there is no licensing of astrologers or established professional criteria. However, there are nationwide organizations of serious, committed astrologers that can help you in your search.

Good places to start your investigation are organizations such as the American Federation of Astrologers or the National Council for Geocosmic Research (NCGR), which offer a program of study and certification. If you live near a major city, there is sure to be an active NCGR chapter or astrology club in your area—many are listed in astrology magazines available at your local newsstand. In response to many requests for referrals, the NCGR has compiled a directory of professional astrologers, which includes a glossary of terms and an explanation of specialties within the astrological field. Contact the NCGR headquarters (see Chapter 10, "The Sydney Omarr Yellow Pages") for information.

Be Aware of When to Beware

As a potentially lucrative freelance business, astrology has always attracted self-styled experts who may not have the knowledge or the counseling experience to give a helpful reading. These astrologers can range from the well-meaning amateur to the charlatan or street-corner gypsy who has for many years given astrology a bad name. Be very wary of astrologers who claim to have occult powers or who make pretentious claims of celebrated clients or miraculous achievements. You can often tell from the initial phone conversation if the astrologer is legitimate. He or she should ask for your birthday time and place and conduct the conversation in a professional manner. Any astrologer who gives a reading based only on your sun sign is highly suspect.

When you arrive at the reading, the astrologer should be prepared. The consultation should be conducted in a private, quiet place. The astrologer should be interested in your problems of the moment. A good reading involves feedback on your part, so if the reading is not relating to your concerns, you should let the astrologer know. You should feel free to ask questions and get clarifications of technical terms. The more you actively participate, rather than expecting the astrologer to carry the reading or come forth with oracular predictions, the more meaningful your experience will be. An astrologer should help you validate your current experience and be frank about possible negative happenings, but suggest a positive course of action.

In their approach to a reading, some astrologers may be more literal, others more intuitive. Those who have had counseling training may take a more psychological approach. Though some astrologers may seem to have an almost psychic ability, extrasensory perception or any other parapsychological talent is not essential. A very accurate picture can be drawn from the data in your horoscope chart.

An astrologer may do several charts for each client, including one for the time of birth and a "progressed chart," showing the evolution from birth to the present time. According to your individual needs, there are many other possibilities, such as a chart for a different location, if you are contemplating a change of place. Relationships between any two people, things, or events can be interpreted with a chart which compares one partner's horoscope with the other's. A composite chart, which uses the midpoint between planets in two individual charts to describe the relationship, is another commonly used device.

An astrologer will be particularly interested in transits—times when planets will pass over the planets or sensitive points in your birth chart, which signal important events in your life.

Many astrologers offer tape-recorded readings, another option to consider. In this case, you'll be mailed a taped reading based on your birth chart. This type of reading is more personal than a computer printout and can give you valuable insights, though it is not equivalent to a live dialogue with the astrologer, when you can discuss your specific interests and issues of the moment.

Phone Readings—Real or Phony?

Telephone readings come in two varieties, a dial-in taped reading, usually recorded in advance by an astrologer or a live consultation with an "astrologer" on the other end of the line. The taped readings are general daily or weekly forecasts, applied to all members of your sign and charged by the minute. The quality depends on the astrologer. *One caution*: Be aware that these readings can run up quite a telephone bill, especially if you get into the habit of calling every day. Be sure that you are aware of the per-minute cost of each call beforehand.

Live telephone readings also vary with the expertise of the astrologer. Ideally, the astrologer at the other end of the line enters your birth data into a computer, which calculates your chart. This chart will then be referred to during the consultation. The advantage of a live telephone reading is that your individual chart is used and you can ask about a specific problem. However, before you invest in any reading, be sure that your astrologer is qualified and that you fully understand in advance how much you will be charged. There should be no unpleasant financial surprises later.

About Computer Readings

Companies which offer computer programs (such as ACS, Matrix, Astrolabe) also offer a variety of computer-generated horoscope readings. These can be quite comprehensive, offering a beautiful printout of the chart plus many pages of detailed information about each planet and aspect of the chart. You can then study it at your convenience. Of course, the interpretations will be general, since there is no personal input from you, and may not cover your immediate concerns. Since computer-generated horoscopes are much lower in cost than live consultations, you might consider them as either a supplement or preparation for an eventual live reading. You'll then be more familiar with your chart and able to plan specific questions in advance. They also make a terrific gift for astrology fans. There are several companies in our "Yellow Pages" chapter which offer computerized readings prepared by reputable astrologers.

Whichever option you decide to pursue, may your reading be an empowering one!

CHAPTER 9

The "In" Sites Online

If you're curious to see a copy of your chart (or someone else's), want to study astrology in depth, or chat with another astrology fan, log on to the Internet! There you'll find a whole new world of astrology waiting for a click of your mouse. Thousands of astrological sites offer you everything from chart services to chat rooms to individual readings. Even better, you'll find *free* software, *free* charts, and *free* articles to download. You can virtually get an education in astrology from your computer screen, share your insights with new astrology-minded pals in a chat room or on a mailing list, then later meet them in person at one of the hundreds of conferences around the world.

The following sites were chosen for general interest from vast numbers of astrology-oriented places on the Net. Many have their own selection of links to other sites for further exploration. *One caveat*: Though these sites were selected with longevity in mind, the Internet is a volatile place where sites can disappear or change without notice. Therefore, some of our sites may have changed addresses, names, or content by the time this book is published.

Free Charts

Astrolabe Software at *http://www.alabe.com* distributes some of the most creative and user-friendly programs now available, like "Solar Fire," a favorite of top astrologers. Visitors to their site are greeted with a chart of the time you log on. You can get your chart calculated, with a mini-interpretation, e-mailed to you.

For an instant chart, surf to this address: *http://www.astro.ch* and check into ASTRODIENST, one of the first and best astrology sites on the Internet. Its world atlas will give you the accurate longitude and latitude of your birthplace for setting up your horoscope. You can print out your chart in a range of easy-to-read formats. One handy feature for beginners: The planetary placement is listed in words, rather than glyphs, alongside the chart (a real help for those who haven't yet learned to read the astrology glyph).

There are many other attractions at this site, such as a list of your astro-twins (famous people born on your birthdate). The site even sorts the "twins" to feature those who also have your identical rising sign. You can then click on their names and get instant charts of your famous sign-mates.

Free Software

Software manufacturers on the Web are generous with free downloads of demo versions of their software. You may then calculate charts using their data. This makes sense if you're considering investing serious money in astrology software, and want to see how the program works in advance. You can preview ASTROLABE Software programs favored by many professional astrologers at *http://www.alabe.com*. Check out the latest demo of "Solar Fire," one of the most user-friendly astrology programs available—you'll be impressed.

For a Fully Functional Astrology Program:

Walter Pullen's amazingly complete ASTROLOG program is offered absolutely free at this site: *http://www.magitech.com/~cruiser1/astrolog.htm*.

ASTROLOG is an ultrasophisticated program with all the features of much more expensive programs. It comes in versions for all formats—DOS, Windows, MAC, UNIX—and has some cool features such as a revolving globe and a constellation map. A "must" for those who want to get involved with astrology without paying big bucks for a professional-caliber program. Or for those who want to add ASTROLOG's unique features to their astrology software library. This program has it all!

Another good resource for software is Astro Computing Services. Their Web site has free demos of several excellent programs. Note especially their "Electronic Astrologer," one of the most effective and reasonably priced programs on the market. It's very easy to use, a bonus for nontechies. Go to *http://www.astrocom.com* for ACS software, books, readings, chart services, and software demos. At this writing, there are free new moon and full moon reports.

Surf to *http://www.astroscan.ca* for a free program called ASTROSCAN. Stunning graphics and ease of use make this a winner.

At Halloran Software's site, *http://www.halloran.com,* there are four levels of Windows astrology software from which to choose. The "Astrology for Windows" shareware program is available in unregistered demo form as a free download and in registered form for $26.50, at this writing. The calculations in this program may be all that an astrology hobbyist needs. The price for the full-service program is certainly reasonable.

Free Screen Saver and More

The Astrology Matrix offers a way to put your sign in view with a downloadable graphic screensaver. There are also many other diversions at this site, where you may consult the stars, the I Ching, the runes, and the tarot. Here's where to connect with news groups and online discussions. Their almanac helps you schedule the best day to sign on the dotted line, ask for a raise, or plant your rosebush. Address: *http://thenewage.com*.

Free Astrology Course

Schedule a long visit to *http://www.panplanet.com*, where you will find the Canopus Academy of Astrology, a site loaded with goodies. For the experienced astrologer, there is a collection of articles from top astrologers. They've done the work for you when it comes to picking the best astrology links on the Web, so be sure to check out those bestowed with the Canopus Award of Excellence.

Astrologer Linda Reid, an accomplished astrology teacher and author, offers a complete online curriculum for all levels of astrology study plus individual tutoring. To get your feet wet, Linda is offering an excellent beginners' course at this site, a terrific way to get off and running in astrology.

Visit an Astro-Mall

Surf to *http://www.astronet.com* for the Internet's equivalent of an Astrology Mall. ASTRONET offers interactive fun for everyone. At this writing, there's a special area for teenage astrology fans, access to popular astrology magazines like *American Astrology,* advice to the lovelorn, as well as a grab bag of horoscopes, featured guests, and a shopping area for books, reports, software, and even jewelry.

Swoon.com is another mall-like site aimed at dating, mating, and relating. It has fun features to spark up your love life, plenty of advice for the lovelorn, as well as links to all the popular fashion magazine astrology columns. Address: *http://www.swoon.com*.

Find An Astrologer Here

Metalog Directory of Astrology
http://www.astrologer.com

Looking for an astrologer in your local area? Perhaps you're planning a vacation in Australia or France and would like to meet astrologers or combine your activities with an astrology conference there? Go no further than this well-maintained resource. Here is an extensive worldwide list of astrologers and astrology sites. There is also an agenda of astrology conferences and seminars all over the world.

The A.F.A. Web Site
http://www.astrologers.com

This is the interesting Web site of the prestigious American Federation of Astrologers. The A.F.A. has a very similar address to the *Metalog Directory* and also has a directory of astrologers, restricted to those who meet their stringent requirements. Check out their correspondence course if you would like to study astrology in depth.

Tools Every Astrologer Needs Are Online

Internet Atlas
http://www.astro.ch/atlas

Find the geographic longitude and latitude and the correct time zone for any city worldwide. You'll need this information to calculate a chart.

The Exact Time, Anywhere in the World
http://www.timeticker.com

A fun site with fascinating graphics which give you the exact time anywhere in the world. Click on the world map and the correct time and zone for that place lights up.

Check the Weather Forecast
http://www.weathersage.com

More accurate than your local TV forecast is the Weathersage, which uses astrology to predict snowstorms and hurricanes. Get your long-range local forecast at this super site.

Celebrate the Queen's Birthday
http://www.zodiacal.com

A great jumping-off place for an astrology tour of the Internet, this site has a veritable Burke's Peerage of royal birthdays. There's a good selection of articles, plus tools such as a U.S. and world atlas and information on conferences, software, and tapes. The links at this site will send you off in the right direction.

Astrology World
http://astrology-world.com

Astrologer Deborah Houlding has gathered some of the finest European astrologers on this super Web site, as well as a comprehensive list of links and conferences.

Astrology Alive
http://www.astrologyalive.com

Barbara Schermer has one of the most innovative approaches to astrology. She was one of the first astrologers to go online, so there's always a "cutting edge" to this site. Great list of links.

National Council for Geocosmic Research (NCGR)
http://www.geocosmic.org

A key stop on any astrological tour of the Net. Here's where you can find local chapters in your area, get information on the NCGR testing and certification programs, and get a conference schedule. You can also order lecture tapes from their nationwide conferences, or get complete lists of conference topics to study at home. Good links to resources.

Where to Find Charts of the Famous

When the news is breaking, you can bet Lois Rodden will be the first to get accurate birthdays of the headline makers, and put up their charts on her Web site: *www.astrodatabank.com*. Rodden's research is astrology's most reliable source for data of the famous and infamous. Her Web site specializes in birthdays and charts of current newsmakers, political figures, and international celebrities. You can purchase her database program, a wonderful research tool, which gives you thousands of birthdays sorted into categories.

Another site with birthdays and charts of famous people to download is *http://www.astropro.com*.

You can get the sun and moon sign, plus a biography of the hottest new film stars here: *http://www.mrshowbiz.com*. Or go to *http://www.imdb.com* for a comprehensive list of film celebrities including bios, plus lists of famous couples from today and yesteryear.

Yet another good source for celebrity birthdates is *http://www.metamaze.com/bdays*. You can find some interesting offbeat newsmakers here.

For Astrology Books

National Clearinghouse for Astrology Books

A wide selection of books on all aspects of astrology, from basics to advanced. Many hard-to-find books. Surf to: *http://www.astroamerica.com*.

These addresses also have a good selection of astrology books, some which are unique to the site:
http://www.panplanet.com
http://thenewage.com
http://www.astrocom.com

Browse the huge astrology list of online bookstore Amazon.com at *http://www.amazon.com*.

Astrology Tapes at Pegasus Tapes
http://www.pegasustape.com

You can study at home with world-famous astrologers via audiocassette recordings from Pegasus Tapes. There's a great selection taped from conferences, classes, lectures, and seminars. An especially good source for astrologers who emphasize psychological and mythological themes.

For History and Mythology Buffs

Be sure to visit the astrology section of this gorgeous site, dedicated to the history and mythology of many traditions. One of the most beautifully designed sites we've seen. Address: *http://www.elore.com*.

The leading authority on the history of astrology, Robert Hand, has an excellent site which features his cutting-edge research. See what one of astrology's great teachers has to offer. Address: *http://www.robhand.com*.

The Project Hindsight group is devoted to restoring the astrology of the Hellenistic period (300 B.C. to about

600 A.D.), the primary source for all later Western astrology. Some fascinating articles for astrology fans. Address: *http://www.projecthindsight-tghp.com/index.html.*

C.U.R.A. is a European site for historical researchers. Address: *http://cura.free.fr.*

Readers interested in mythology should also check out *http://pantheon.org/mythical/* for stories of gods and goddesses.

Astrology Magazines

The Mountain Astrologer
http://www.mountainastrologer.com

A favorite magazine of astrology fans, *The Mountain Astrologer* has an interesting Web site featuring the latest news from an astrological point of view, plus feature articles from the magazine.

Financial Astrology

Find out how financial astrologers play the market. Here are hot picks, newsletters, specialized financial astrology software, and mutual funds run by astrology seers. Go to *www.afund.com* or *www.alphee.com* for tips and forecasts from two top financial astrologers.

CHAPTER 10

The Sydney Omarr Yellow Pages

Enter the world of astrology! If you want to find an astrology program for your computer, connect with other astrology fans, study advanced techniques, or buy books and tapes, consider this chapter "Astrology Central." Here you'll find the latest products and services available, as well as the top astrology organizations which hold meetings and conferences in your area.

There are organized groups of astrologers all over the country who are dedicated to promoting the image of astrology in the most positive way. The National Council for Geocosmic Research (NCGR) is one nationwide group that is dedicated to bringing astrologers together, promoting fellowship and high-quality education. Their accredited course system promotes a systematized study of all the different facets of astrology. Whether you'd like to know more about such specialties as financial astrology or techniques for timing events, or if you'd prefer the psychological or mythological approach, you'll find the leading experts at NCGR conferences.

Your computer can be a terrific tool for connecting with other astrology fans at all levels of expertise, as we explored in the Internet chapter in this book. Even if you are using a "dinosaur" from the 1980s, there are still calculation and interpretation programs available for DOS and MAC formats. They may not have all the bells and whistles or the exciting graphics, but they'll get the job done!

Newcomers to astrology should learn some of the basics, including the glyphs (astrology's special shorthand language) before you invest in a complex computer program. Use the chapter in this book to help you learn the symbols easily, so you'll be able to read the charts without consulting the "help" section of your program every time. Several programs, such as Astrolabe's "Solar Fire," have pop-up definitions to help you decipher the meanings of planets and aspects. Just click your mouse on a glyph or an icon on the screen, and a window with an instant definition appears.

You don't have to spend a fortune to get a perfectly adequate astrology program. In fact, if you are connected to the Internet, you can download one free. Astrology software is available at all price levels, from a sophisticated free application like *Astrology,* which you can download from a Web site, to inexpensive programs for under $100 such as Halloran's "Astrology for Windows," to the more expensive astrology programs such as "Winstar," "Solar Fire," or "Io" (for the Mac), which are used by serious students and professionals. Before you make an investment, it's a good idea to download a sample from the company's Web site or order a demo disk.

If you're baffled by the variety of software available, most of the companies on our list will be happy to help you find the right application for your needs.

Students of astrology who live in out-of-the-way places or are unable to fit classes into your schedule have several options. There are online courses offered at astrology Web sites, such as *www.panplanet.com,* and at the NCGR and AFA Web sites. Some astrology teachers will send you a series of audiotapes or you can order audiotaped seminars of recent conferences; other teachers offer correspondence courses that use their workbooks or computer printouts.

The Yellow Pages

Nationwide Astrology Organizations and Conferences

Contact these organizations for information on conferences, workshops, local meetings, conference tapes, and referrals:

National Council for Geocosmic Research

Educational workshops, tapes, conferences, and a directory of professional astrologers are available from this nationwide organization devoted to promoting astrological education. For a $35 annual membership fee, you get their excellent publications and newsletters, plus the opportunity to network with other astrology buffs at local chapter events (there are chapters in twenty states).
For general information about NCGR, contact:

NCGR
P.O. Box 38866
Los Angeles, CA 90038
Phone: 818-705-1678

Or visit their Web page, *http://www.geocosmic.org*, for updates and local events.

American Federation of Astrologers (A.F.A.)

One of the oldest astrological organizations in the United States, established in 1938. Conferences, conventions, and a correspondence course. Will refer you to an accredited A.F.A. astrologer.

A.F.A.
P.O. Box 22040
Tempe, AZ 85382

Phone: 602-838-1751
Fax: 602-838-8293

A.F.A.N. (Association for Astrological Networking)

(Networking, Legal Issues)
Did you know that astrologers are still being arrested for practicing in some states? AFAN provides support and legal information, and works toward improving the public image of astrology. Here are the people who will go to bat for astrology when it is attacked in the media. Everyone who cares about astrology should join!

A.F.A.N.
8306 Wilshire Blvd., Suite 537
Beverly Hills, CA 90211

ARC Directory

(Listing of astrologers worldwide)
2920 E. Monte Vista
Tucson, AZ 85716
Phone: 602-321-1114

Pegasus Tapes

(Lectures, conference tapes)
P.O. Box 419
Santa Ysabel, CA 92070

International Society for Astrological Research

(Lectures, workshops, seminars)
P.O. Box 38613
Los Angeles, CA 90038

ISIS Institute

(Newsletter, conferences, astrology tapes, catalog)
P.O. Box 21222
El Sobrante, CA 94820-1222
Phone: 888-322-4747
Fax: 510-222-2202

Astrology Software

Astrolabe

Box 1750-R
Brewster, MA 02631
Phone: 800-843-6682

Check out the latest version of their powerful "Solar Fire" software for Windows—it's a breeze to use and will grow with your increasing knowledge of astrology to the most sophisticated levels. This company also markets a variety of programs for all levels of expertise, a wide selection of computer astrology readings, and Mac programs. A good resource for innovative software as well as applications for older computers.

Matrix Software

407 N. State Street
Big Rapids, MI 49307
Phone: 800-PLANETS

A wide variety of software in all price ranges, demo disks, student and advanced levels, and lots of interesting readings. Check out "Winstar," their powerful professional software, if you're planning to study astrology seriously.

Astro Communications Services

Dept. AF693, PO Box 34487
San Diego, CA 92163-4487
Phone: 800-888-9983

Books, software for MAC and IBM compatibles, individual charts, and telephone readings. Find technical astrology materials here, such as "The American Ephemeris." They will calculate charts for you if you do not have a computer.

Air Software

115 Caya Avenue
West Hartford, CT 06110
Phone: 800-659-1247

Powerful, creative astrology software, like their millennium "Star Trax 2000." For beginners, check out "Father Time," which finds your best days. Or "Nostradamus," which answers all your questions. Financial astrology programs for stock market traders are a specialty.

Time Cycles Research—For Mac Users!!!

375 Willets Avenue
Waterford, CT 06385
Fax: 869-442-0625
E-mail: *astrology@timecycles.com*
Internet: *http://www.timecycles.com*

Where MAC users can find astrology software that's as sophisticated as it gets. If you have Mac, you'll love their beautiful graphic "IO Series" programs.

Astro-Cartography

(Charts for location changes)
Astro-Numeric Service Box 336-B
Ashland, OR 97520
Phone: 800-MAPPING

Astro-cartography is a sophisticated technique which superimposes an astrology chart on a map of the world. A fascinating study for serious students of astrology.

Astrology Magazines

In addition to articles by top astrologers, most have listings of astrology conferences, events, and local happenings.

AMERICAN ASTROLOGY
Dept. 4
P.O. Box 2021
Marion, OH 43306-8121

DELL HOROSCOPE
P.O. Box 53352
Boulder, CO 89321-3342

THE MOUNTAIN ASTROLOGER
P.O. Box 970
Cedar Ridge, CA 95924

Astrology Schools

Though there are many correspondence courses available through private teachers and astrological organizations, up until now, there has never been an accredited college of astrology. That is why the following address is so important.

Kepler College of Astrological Arts and Sciences

Kepler College, the first institution of its kind to combine an accredited liberal arts education with extensive astrological studies, is now in operation, after many years in planning. A degree-granting college that is also a center of astrological studies has long been the dream of the astrological community and will be a giant step forward in providing credibility to the profession. The Kepler College faculty comprises some of the most creative leaders in the astrology community.

For more information, contact:

Kepler College of Astrological Arts and Sciences
Business Office
4630 200th St. SW
Suite L-1
Lynnwood, WA 98036
Phone: 435-673-4292
Fax: 425-673-4983
Internet: *www.kepler.edu*

Your Gemini Home Pages—All About Your Life, Friends, Family, Work, and Style!

If you're a typical Gemini, you have an insatiable appetite for knowledge, a mind in perpetual motion, and a constant craving for innovation. Though some may question your staying power, others will benefit from your inquiring mind, your love of conveying information, and your need for constant stimulation. You enjoy variety in life and love, and can be happy single or married, provided you do not become bored. Because you're an air sign, social interaction is key, and you shine in the role of teacher, confidante, lover, confessor, or gossip (it's no accident that two of the most famous gossip columnists, Hedda Hopper and "Suzy" [Aileen Mehle] were born under your sign).

You'll find that the qualities associated with Gemini resonate through the many roles you play in life. And if there are other Gemini planets in your horoscope, or if your rising sign is Gemini, these conditions will intensify your Gemini-type personality. There'll be no mistaking you for another sun sign! For example, someone with a Gemini sun, Mars, and rising sign (ascendant) is likely to be much more obviously a "Gemini" type than someone whose Gemini sun is combined with a less talkative Scorpio ascendant and a slower-moving Mars in Taurus. However, even if you have a different personality from the typical Gemini, you'll find that many of the traits and preferences described below will still apply to you.

CHAPTER 11

Are You True to Type?

The Gemini Man—
The Great Communicator

"What's new?" is the constant question of the Gemini man. You're on a perpetual journey in search of the extraordinary, the startling, the intrigue of life. You can't bear boredom—any amount of activity is preferable to being stuck in a rut, so you're forever in motion. Even when you appear to be sitting still, chances are your mind is racing.

You're a lover of games on every level; the most complicated situations are like catnip to your agile mind. On the negative side, it is difficult for you to take anything or anyone too seriously. Weighty matters drag you down. You'd rather dabble in lots of different projects and fly off when things get too sticky.

In childhood, you were the bright funny little boy who talked early. A "quick study," you were often bored in school at the slowness of others—and could devise some jolly pranks to amuse yourself. You had many interests and hobbies, which kept changing constantly. Perhaps you learned self-discipline and the satisfaction of setting goals and reaching them in your early years; otherwise, you could have the tendency to skim the surface of life, with much activity, but few real accomplishments.

The young Gemini man tends to be a job-hopper, who rarely stays in your first position for long, unless it provides an outlet for your restless mind. Young adulthood is your time to experiment, and you're not about to deny yourself any adventures. A natural flirt and a charming chameleon who can't resist an exciting affair of the heart, you rarely get deeply involved at this stage and usually opt for several romantic experiences at once. This could lead to becoming a perennial playboy or to leading a double life, both hazards of the ever-curious and charming Gemini man.

In a Relationship

The woman who succeeds in tying Gemini down would be well advised to give him a lot of rope and keep an open mind. This is likely to be a nontraditional marriage: exciting, but not particularly stable. Though Gemini is not naturally inclined to be monogamous, he will stick with a woman who is bright, entertaining, sociable, and an interesting companion. Mental compatibility and stimulation are the keys to success. It would help if she is involved in his professional life, too, as well as having strong interests of her own. His hot-cold temperament and roving eye could cause his wife a great deal of insecurity, unless she is an independent person as well.

The Gemini Woman—
Many Sparkling Facets

The Gemini woman has a mind of her own and many different facets to her personality. You're not likely to fulfill any roles in the traditional way. Even the Geminis with a conservative, maternal facade, such as Barbara Bush, are up to date and with it, and probably know a little bit about almost everything. Even if you don't have a college education, you've probably done an excellent job of educating yourself. Your mind races so fast that you often know the answer before the question is asked!

You have the advantage of being a quick study who can match wits and "spin on a dime," like Geminis Joan Rivers, Joan Collins, and Elizabeth Hurley, all of whom carry on multiple careers at once. You rarely get too attached to anything or anyone, and you can adapt to a new situation quickly.

Face it—you'd be miserable in a life of routine. Often you'll do two things at once—hold down two jobs, combine a job with a personal interest, talk on two telephones, have two love affairs simultaneously. But this keeps you from getting too attached to anything or anyone. It's more fun to keep your options open, isn't it? After all, something or someone more exciting might appear.

At some point, you've got to figure out where you're going and get some "grounding." Otherwise, you could become like those lost Gemini girls, always looking for love somewhere "Over the Rainbow," like the characters Judy Garland and Marilyn Monroe portrayed. It is important for you to reconcile the twins within—that is, your feminine feelings with your detached "masculine" intelligence. When you're using your excellent mind in the right way, you can find the combination of stimulation and security that is your real "pot of gold."

In a Relationship

The Gemini woman usually prefers to keep working after marriage and to delegate the more mundane household chores to someone else. And an interesting job is essential to provide the change of scene and social contact she needs to keep from getting bored.

Geminis often marry more than once, since it's not easy to find a man who can match your wit and intelligence, allow you the space you need, as well as contribute solid financial and emotional support.

Gemini is rarely the sentimental wife—you like a full social life with some games, frivolity, and style. You love to flirt, so your mate must not be the jealous type. But if you can negotiate enough room in your marriage for personal freedom, you'll provide a life of sparkle and variety.

Gemini in the Family

As a Parent

Geminis take a great interest in their child's different stages, as the young personality unfolds. You may find the early babyhood years most difficult, when the child is dependent and needs steady, routine care. After the child learns to communicate, you'll take on the role of teacher, introducing the child to the world of ideas and mental pursuits, helping with homework and making difficult subjects easier to understand. One of your greatest assets as a parent is your own insatiable curiosity about the world, which you can communicate to your children by introducing them early to the world of ideas and books. You are also an excellent coach, teaching your child social skills at an early age. As your child matures, your youthful, ever-fresh outlook makes you a wonderful friend and companion through the years.

The Gemini Stepparent

Your sense of humor will often come to the rescue in the initial stages of starting up a new family. You're a communicator who can quickly get shy youngsters to open up and difficult personalities to respond. Gemini's talk power and natural sociability encourage everyone to have fun, making family get-togethers seem more like parties. Since you'll have many outside activities and interests, the children will be able to have as much time as they need alone with their parent. Soon your new family will find that you are a fun-loving addition to their lives, a wise adviser, and an excellent noncompetitive companion.

The Gemini Grandparent

You're an upbeat senior who still finds life an interesting adventure. You'll be the life of the family party, up on all the latest gossip, as well as what's happening with the rest of the world. Your visits are full of laughter and good stories! You'll take a special interest in your grandchildren's education (like Barbara Bush, you may have a large extended family which reaches out to the children of your community) and support them in whatever career path they choose. You'll give your own children plenty of space to rear the grandchildren as they please, never interfering with Mother's rules or taking over the grandchildren's upbringing. "Never complain" was the motto of the Duchess of Windsor (a Gemini), and it could be yours, too. You accentuate the positive and keep a cheerful attitude. After all, Norman Vincent Peale, the author of *The Power of Positive Thinking,* was a Gemini!

CHAPTER 12

"In Style" the Gemini Way

The key to looking and feeling your best is to go with the style that best suits your Gemini personality, which favors specific colors, surroundings, and attitudes. Follow these tips to maximize your own Gemini star quality.

Gemini's Atmospheric Conditions

"Flexible" is the word for the perfect Gemini environment. You need a place that accommodates all your different interests, with plenty of storage space, so you can sweep your projects quickly out of sight when friends drop in. A light, neutral background allows you to achieve different effects by changing color accents and accessories with your mood. Lots of bookcases, a telephone or three, and furniture you can rearrange in many different ways would provide you with enough variety. You're the sign with a telephone on both sides of the bed and alongside the bathtub. Have a separate room or corner with a desk where you can organize all your lists, fax machine, Palm Pilot, Rolodexes, and appointment books, so you won't waste time looking for them. Many Geminis enjoy having houses in more than one place (you're often bicoastal) and keep residences in different cities or a country house, so they can switch environments when bored.

Gemini's Music Mix

You're a natural disk jockey, who can juggle the beat according to the mood of the moment. Your music tastes are usually eclectic, with a wide variety of sounds, but you also pay attention to the words as well as the melody, so the witty lyrics of Cole Porter and the poetry of Bob Dylan appeal. So does abstract classical music—nothing too heavy or loud that might distract from conversation or bring on the blues. Create your own mix of sounds on tapes, so you can change moods frequently, perhaps mixing Paula Abdul, Miles Davis, Alanis Morrisette, some rap music, Cole Porter, Judy Garland, and some continental tunes from Charles Aznavour.

Stimulating Vacations for Gemini

Stay away from desert islands, unless you need some peace and quiet to write your novel. Stick to places where there's a lively social scene, some interesting scenery, local characters to provide good conversation, and an Internet café to keep up with your e-mail. Improve your language skills by visiting a foreign country—you'll have no trouble communicating in sign language, if necessary. Consider a language school in the south of France or Switzerland, where you'll mix with fellow students of many nationalities, while you perfect your accent.

Lightness is the key to Gemini travel. Don't weigh yourself down with luggage. Dare to travel with an empty suitcase and acquire clothes and supplies at your destination. (Imagine how fast you'll speed through the airport!)

Keep a separate tiny address book for each city, so the right numbers are always handy. Invest in beautifully designed travel cases and briefcases, since you're on the go so much. Spend some time looking for the perfect luggage, portable notebook computers (with a modem), and cellular telephones to keep you in touch at all times.

The Shades of Gemini

Soft silvery gray, pale yellow, and airy Wallis Windsor blue are Gemini colors. Sound bland? That's because these are great background colors, the ones you can live with over a period of time. They'll adapt to different seasons and climates, and won't compete with your personality or distract from your total image. You can change the look of these colors at will, accenting them with bright touches or blending with other pastels. And they can tolerate a frequent change of accessories, according to your mood of the moment.

Gemini Fashion Tips

You have fun with fashion and never take your fashion image too seriously. Some great fashion icons, like the Duchess of Windsor, were born under your sign and you couldn't find better inspiration than this legendary fashion devotee. We remember Wallis Simpson for her witty way with accessories, like those fabulous jewels she wore with casual aplomb (some engraved with secret messages from the Duke). Yet she never varied her signature swept-back hairdo or her elegantly simple style of dressing.

Gemini always likes to do something interesting

with your clothes, to get them talking about you! Nicole Kidman dresses with great Gemini flair, in clothes that get people talking. Annette Bening opts for simple elegant clothes that set off her delicate beauty. Other Gemini beauties—like Elizabeth Hurley, who attended the Academy Awards in a gown held together with safety pins, and Angelina Jolie—enjoy being downright outrageous, keeping their fans guessing! Some Geminis, like Elizabeth Hurley or Marilyn Monroe, love to flaunt their sex appeal, making a game of it. Play up your expressive hands with a perfect manicure and beautiful rings. A hairstyle that you can wear several different ways could satisfy your need for variety. Joan Rivers transforms her classic style into a tumble of curls with a few hot rollers.

Double-duty clothes that can work all day and dash to a party at night are perfect for busy Geminis. Add a witty, scene-stealing jewel or two, a dramatic scarf, or trendy shoes and handbag to quick-change your outfit's personality and you're ready to go!

Let Gemini Fashion Leaders Inspire You

Since you have such a changeable personality, you'll probably experiment with every kind of look before you settle on the style that has your name on it. Usually you're up to the minute, however, with a touch of the newest trend coming down the runway. The fashion duo Dolce & Gabbana, the with-it looks of Anna Sui, or the newest androgynous menswear styles would be fun for you to try on for size. Gemini models who express your flair, like Naomi Campbell, Elizabeth Hurley, and Brooke Shields, have the ability to change their image with their hairstyle, be a vamp one moment, an innocent girl next door the next.

Gemini Food for Thought

No matter what you order, you'll always want a bit of what everyone else is eating. Buffet tables are ideal ways for Geminis to sample a little bit of everything. Though your sign rarely has to worry about weight, try ordering a meal of appetizers to keep down calorie intake while you sample the menu, which is your favorite way to dine!

CHAPTER 13

The Healthy Gemini

One of the most social signs, Gemini rules the nerves, our body's lines of communication. If your nerves are on edge, you may be trying to do too many things at once, leaving no time for fun and laughter. When you've overloaded your circuits, it's time to get together with friends, go out to parties, do things in groups to bring perspective into your life. Investigate natural ways to relieve tension such as yoga or meditation. Doing things with your hands—playing the piano, typing, doing craftwork—is also helpful.

Since Gemini also rules the lungs, yours are especially sensitive, so if you smoke, please consider quitting. Deep breathing exercises which fill your lungs with oxygen are very beneficial. Yoga, which incorporates deep breathing into physical exercise, is a wonderful exercise system for Geminis. Among its many benefits are the deep relaxation and tranquility so needed by your sign.

Diet-wise, you belong to one of the naturally skinny signs. However, parties and restaurant meals can pile on the pounds, if you hang around the buffet table instead of the dance floor. Your curiosity leads you to sample a bit of everything, which could add up calories before you realize it. Your challenge is to find a diet with plenty of variety, so you won't get bored. Develop a strategy for eating in restaurants and coping with buffets (pile the plate with salad and veggies).

Social activity is most therapeutic for you, so combine your healthy activities with social get-togethers for fun and plenty of fringe benefits for everyone. Include friends in your exercise routines; join an exercise class or jogging club. Gemini excels at sports which require good timing and manual dexterity as well as communication with others, like tennis (Steffi Graf) or golf. Those of you who jog may want to add hand weights or upper body exercises to your daily routine, for benefits to the Gemini-ruled arms and hands. If you spend long hours at the computer, be sure you have an ergonomic keyboard for comfort and protection against carpal tunnel syndrome.

CHAPTER 14

Gemini at Work!

Gemini has many winning cards to play in the career game. Your quick mind works best in a career where there is enough mental stimulation to keep you from getting bored. High-pressure situations that would be stressful to others are stimulating to you. Many things happening simultaneously—phones ringing off the hook, daily client meetings, constant changes—are all exciting to you. Your ability to communicate with a variety of people works well in sales, journalism, public relations, agent or broker work, personnel or consulting, literally any job that requires verbal or writing skills. You who learn languages easily could be a language teacher or interpreter. Manual dexterity is another Gemini gift that can find craft, musical, or medical expression (especially surgery or chiropractic).

What to avoid: a job that is too isolated, routine, detail-oriented, or confining. Stay away from companies that are hidebound, with rigid rules. Instead, look for a place that gives you strong backup as well as free rein. Gemini often succeeds in a freelance position, provided they have a solid support system to help with the details and routine chores.

The Gemini Leader

You operate best as a dealmaker or an entrepreneur, rather than a designer or a producer. (Flamboyant

Gemini Donald Trump wrote the book on wheeling and dealing—*The Art of the Deal.*) You often change your mind, so you should hire assistants who are adaptable enough to keep up with you, yet who are organized to provide direction and structure. If a project gets bogged down, you will change course rapidly, rather than see it through. Sometimes you have so many projects going on at once that others are dizzy, yet you are known for innovative ideas and your cool analysis of problems. You are especially gifted in making a deal, coordinating the diverse aspects of a project.

Gemini is fun to work for—sociable, witty, and clever. Your office will be a beehive of activity, with telephone lines buzzing and clients coming and going. What is lacking in job security you make up in opportunities for others to experiment, to develop flexibility and a sense of gamesmanship.

Gemini Teamwork

The Gemini worker shines in a job full of variety and quick changes. The key: You must be stimulated mentally. Financial security alone rarely motivates you. You can learn a job quickly, but you leave it just as quickly once it becomes routine. You work beautifully in a team, where your light sense of humor and friendliness and ability to express yourself clearly are appreciated. Your position should be dealing with the public in a sales or communications position. You are also skilled at office politics. It's all part of the game to you. You rarely get emotionally involved. Let someone else do the record keeping, financial management, or accounting. Or you can handle a position where you report to several different people or juggle several different assignments, though you may do less well if the job requires intense concentration, patience, and perseverance.

Your Gemini Career Strategy

To get ahead fast, pick a job with variety and mental stimulation. Play up your best attributes, especially the following:
- Verbal and written communication skills
- Ability to handle several tasks at once
- Charm and sociability
- Manual dexterity
- Ability to learn quickly
- Analytical ability

Gemini Career Role Models

Study the careers of these colorful Geminis, some of them legends in their own time. Most are featured in biographies, business magazine profiles, or reference books. You might get some valuable tips on what to do—and what not to do—to make the most of your sign's moneymaking potential:

Donald Trump
Mortimer Zuckerman
Sam Wanamaker
Katharine Graham (*Washington Post*)
Charles and Maurice Saatchi (advertising)
Laurence Rockefeller
Baron Guy de Rothschild
Paul Mellon

CHAPTER 15

Gemini Rich and Famous!

We're fascinated by reading tabloids and gossip items about the rich, famous, and infamous in the post-Millennium, but astrology can tell you more about your heroes than most magazine articles. Like what really turns them on (check their Venus). Or what makes them rattled (scope their Saturn). Compare similarities and differences between the celebrities who embody the typical Gemini sun sign traits and those who seem atypical. Then look up other planets in the horoscope of your favorites, using the charts in this book, to see how other planets influence the horoscope. It's a fun way to get your education in astrology.

Naomi Campbell (5/22/70)
Douglas Fairbanks (5/23/1883)
Roseanne Cash (5/24/50)
Bob Dylan (5/24/41)
Patti LaBelle (5/24/44)
Priscilla Presley (5/23/45)
Miles Davis (5/23/26)
Dixie Carter (5/25/39)
Connie Selleca (5/25/55)
Ian McKellen (5/25/39)
Anne Heche (5/25/63)
Helena Bonham Carter (5/26/66)

John Wayne (5/26/07)
Peggy Lee (5/26/20)
Stevie Nicks (5/26/48)
Philip Micheal Thomas (5/26/49)
Louis Gossett Jr. (5/27/36)
Tony Hillerman (5/27/25)
Siouxie Sioux (5/27/57)
Vincent Price (5/27/11)
Gladys Knight (5/28/44)
Sondra Locke (5/28/47)
Annette Bening (5/29/58)
Anthony Geary (5/29/47)
Kevin Conway (5/29/42)
Bob Hope (5/29/03)
Rupert Everett (5/29/59)
John F. Kennedy (5/29/17)
Benny Goodman (5/30/09)
Prince Rainier (5/31/23)
Joe Namath (5/31/50)
Clint Eastwood (5/31/30)
Brooke Shields (5/31/65)
Lea Thompson (5/31/61)
Sharon Gless (5/31/43)
Peter Yarrow (5/31/38)
Tom Berenger (5/31/50)
Morgan Freeman (6/1/37)
Andy Griffith (6/1/26)
Jonathan Pryce (6/1/47)
Ron Wood (6/1/47)
Edward Woodward (6/1/30)
Pat Boone (6/1/34)
Rene Auberjonois (6/1/40)
Marilyn Monroe (6/1/26)
Hedda Hopper (6/2/1890)
Sally Kellerman (6/2/37)
Stacey Keach (6/2/41)
Marvin Hamlisch (6/2/44)
Curtis Mayfield (6/3/42)

Tony Curtis (6/3/25)
Deniece Williams (6/3/51)
Michelle Phillips (6/4/44)
Dr. Ruth Westheimer (6/4/28)
Parker Stevenson (6/4/52)
Bruce Dern (6/4/36)
Mark Wahlberg (6/5/71)
Bill Moyers (6/5/34)
Sandra Bernhard (6/6/55)
Jessica Tandy (6/7/09)
Tom Jones (6/7/40)
James Ivory (6/7/28)
Liam Neeson (6/7/52)
Prince (6/7/58)
Kathy Baker (6/8/50)
Barbara Bush (6/8/25)
Joan Rivers (6/8/33)
Michael J. Fox (6/9/61)
Johnny Depp (6/9/63)
Elizabeth Hurley (6/10/65)
Tara Lipinski (6/10/82)
Grace Mirabella (6/10/30)
Lionel Jeffries (6/10/26)
Prince Philip (6/10/21)
Gene Wilder (6/11/35)
Chad Everett (6/11/37)
Adrienne Barbeau (6/11/45)
George Bush (6/12/24)
Timothy Busfield (6/12/57)
Tim Allen (6/13/53)
Ally Sheedy (6/13/62)
Christo (6/13/35)
Basil Rathbone (6/13/1892)
Donald Trump (6/14/46)
Boy George (6/14/61)
Steffi Graf (6/14/69)
Waylon Jennings (6/15/37)
Mario Cuomo (6/15/32)

Courteney Cox Arquette (6/15/64)
Helen Hunt (6/15/63)
Yasmine Bleeth (6/16/68)
Corin Redgrave (6/16/39)
Dean Martin (6/17/17)
Joe Piscopo (6/17/51)
Roger Ebert (6/18/42)
Isabella Rossellini (6/18/52)
E. G. Marshall (6/18/10)
Paul McCartney (6/18/41)
Paula Abdul (6/19/63)
Kathleen Turner (6/19/54)
Danny Aiello (6/20/33)
John Goodman (6/20/52)

CHAPTER 16

Gemini Pairs—How You Get Along with Every Other Sign

Before you commit or sign on the dotted line, check this tip list of pluses and minuses of every combination, so you'll know what to expect before you leap into love (or any other relationship).

Gemini/Aries

PLUSES:
There is fast-paced action here. Gemini gets a charge of excitement. Aries gets constant changes to keep up with. Both are spontaneous, optimistic, and energetic. Differences of opinion only keep the atmosphere stimulating.

MINUSES:
Juggling life with you could have Aries seeing double. Aries is direct and to the point, but you can't or won't be pinned down. This hyperactive combination could get on both your nerves unless you give each other plenty of space. Gemini, tone down the flirting—Aries must be number 1!

Gemini/Taurus

PLUSES:
Next-door signs may be best friends as well as lovers. In this case, you drag Taurus out of the house and into social life, adding laughter to love. Taurus has a soothing, stabilizing quality that supports your restlessness and allows you to be more creative than ever.

MINUSES:
Homebody Taurus usually loves one-on-one relations, while social Gemini loves to flirt with a crowd. You will have to curb roving eyes and bodies and plan to spend more time at home, which might cramp your style and leave you gasping for air. Infidelity can be serious business with Taurus—but taken lightly by Gemini. The balance scales between freedom and license swing and sway here.

Gemini/Gemini

PLUSES:
When Gemini Twins find each other, you know you'll never be bored. Here are enough multifaceted mental activity, games, and delightful social life to double your pleasure. You'll understand the complexities of your sign as only fellow Geminis can.

MINUSES:
When the realities of life hit, you may go off in five directions at once. This combination lacks focus and functions best in a light, creative atmosphere, where there are no financial concerns. Serious practical problems could split your personalities and send you running elsewhere for protection and guidance.

Gemini/Cancer

PLUSES:
This is a very public pair with charisma to spare. Your sparkling wit sets off Cancer's poise with the perfect light touch. Cancer adds warmth and caring to Gemini. This sign's shrewd insight can make your ideas happen. You can go places together.

MINUSES:
It's not easy for Gemini to deliver the kind of devotion Cancer needs. There are too many other exciting options. Nor do you react well to Cancer's need to mother you or pleas for sympathy. Their up-and-down moods also get on your nerves . . . why can't they learn to laugh away their troubles or find new interests? When Cancer clings, Gemini does a vanishing act. You need to have strong mutual interests or projects to hold this combo together. (But it has been done!)

Gemini/Leo

PLUSES:
Gemini's good humor, ready wit, and social skills delight and complement Leo. Here is someone who can share the spotlight without trying to steal the show from the regal Lion. This is one of the most entertaining combinations. Steady Leo provides the focus Gemini often lacks and directs the Twins toward achieving goals and status.

MINUSES:
Gemini loves to flirt and flit among many interests, romantic and otherwise, which is sure to irritate the Lion, who does one thing at a time and does it well.

Gemini might be a bit bored with Leo's self-promotion and might poke fun at this sign's notorious vanity. The resulting feline roar will be no laughing matter.

Gemini/Virgo

PLUSES:
Both Mercury-ruled, your deepest bond will be mental communication and appreciation of each other's intelligence. Virgo's Mercury is earthbound and analytical, while Gemini's Mercury is a jack-of-all-trades. Gemini shows Virgo the big picture; Virgo takes care of the details. Your combined talents make a stimulating partnership. Virgo becomes the administrator here, Gemini the "idea" person.

MINUSES:
Your different priorities can be irritating to each other. Virgo needs a sense of order. Gemini needs to experiment and is forever the gadabout. An older Gemini who has slowed down somewhat makes the best partner here.

Gemini/Libra

PLUSES:
Air signs Gemini and Libra have both mental and physical rapport. This is an outgoing combination, full of good talk. You'll never be bored. Libra's good looks and charm, as well as fine mind, could keep restless Gemini close to home.

MINUSES:
Both of you have a low tolerance for boredom and practical chores. The question of who will provide, do

the dirty work, and clean up can be the subject of many a debate. There could be more talk than action here, leaving you turning elsewhere for substance.

Gemini/Scorpio

PLUSES:
You're a fascinating mystery to each other. Gemini is immune from Scorpio paranoia, laughs away dark moods, and matches wits in power games. Scorpio's intensity, focus, and sexual magnetism draw Gemini like a moth to a flame. You're intrigued by their secrets . . . here's a puzzle that would be fun to solve. And steamy Scorpio brings intensity and a new level of thrills to your sex life.

MINUSES:
Scorpio gets "heavy," possessive, and jealous, which Gemini doesn't take seriously. To make this one last, Gemini needs to treat Scorpio like the one and only, while Scorpio must use a light touch, and learn not to take Gemini's flirtations to heart.

Gemini/Sagittarius

PLUSES:
These polar opposites shake each other up—happily. Sagittarius helps Gemini see higher truths, to look beyond the life of the party and the art of the deal. Gemini adds mental challenge and flexibility to Sagittarius.

MINUSES:
Gemini pokes holes in Sagittarius's theories. Sagittarius can brand Gemini as a superficial party animal.

Work toward developing nonthreatening, nonjudgmental communication. However, you can't talk away practical financial realities—you need a well-thought-out program to make things happen.

Gemini/Capricorn

PLUSES:
Capricorn benefits from Gemini's abstract point of view and lighthearted sense of fun. Gemini shows Capricorn how to enjoy the rewards of hard work. Support and structure are Capricorn's gifts to Gemini. (Taking that literally, Capricorn Howard Hughes designed the famous bra that supported Gemini Jane Russell's physical assets.)

MINUSES:
Capricorn can be ultraconservative and tightfisted with money, which Gemini will not appreciate. Gemini's free-spirited, fun-loving attitude could grate against Capricorn's driving ambition. Gemini will have to learn to take responsibility and to produce solid results.

Gemini/Aquarius

PLUSES:
In this open, spontaneous relationship, the pressure's off, and two air signs have room to breathe freely. At the same time, you can count on each other for friendship, understanding, and mental stimulation, plus highly original romantic ideas. You'll keep each other entertained and your love life fresh and stimulated.

MINUSES:
Be sure to leave time in your busy schedule for each other. If there is no commitment, you could both fly off, but sharing causes, projects, or careers could hold you together.

Gemini/Pisces

PLUSES:
You are both dual personalities in mutable, freedom-loving signs, who fascinate each other with ever-changing facets. You keep each other from straying by providing constant variety and new experiments to try together.

MINUSES:
At some point, you'll need a frame of reference for this relationship to hold together, but since neither likes structure, this could be a problem. Overstimulation is another monster which can surface. Pisces's sensitive feelings and Gemini's hyperactive nerves could send each other searching for more soothing, stabilizing alternatives.

CHAPTER 17

Astrological Outlook for Gemini in 2002

There will be lots of soul-searching for you this year. Some will call it karma; others claim that you are being too hard on yourself. The combination of number 7, Neptune, and Saturn could bring you to your knees, if not prepared to accept bittersweet decisions.

Pisces and Virgo will play instrumental roles in your life this year. This will be true even if you don't know them during the early part of this period. With Pisces, there will be much social activity. You both will participate in political-charitable campaigns. You'll have so much in common that both of you wonder out loud, "Could we be part of the same family?"

With Virgo, the business at hand will achieve top priority. This could mean investments, including the Stock Market. Virgo relates to that part of your horoscope associated with land, real estate, and your family home.

In matters of speculation, stick with number 7. You will be drawn to water. Be careful, don't overdo it.

January and October will be your most memorable months of the year.

You could be involved in areas of spirituality and mysticism. You learn more about major religions. You also learn not to dismiss any subject prior to investigation.

Regard the following pages as your "diary in advance." You will find numerous subjects, including matters of speculation such as horse racing, special relationships, and love sparks.

During these months, you could be the prime target for "con people." If a proposition sounds too good to be true, it probably is not true. With your Gemini wit and wisdom, you'll detect who is sincere and who is full of "malarkey."

Get ready for the adventure of knowing your future. Check each day as provided in your "diary in advance."

CHAPTER 18

Eighteen Months of Day-by-Day Predictions—July 2001 to December 2002

JULY 2001

Sunday, July 1 (Moon in Scorpio to Sagittarius 11:13 p.m.) On this Sunday, plans will revolve around the upcoming holiday—the Fourth of July. Be open to changes and suggestions that you might not agree with, at least not at first. Virgo, Sagittarius, and another Gemini play outstanding roles.

Monday, July 2 (Moon in Sagittarius) Attention revolves around your home, the protection of your family, a domestic adjustment that could include where you live, the settlement of a dispute over the budget. Diplomacy is necessary if anything is going to get done. Taurus and Libra play top roles, and have these letters in their names—F, O, X.

Tuesday, July 3 (Moon in Sagittarius) Check your invitation list. Stick to rules concerning firecrackers and explosives. The Sagittarian moon relates to public relations, publicity, your marital status. A product you sent for will arrive later tonight.

Wednesday, July 4 (Moon in Sagittarius to Capricorn 8:21 a.m.) Happy holiday, happy Fourth! Take charge. Celebrate not only with noise but with the knowledge that the founders of the nation will be happy if you are happy celebrating the birth of this nation. Capricorn and Cancer figure in this dynamic holiday. Your lucky number is 8.

Thursday, July 5—Lunar Eclipse (Moon in Capricorn) The full moon, lunar eclipse falls in Capricorn. This means what was hidden will be revealed. You garner attention because of the unique way in which you celebrated the holiday. The spotlight falls on romance, creativity, the ability to withstand the pangs of falling madly in love!

Friday, July 6 (Moon in Capricorn to Aquarius 7:32 p.m.) Memory blends with your ability to predict the future. The spotlight is on accounting procedures, learning more about tax and license requirements. A project started three months ago is near completion. A relationship is intense. You make a fresh start in a new direction. Love will find its way.

Saturday, July 7 (Moon in Aquarius) Go slow. Your future prospects will be bright if you are thorough in your research. The lunar position highlights preparation for a journey and special study. Your relationship blends with travel and investigative reports. Cancer, Capricorn will play stunning roles, and will have these initials in their names—B, K, T.

Sunday, July 8 (Moon in Aquarius) Today you might be welcoming a visitor from a foreign country. Shared interests prove stimulating. Learn more about foreign exchange rates, about the philosophy and theology of a visitor's country. Plan for a social occasion honoring a distinguished guest.

Monday, July 9 (Moon in Aquarius to Pisces 8:04 a.m.) Within 24 hours, your career gets a boost. Writings that remained in a drawer for some time will find publication. Those who said your work was worth next to nothing will be biting their tongues. Opening lines of communication is a wise course. This scenario relates to distance and financial aid.

Tuesday, July 10 (Moon in Pisces) Keep your plans flexible. Confer with a superior. Do not sell yourself cheap! Once again, the written word impresses, and will be responsible for a possible promotion. A flirtation that lends spice involves Virgo and Sagittarius. Have luck with number 5.

Wednesday, July 11 (Moon in Pisces to Aries 8:34 p.m.) Lucky lottery: 3, 6, 12, 18, 19, 22. The spotlight is on music, style, fashion, reinforcing the feeling of being in love. Be diplomatic and confident enough to relax while engaged in serious research. Taurus, Libra, and Scorpio command attention.

Thursday, July 12 (Moon in Aries) Slow down! A Pisces is in a position to manipulate, to be in charge of whether or not to advance your career. Define terms, outline boundaries, and see people and relationships in a realistic light. An element of deception exists. Don't fool yourself by manipulating figures so that they come out just right.

Friday, July 13 (Moon in Aries) Talk and interest revolve around a game of chess. You might be asking, "What took me so long to learn about this game?" The Aries moon relates to your eleventh house, which means many of your dreams become realities. Take note of the dream you dreamed last night!

Saturday, July 14 (Moon in Aries to Taurus 7:12 a.m.) Focus on universal appeal. Learn more about language and foods imported from foreign countries. Speak up at a social affair, wear shades of red, reject a scheme for shortcuts and easy profit. Aries and Libra play outstanding roles, and have these letters in their names—I and R.

Sunday, July 15 (Moon in Taurus) This Sunday features a new hobby, new people in your life. The Taurus moon relates to hospital visits, much needed privacy, a possible romantic involvement with Leo. Stress your originality and independence. Avoid heavy lifting. Share what you know about back injuries.

Monday, July 16 (Moon in Taurus to Gemini 2:23 p.m.) Focus on your marital status, partnership, public relations, legal rights and permissions. The lunar position relates to secrets. Doors previously shut tight will now open at your touch. A gift is received of a luxury item or art object or both! Your lucky number is 2.

Tuesday, July 17 (Moon in Gemini) For racing luck at all tracks: Post position special—number 3 p.p. in the third race. Pick six: 1, 2, 3, 8, 7, 8. Look for these letters or initials in the names of potential winning horses or jockeys: C, L, U. Hot daily doubles: 1 and 2, 3 and 3, 5 and 6. Long-shot prices are paid. Speed horses get out in front and never look back!

Wednesday, July 18 (Moon in Gemini to Cancer 5:55 p.m.) Lucky lottery: 1, 3, 8, 12, 16, 33. Check details, make mathematical corrections, complete repair work on your automobile and home. A Scorpio says, "You can do without me, but I could never survive without you!" Taurus also plays an exciting role.

Thursday, July 19 (Moon in Cancer) An exciting Thursday! Money is available for a project or surprise party. Keep your plans flexible. A bit of creative thinking is much desired. The spotlight is on reading, writing, and spreading information. A flirtation lends spice. Know when to say, "It's been fun, but enough is enough!"

Friday, July 20 (Moon in Cancer to Leo 6:42 p.m.) The new moon in Cancer relates to your income, locating lost articles, preparing and consuming a sumptuous dinner tonight. Attention revolves around design, color coordination, and home beautification. Be receptive and diplomatic without being weak. Libra is in the picture.

Saturday, July 21 (Moon in Leo) A mysterious Saturday! Relatives are involved. A colorful Leo is argumentative, and possibly consumed too much adult beverage. Stay calm, despite a foolish accusation by a confused person. Pisces and Virgo figure in this dramatic scenario, and could have these letters or initials in their names—G, P, Y.

Sunday, July 22 (Moon in Leo to Virgo 6:28 p.m.) A unique situation exists, which involves your family. Major questions concern: "Can we afford this trip and learning institution?" Do not let a clash of ideas disintegrate into a common argument. Capricorn and Cancer will play sensational roles.

Monday, July 23 (Moon in Virgo) Let go of an unsavory situation. Flirting with the law can go only so far—you might be asking to get caught. Love and romance are involved, along with travel, a unique publication, discovering hidden values.

Tuesday, July 24 (Moon in Virgo to Libra 7:07 p.m.)   You find a new voice. Imprint your style and don't follow others. You are going places, especially where there is sun. Get ready for a barrage of questions. Answer from your heart, rather than from statistics. Leo and Aquarius will play fascinating roles.

Wednesday, July 25 (Moon in Libra)   Count your blessings and lucky stars! A Libra moon relates to your fifth house, which involves creativity, challenge, a variety of sensations. One person makes you proud. You are respected and loved. Cancer and Capricorn are ready to play creative, dynamic roles.

Thursday, July 26 (Moon in Libra to Scorpio 10:17 p.m.)   Social activities accelerate. You exude an aura of sensuality and sex appeal. Your popularity zooms. Diversify, show off your versatility, your ability to make people laugh through their tears. Sagittarius and another Gemini will play outstanding roles. Your lucky number is 3.

Friday, July 27 (Moon in Scorpio)   Hold up—do not equate delay with defeat! A practical method helps repair physical and emotional injuries. You'll be asked to take a physical examination. The final report varies from good to excellent. Taurus, Leo, and Scorpio figure in this scenario.

Saturday, July 28 (Moon in Scorpio to Sagittarius 4:44 a.m.)   There's plenty of passion and dealings with persons who have young ideas, who are willing to explore and experiment. Be confident; deliberately tear down to rebuild on a solid structure. Virgo, Sagittarius, and another Gemini will play featured roles. Your lucky number is 5.

Sunday, July 29 (Moon in Sagittarius) The Venus keynote helps assuage a minor disappointment. A promise will be fulfilled, but not tonight. The emphasis is on beauty, style, and clever arrangements. Taurus, Libra, and Scorpio will top today's interesting scenario. A domestic situation will no longer be scrambled. Thank your lucky stars!

Monday, July 30 (Moon in Sagittarius) The Sagittarian moon relates to publicity, publishing, advertising, exploiting the exploitable. Some degree of restraint is necessary. Let it be known, "I am here to stay and to serve you—of course, any suggestions will be welcomed." Virgo is represented.

Tuesday, July 31 (Moon in Sagittarius to Capricorn 2:16 p.m.) Goodbye Tuesday! A decision relates to a partnership, legal agreements, and marriage. The emphasis is on time, surprise, meeting and beating a deadline. The Sagittarius moon clearly indicates victory in court! Cancer and Capricorn will command your attention.

AUGUST 2001

Wednesday, August 1 (Moon in Capricorn) Learn more about money, payments, and collections, how and where money is spent. On this first day of August, you realize that you have an abundance of personal magnetism and sex appeal. Lucky lottery: 9, 12, 13, 18, 29, 42.

Thursday, August 2 (Moon in Capricorn) For racing luck at all tracks: post position special—number 1 p.p. in the sixth race. Pick six: 1, 1, 2, 3, 6, 1. Be alert for these letters or initials in the names of potential winning horses or jockeys: G, P, Y. Hot daily doubles: 1 and 1, 7 and 1, 4 and 6. Horses that run well on off-tracks will be in the money. Leo jockeys shine.

Friday, August 3 (Moon in Capricorn to Aquarius 1:52 a.m.) Within 24 hours, you receive news about travel, about assignments that include writing, photography, and history. Whether or not you write professionally about these subjects, you will be interested and will round out your general knowledge. Capricorn plays a role.

Saturday, August 4 (Moon in Aquarius) You will be immersed in information about people who request a last fling before marriage or commitment. As a Gemini, the subject itself fascinates. You instinctively know that people are interested in that crucial moment when others say in effect, "I love you but I want permission for one last fling."

Sunday, August 5 (Moon in Aquarius to Pisces 2:29 p.m.) The emphasis is on your ability to win friends and influence people. A romantic entanglement is just around the corner! Focus on speculation, winning ways, and overcoming obstacles—human and otherwise. Leo and Aquarius figure in this scenario, and have these letters in their names—A, S, J.

Monday, August 6 (Moon in Pisces) The focus is on your marital status, proposals that include business, career, and marriage. The Pisces moon relates to methods that result in promotion, more money, and added prestige. Pisces, Capricorn, and Cancer figure in today's dynamic, complex scenario, and could have these letters or initials in their names: B, K, T.

Tuesday, August 7 (Moon in Pisces) On this Tuesday, social activities accelerate. You confer with executives, people among the high and mighty. The Jupiter keynote blends with your Mercury. You'll be dubbed a "hale fellow well met!" People note that your humor can be translated into profundity.

Wednesday, August 8 (Moon in Pisces to Aries 3:03 a.m.) Attend to details early; fix things in need of repairs in your automobile and home. You will breathe a sigh of relief, as a mathematical problem is solved. Taurus, Leo, and Scorpio play meaningful roles, and have these initials in their names: D, M, V. Your lucky number is 4.

Thursday, August 9 (Moon in Aries) Regard these as lucky numbers: 5, 0, 5. The emphasis is on reading and writing, disseminating information, a flirtation that grows hot and heavy. Be aware of various implications and possible complications. It might be time to say, "Enough is enough!"

Friday, August 10 (Moon in Aries to Taurus 2:21 p.m.) The Aries moon in your eleventh house equates to good fortune in finance and romance. Be aggressive when listing grievances, pleasures, future desires, and in a willingness to cooperate and produce. The accent is on domestic issues, music, decorating, and remodeling.

Saturday, August 11 (Moon in Taurus) You'll regard today as puzzling. Blueprints are out of the question; almost everything is under the heading of unorthodox. Your intuitive intellect is at work. You'll encounter people versed in the mantic arts and sciences, including astrology. Have luck with number 7.

Sunday, August 12 (Moon in Taurus to Gemini 10:56 p.m.) A power play! The moon's position in Taurus relates to institutions, hospitals, theater, a romance that is kept quiet. Get ready for extra responsibility, the pressure of playing two games simultaneously. The spotlight is on your marital status and professional advancement.

Monday, August 13 (Moon in Gemini) Look beyond the immediate. Your cycle is moving up. Circumstances turn in your favor. What appeared to be lost will be found practically at your doorstep. Let go of an obligation that's not really your own. Be finished with an unsavory situation. Don't associate with those who take you for granted.

Tuesday, August 14 (Moon in Gemini) The moon in your sign highlights independence, originality, the courage of your convictions. Imprint your style; do not follow others. Turn on your Gemini charm. Use your ability to make people laugh. Leo and Aquarius play astonishing roles.

Wednesday, August 15 (Moon in Gemini to Cancer 3:53 a.m.) The spotlight is on your home, partnership, public relations, and the sale or purchase of property. The question of marriage will loom large. A gift that adds to your wardrobe makes you realize your love is not unrequited. Cancer and Capricorn are loyal and will prove it.

Thursday, August 16 (Moon in Cancer) On this Thursday, you receive accolades based on past performances. The moon in Cancer relates to money, payments, collections, and increased income. A family member appears with necessary material at practically the last minute. A night of love and laughter is in store!

Friday, August 17 (Moon in Cancer to Leo 5:24 a.m.) The moon in its own sign helps in connection with search, exploration, independence, and sex appeal. A Cancer invites you to "have dinner with us." Look forward to something special, including broiled lobster or swordfish. Scorpio plays a fascinating role.

Saturday, August 18 (Moon in Leo) Focus on trips, visits, relatives, people who are capable of making you laugh and cry at almost one and the same time. Special note: Take extra care in traffic. People tend to speed and drive carelessly. The emphasis is on children, challenge, a change of scene. Your lucky number is 5.

Sunday, August 19 (Moon in Leo to Virgo 4:52 a.m.) The new moon in your third house means finally you make peace with a difficult relative. The funny part is that both of you have secret admiration for each other. Tonight, you could both laugh at each other's foolishness. Taurus, Libra, and Scorpio figure in today's memorable scenario.

Monday, August 20 (Moon in Virgo) Define terms, accept constructive criticism, highlight good nature, humor, and wisdom. Focus on mystery and intrigue, the possibility of deception, deliberate or otherwise. Look behind the scenes. Someone is pulling a rabbit out of a hat and it is magic laced with trickery.

Tuesday, August 21 (Moon in Virgo to Libra 4:18 a.m.) The Virgo moon relates to property, critical appraisal of your basic values. An article once presented could now be quickly accepted. Capricorn and Cancer figure in today's dynamic scenario, and could have these letters or initials in their names: H, Q, Z. Your lucky number is 8.

Wednesday, August 22 (Moon in Libra) For racing luck at all tracks: post position special—number 8 p.p. in the first race. Pick six: 8, 1, 5, 3, 6, 8. Watch for these letters or initials in names of potential winning horses or jockeys: I and R. Hot daily doubles: 8 and 1, 8 and 5, 4 and 4. Foreign horses win. Aries jockeys get through heavy traffic to win photo finishes.

Thursday, August 23 (Moon in Libra to Scorpio 5:49 a.m.) Your kind of day! You exude personal magnetism, sensuality, and sex appeal. Let go of the past; make a fresh start in a new direction. The Libra moon relates to challenge, adventure, and exploration. Turn down a tempting offer if it is not completely legal. An Aquarian is involved.

Friday, August 24 (Moon in Scorpio) Progress is made. A minor legal obstacle remains. The focus is on food, restaurant management, a paid consultation during which your opinions are noted. A dream tonight revolves around a sexual encounter with an older person who is an excellent cook. The dream is jumbled, but meaningful.

Saturday, August 25 (Moon in Scorpio to Sagittarius 10:59 a.m.) Lucky lottery: 8, 12, 13, 22, 42, 51. The emphasis is on cooperation in a public community project. Look forward tonight to an excellent motion picture or stage production. The spotlight is on entertainment, intellectual curiosity, the temptation to write a review.

Sunday, August 26 (Moon in Sagittarius) The moon in Sagittarius relates to public relations, legal rights and permissions, your marital status. Go slow, and encourage a clash of ideas. People note your enthusiasm and creativity. You'll hear this remark, "You really are something, Gemini!" Scorpio is involved.

Monday, August 27 (Moon in Sagittarius to Capricorn 8:01 p.m.) One of your hidden talents is writing, so get going; write first and think about a possible market later. A flirtation lends spice. You could find a collaborator. In turn, a physical attraction results in mutual admiration and, after that, who knows! Virgo is represented.

Tuesday, August 28 (Moon in Capricorn) You took notes after viewing TV clips of Maria Callas. You enjoyed her performance and said, "She really could sing, she had a lovely smile and beautiful eyes." Then you inserted these notes: "She was tempestuous and had a big nose!" Very interesting, Gemini!

Wednesday, August 29 (Moon in Capricorn) Much that happens remains shrouded in mystery. You know what happened, but you do not know why or how. Deception is involved, but so is magic, mystery, and intrigue. Play a quiet role, and be a shrewd observer. Pisces and Virgo will play dominant roles, and have these initials in their names: G, P, Y.

Thursday, August 30 (Moon in Capricorn to Aquarius 7:47 a.m.) What begins as adversity will be transformed into a rousing victory. The emphasis is on the occult, hidden affairs, a tendency to make things difficult for yourself. Capricorn and Cancer play outstanding roles, and could have these letters or initials in their names: H, Q, Z.

Friday, August 31 (Moon in Aquarius) A project is completed. A long-distance communication verifies your views. You will receive more money than you originally anticipated. Focus on construction, language, learning how people in foreign countries live and love. Aries will play a sensational role. Your lucky number is 9.

SEPTEMBER 2001

Saturday, September 1 (Moon in Aquarius to Pisces 8:31 p.m.) Be realistic. A friendship or love relationship is temporarily on the rocks. But the good news on this first day of September is that what was broken will be repaired. Deception is involved, deliberate or otherwise. Pisces plays a major role.

Sunday, September 2 (Moon in Pisces) The full moon in your tenth house equates to career, pulling out of a crisis in a dramatic way. Capricorn and Cancer will play fascinating roles. You will be thanking your lucky stars. The lunar position accents an unusual climb out of a morass.

Monday, September 3 (Moon in Pisces) Open lines of communication. A favor you requested will be fulfilled. In matters of speculation, stick with number 9. Aries and Libra will figure prominently and, as a result you'll be flirting with a special person in another country.

Tuesday, September 4 (Moon in Pisces to Aries 8:57 a.m.) For racing luck at all tracks: post position special—number 7 p.p. in the third race. Pick six: 1, 7, 7, 4, 2, 8. Watch for these letters or initials in the names of potential winning horses or jockeys: A, S, J. Hot daily doubles: 1 and 7, 4 and 4, 5 and 8. Long shots will be in the money. Leo jockeys win photo finishes.

Wednesday, September 5 (Moon in Aries) Lucky lottery: 1, 2, 3, 6, 9, 12. An opportunity exists for a fresh start in a new direction. A love relationship that went cold will again be hot. Focus on your marital status, direction, motivation, gourmet dining tonight. Cancer and Capricorn figure prominently.

Thursday, September 6 (Moon in Aries to Taurus 8:16 p.m.) Forces are scattered, so don't attempt to please everyone—that would be a sure road to madness. Highlight versatility, diversification, a willingness to bring your material up-to-date. Sagittarius and another Gemini will play fascinating roles. Your lucky number is 3.

Friday, September 7 (Moon in Taurus) Within 24 hours a well-kept secret will no longer be secret. Check your source material. Someone is holding something back. Originally, it was a joke, but is no longer funny. Taurus, Leo, and Scorpio play quixotic roles. These letters are likely to be in their names: D, M, V.

Saturday, September 8 (Moon in Taurus) Lucky lottery: 2, 5, 7, 9, 18, 20. The Leo moon relates to surprise visits, dealings with a quarrelsome relative, writing your way in and out of a tight spot. Virgo, Sagittarius, and another Gemini figure in today's unusual scenario, and have these letters in their names: E, N, W.

Sunday, September 9 (Moon in Taurus to Gemini 5:40 a.m.) Attention revolves around your family and home. There is more financial security. With music in your life, the Taurus moon tells of romance, the necessity for discretion. Keep to yourself the fact that money has come from a bolt out of the blue. Libra plays a dominant role.

Monday, September 10 (Moon in Gemini) Define plans, make it crystal clear that you are aware of attempted deception. Perfect techniques and streamline procedures. People regarded as important are observing, perhaps testing you. You might be sighing, "What next could happen to me?"

Tuesday, September 11 (Moon in Gemini to Cancer 12:07 p.m.) An unusual occurrence takes place in connection with names. A family member reveals that when a youngster, your name was changed. Ride with the tide. In plain words: "Don't make a federal case of it!" A Capricorn figures prominently.

Wednesday, September 12 (Moon in Cancer) You'll be credited with performing an impossible task. Strive for universal appeal, look beyond the immediate, and get rid of emotional debris. A question exists whether or not to go forward. The key is to take a cold plunge into the future. Lucky lottery: 1, 5, 7, 10, 12, 18.

Thursday, September 13 (Moon in Cancer to Leo 3:14 p.m.) Make a fresh start. Highlight independence of thought and action. A Leo relative declares, "Let me entertain; I will do everything possible to make your party a success!" The sun keynote provides light where previously there was darkness.

Friday, September 14 (Moon in Leo) A close call in traffic! Be wary of someone on the road who has been drinking heavily. Highlight color coordination, showmanship, and dealings with those who are starved for attention. Serious discussions take place regarding your martial status. A Cancer is involved.

Saturday, September 15 (Moon in Leo to Virgo 3:38 p.m.) For racing luck at all tracks: post position special—number 3 p.p. in the third race. Pick six: 7, 1, 3, 4, 4, 8. Watch for these letters or initials in the names of potential winning horses or jockeys: C, L, U. Hot daily doubles: 7 and 1, 3 and 3, 5 and 7. Luck rides with Sagittarian jockeys who survive falls and escape injuries.

Sunday, September 16 (Moon in Virgo) Be willing to revise, review, rewrite, and to tear down for the ultimate purpose of rebuilding on a solid structure. By meditating you will come up with the correct answers. People ask, "How did you do it?" Respond: "I put possible defeat far away and pictured myself doing the right thing at the right time."

Monday, September 17 (Moon in Virgo to Libra 2:59 p.m.) A fascinating Monday! The new moon in your fourth house equates to property values, electricity, furniture recently arrived. The emphasis is on change, travel, variety, and flirtation. A member of the opposite sex builds your ego as a result of intense flattery.

Tuesday, September 18 (Moon in Libra) The Libra moon emphasizes music, romance, a decision relating to a business partnership, career, and marriage. Lost items will be found; it's possible they were never moved from your hiding place. The lunar position accents your writing ability, creativity, and sex appeal. Aries plays a role.

Wednesday, September 19 (Moon in Libra to Scorpio 3:27 p.m.) Lucky lottery: 6, 7, 11, 12, 17, 22. A mysterious individual from a foreign country will play an important role in your life. Pisces and Virgo are in this picture, and will have these letters or initials in their names: G, P, Y. The Neptune keynote coincides with hidden values, deception, and salesmanship.

Thursday, September 20 (Moon in Scorpio) The emphasis is on a deadline, and on elements of timing and surprise. The Scorpio moon tells of catching up with work that previously was shunted aside. Take special care in connection with your lower abdomen. What begins as a sports activity could end in injury unless you are ultracareful.

Friday, September 21 (Moon in Scorpio to Sagittarius 7:02 p.m.) Look beyond the immediate, finish what you start, and ignore persons who say, "It is impossible!" Recall what Napoleon is purported to have said: "Impossible is a word used by fools!" Overcome distance and language obstacles—you can and will do it!

Saturday, September 22 (Moon in Sagittarius) The answer to your question: Be knowledgeable about fashion, the latest humor, and color coordination. The lunar position verifies that you will receive offers that include a marriage proposal. Leo and Aquarius figure in this dramatic scenario. Your lucky number is 1.

Sunday, September 23 (Moon in Sagittarius) Your views are verified. You'll long remember this Sunday. You win a legal battle and tonight you will wonder, "It happened in a strange way, especially on a Sunday!" As you face the crossroads, don't turn right or left. Stick to familiar ground; fulfill family obligations.

Monday, September 24 (Moon in Sagittarius to Capricorn 2:48 a.m.) Your cycle is such that you have a night of love and laughter. The green light flashes for experimentation, exploration, and romance. Let go of a burden you had no right to carry in the first place. Sagittarius and another Gemini figure in this fantastic scenario.

Tuesday, September 25 (Moon in Capricorn) All indications point to temporary restrictions. The spotlight is on accounting methods, detecting and correcting a bank error. The Capricorn moon relates to mystery, intrigue, digging deep for information and coming up with a possible gold mine. Scorpio is involved.

Wednesday, September 26 (Moon in Capricorn to Aquarius 2:04 p.m.) For racing luck at all tracks: post position special—number 5 p.p. in the fifth race. Pick six: 3, 1, 7, 2, 5, 1. Be alert for these letters or initials in the names of potential winning horses or jockeys: E, N, W. Hot daily doubles: 3 and 1, 5 and 5, 2 and 8. Horses that get out in front win, and pay excellent prices.

Thursday, September 27 (Moon in Aquarius) Attention revolves around your home, family, music, entertainment, and color coordination. Taurus and Libra play instrumental roles, and will help you over rough spots. Don't force issues. If you are willing to be patient, you'll improve your income potential.

Friday, September 28 (Moon in Aquarius) Hold off on a financial decision relating to where you live, whether or not your plumbing is actually repaired. A dream proves prophetic, so be familiar with various symbols. Psychic impressions should be taken seriously. Pisces and Virgo are in this picture.

Saturday, September 29 (Moon in Aquarius to Pisces 2:49 a.m.) Under much pressure, this will be a night to remember. You meet someone who will play an important role in your destiny. Keep your emotional equilibrium; avoid bragging. Within 24 hours, your career gets a boost. Though pride is elevated, keep in mind, "Pride goeth before a fall!"

Sunday, September 30 (Moon in Pisces) On this last day of September, you will be in touch with people from your past as well as with those in the current action. The Pisces moon relates to career, promotion, production, the possibility of a raise in pay. A relationship could get too hot not to cool down. Aries is in this picture.

OCTOBER 2001

Monday, October 1 (Moon in Pisces to Aries 3:06 p.m.) Don't take offense at a careless remark made by a lifelong friend. If you're careful and analytical, you'll discover that no harm is meant. Capricorn and Cancer will play leading roles, and have these letters or initials in their names—H, Q, Z. Study modes of speculation, including the stock market.

Tuesday, October 2 (Moon in Aries) The full moon in Aries relates to your eleventh house, which means many of your most spectacular wishes could come true. Reach beyond the immediate. Libra and Aries play fascinating roles. The full moon suggests a secret love affair. Your lucky number is 9.

Wednesday, October 3 (Moon in Aries) You could invent something that will lead to prosperity. Fight for your rights. On a personal level, give your all and you will be receiving love. Leo and Aquarius play fantastic roles, and have these letters or initials in their names: A, S, J. Your lucky number is 1.

Thursday, October 4 (Moon in Aries to Taurus 1:59 a.m.) What was delayed for approximately two months will be back in action. Within 24 hours, the moon will be in your twelfth house, which signifies the need to be discreet in almost all of your actions. Cancer and Capricorn play leading roles tonight, and have these letters in their names: B, K, T.

Friday, October 5 (Moon in Taurus) Words count for plenty! Read and write, teach, and disseminate information. A flirtation is fine and lends spice, but realize there is a time when enough is enough! A Sagittarius compliments you on your intelligence, your ability to make meanings crystal clear. Your lucky number is 3.

Saturday, October 6 (Moon in Taurus to Gemini 11:10 a.m.) A stubborn streak will be much in evidence. This is not the kind of Saturday night that you dream of. You might be tempted to scream, "Let's stop the playing around; let's get down to business!" Taurus, Leo, and Scorpio are involved.

Sunday, October 7 (Moon in Gemini) On this Sunday, you make exciting contacts, and are praised for your wit and wisdom. A well-known writer is included as part of the scenario. The spotlight is on change, travel, a variety of experiences. You will berate yourself for not getting enough rest!

Monday, October 8 (Moon in Gemini to Cancer 6:18 p.m.) The moon in your sign represents your high cycle. Designate where the action will be. Take the initiative. Trust your judgment and intuitive intellect. You'll be called upon to solve a complex problem—back off at first, then make a head-on rush to resolve the dilemma. Libra is involved.

Tuesday, October 9 (Moon in Cancer) Be near or around water, if possible. Your psychic impressions are valid; a bit of "floating" would be excellent for your nerves. See people and relationships as they exist, not merely as you wish them to be. What is offered as a surefire financial deal is not what it appears to be.

Wednesday, October 10 (Moon in Cancer to Leo 10:52 p.m.) Dig deep for information, including references. Today's scenario boils down to money, payments, dealing with someone who wants something for nothing. Don't be too surprised if at least one check has rubber in it. Lucky lottery: 12, 4, 7, 50, 51, 22.

Thursday, October 11 (Moon in Leo) The message is "get tangled." Someone who appropriates what is not his own will use the excuse: "Apparently, I got the wrong message, I thought it was a green light!" A journey could be necessary to straighten out files. Make it business and pleasure!

Friday, October 12 (Moon in Leo) On this Friday, resolve to make a fresh start in a new direction. The Leo moon tells of seeking cooperation from a relative in connection with display art, color coordination, and showmanship. Be sure that a relative avoids heavy lifting! Your lucky number is 1.

Saturday, October 13 (Moon in Leo to Virgo 12:56 a.m.) For racing luck at all tracks: post position special—number 6 p.p. in the fifth race. Pick six: 2, 2, 1, 5, 6, 8. Be alert for these letters or initials in the names of potential winning horses or jockeys: B, K, T. Hot daily doubles: 2 and 2, 5 and 6, 3 and 7. A veteran Cancer jockey has a superlative ride. Favorites win.

Sunday, October 14 (Moon in Virgo) By playing the waiting game you receive a better offer. Currently forces are scattered. You might be undergoing a reign of confusion. Highlight versatility, entertainment, and fashion notes that can be transformed into a feature story.

Monday, October 15 (Moon in Virgo to Libra 1:25 a.m.) Be willing to revise, review, rewrite, and to put your position forward for appraisal by a superior. Don't endorse a check unless you know what you are signing and why. Taurus, Leo, and Scorpio play dramatic roles, and have these letters or initials in their names—D, M, V.

Tuesday, October 16 (Moon in Libra) The new moon in Libra equates to count your blessings! The lunar position in your fifth house tells of creativity, style, a serious flirtation that could result in who knows? Focus on intellectual activity, writing and reporting, expressing feelings to one who so far has been cold.

Wednesday, October 17 (Moon in Libra to Scorpio 2:02 a.m.) Lucky lottery: 5, 8, 12, 14, 15, 16. Attention revolves around your home, domesticity, increasing your earning power by learning about recipes and cooking. Music plays: catch the rhythm and dance to your own tune. Taurus and Libra attempt to grab the spotlight.

Thursday, October 18 (Moon in Scorpio) Time is on your side, so be alert. Realize someone who wants something for nothing has an eye on you. Avoid self-deception. A Pisces offers a deal that appears to be too good to be true. Answer: It looks too good and it is—get far away, pronto!

Friday, October 19 (Moon in Scorpio to Sagittarius 4:46 a.m.) A power play day. People who formerly were gentle seem now to be transformed into madmen. Memory haunts; stop reviewing past mistakes, unless you do it is a sure road to madness. Capricorn and Cancer will become true allies, just in the nick of time!

Saturday, October 20 (Moon in Sagittarius) The Sagittarian moon relates to legal affairs, public relations, a variety of proposals that include marriage. Look beyond the immediate. Communicate with someone who could represent your talent or product overseas. Lucky lottery: 9, 17, 6, 47, 2, 3.

Sunday, October 21 (Moon in Sagittarius to Capricorn 11:12 a.m.)   Love is in bloom! A spark that brought you together with your current love will reignite. Stress independence, creativity, and confidence. Muse happily, "Yes, I am in love again, and I wouldn't change it for all the world!" Leo will play a dramatic role.

Monday, October 22 (Moon in Capricorn)   The moon in your eighth house relates to mystery, locating an ancient art object. You might find yourself in the middle of a discussion about a treasure map. Check accounting procedures. Learn more about tax and license requirements.

Tuesday, October 23 (Moon in Capricorn to Aquarius 9:26 p.m.)   Give full play to your intellectual curiosity. Volunteer for an entertainment program. You could make contacts that result in a new or second career. The moon in Capricorn encourages mystery, the need to delve into ancient manuscripts.

Wednesday, October 24 (Moon in Aquarius)   Lucky lottery: 7, 8, 10, 11, 13, 41. Within 24 hours, the emphasis will be on travel, religious studies, exploration, the adventure of discovery. Leave behind emotional debris. Wear shades of red, make personal appearances, stand tall, and be proud.

Thursday, October 25 (Moon in Aquarius)   Lucky day! The moon in Aquarius represents your ability to pick winners. Expect the unorthodox. A visiting relative is taking up much more of your time than you can spare. Be gracious, but let it be known, "I have a deadline and if I am going to make it, I must start work immediately!"

Friday, October 26 (Moon in Aquarius to Pisces 9:54 a.m.) For racing luck at all tracks: post position special—number 2 p.p. in the fourth race. Pick six: 1, 3, 5, 2, 7, 7. Be alert for these letters or initials in the names of potential winning horses or jockeys: F, O, X. Hot daily doubles: 1 and 3, 6 and 7, 4 and 6. Hometown jockeys bring horses in the money. The payoffs are good.

Saturday, October 27 (Moon in Pisces) A very romantic Saturday! If lies are told, it is in the spirit of make-believe, romantic interpretations, sights, and sounds. Don't take too seriously an offer for a long-term arrangement. Pisces and Virgo will dominate this scenario, making people laugh!

Sunday, October 28—Daylight Saving Time Ends (Moon in Pisces to Aries 9:13 p.m.) A very active Sunday! The deal is set, which gives you additional authority and more money. A bank error could be disclosed. It's not intentional, but the delay in notification could have proven disastrous. Capricorn and Cancer are powers behind the throne.

Monday, October 29 (Moon in Aries) You possess the secret of universal appeal. Design your product to appeal to many cultures—militaristic music could be involved. Be nice to people without being obsequious. Aries and Libra figure in this scenario.

Tuesday, October 30 (Moon in Aries) Make a fresh start. You are on the verge of making your wishes come true. The spotlight falls on personal magnetism, sensuality, and sex appeal. An Aries says, "You are so very wonderful, and I am happy you are in my life!" To say you are swept off your feet would be putting it mildly.

Wednesday, October 31 (Moon in Aries to Taurus 7:46 a.m.) Magicians throughout the world will be celebrating National Magic Day in honor of Houdini. Most other people will be celebrating Halloween in honor of breaking rules and not going to jail. Favorite costumes: Star Wars, Pirates, Cowboys, and Angels.

NOVEMBER 2001

Thursday, November 1 (Moon in Taurus) On this first day of the month, the full moon relates to clandestine affairs and secret arrangements. Remember resolutions to cheer up someone confined to home or hospital. Aries and Libra play dramatic roles, and have these letters or initials in their names: I and R.

Friday, November 2 (Moon in Taurus to Gemini 4:11 p.m.) The darker areas of your life will receive the benefit of more light. Aries, Leo, and Taurus are in today's dynamic action, with these letters or initials in their names: A, S, J. Dress in bright colors, speak up for your ideals and beliefs.

Saturday, November 3 (Moon in Gemini) For racing luck at all tracks: post position special—number 6 p.p. in the fifth race. Pick six: 3, 3, 1, 6, 6, 7. Be alert for these letters or initials in the names of potential winning horses or jockeys: B, K, T. Hot daily doubles: 3 and 3, 7 and 6, 1 and 1. Leo and Taurus jockeys win in photo finishes, paying good prices.

Sunday, November 4 (Moon in Gemini to Cancer 10:42 p.m.) The moon in your sign equates to your high cycle. Put your faith in judgment and intuition. Focus on your personality, magnetic appeal, the willingness to make a fresh start in a new direction. Another Gemini and Sagittarius play meaningful roles, and have these initials in their names: C, L, U. Your lucky number is 3.

Monday, November 5 (Moon in Cancer) Within 24 hours, funding activities will accelerate. Some people, kidding on the square, will dub you "king of the moneymakers!" Taurus, Leo, and Scorpio figure in this fantastic scenario, and will have these letters or initials in their names: D, M, V.

Tuesday, November 6 (Moon in Cancer) People who claimed to be one step ahead will discover that it is really you who are ahead of the game. There is music in your life. A busy Virgo suggests a color combination, and provides overall help in beautifying your home. The spotlight is on reading and writing, filing information to be found in a variety of sources.

Wednesday, November 7 (Moon in Cancer to Leo 3:32 a.m.) The spotlight is on rhythm, style, special activities, a moneymaking plan. People might laugh, but remember that he who laughs last will laugh best. Others are drawn to you, confiding questions and problems, some of an intimate nature. Have luck with number 6.

Thursday, November 8 (Moon in Leo) The Leo moon relates to the need to be careful in traffic, to avoid arguments with relatives who constantly seek a fight. Someone close to you might announce an official engagement. Look beyond the immediate. See people and places as they are, not merely as you wish they might be.

Friday, November 9 (Moon in Leo to Virgo 6:48 a.m.) Let it be known: "I mean business, and when I say I will do something, I mean it and I will do it!" Capricorn and Cancer will play unusual roles, and have these letters or initials in their names: H, Q, Z. Get ready for more responsibility, overtime, an opportunity to hit the jackpot.

Saturday, November 10 (Moon in Virgo) Lucky lottery: 4, 6, 9, 11, 15, 22. Stress universality, devote time and study to language. A surprise call might find you acting as an interpreter. Some people state, "You most certainly live an exciting life!" Aries and Libra will play dedicated roles.

Sunday, November 11 (Moon in Virgo to Libra 8:52 a.m.) Follow your hunch, participate in a pioneering project. A love relationship is hot and heavy, and could get too hot not to cool down! A Leo declares, "You could give anyone competition in charm, personality, and sex appeal." Have luck with number 1.

Monday, November 12 (Moon in Libra) You might be musing with this question: "Am I here for a purpose, or am I merely marking time!" The answers will be forthcoming following serious meditation. The spotlight is on a variety of proposals, including business, career, and marriage.

Tuesday, November 13 (Moon in Libra to Scorpio 10:44 a.m.) What once got out of hand will be back, and you are glad of it. Show that you, too, also are happy about a reunion. The elements of timing and luck ride with you. Tonight will mark the celebration of a joyous occasion. A Sagittarian will be a master of ceremonies.

Wednesday, November 14 (Moon in Scorpio) For racing luck at all tracks: post position special—number 4 p.p. in the fourth race. Pick six: 2, 3, 1, 4, 5, 6. Watch for these letters and initials in the names of potential winning horses or jockeys: D, M, V. Hot daily doubles: 2 and 3, 3 and 6, 5 and 4. A steady ride by a favorite will be in the money, with a Scorpio jockey aboard.

Thursday, November 15 (Moon in Scorpio to Sagittarius 1:51 p.m.) The new moon in Scorpio relates to a surprise announcement. A family member, returned from college, announces, "No more doubt about it—I am going on the stage!" Take this proclamation in stride; neither encourage nor discourage. Virgo is involved.

Friday, November 16 (Moon in Sagittarius) Suddenly, serious discussions revolve around questions of partnership, business arrangements, and your marital status. What others took for granted, turned out to be exactly the opposite. Fortunately, you were alert and provided protection for valuables.

Saturday, November 17 (Moon in Sagittarius to Capricorn 7:39 p.m.) You meet bright, creative, sensual persons who engage you in a clash of ideas. Many debates involve the advantages and disadvantages of marriage. This is very stimulating, but don't allow it to fall into the category of common arguments. Pisces will take charge!

Sunday, November 18 (Moon in Capricorn) On this Sunday, be realistic about credit, savings accounts, the need to check facts and figures. Within 24 hours, the moon will be in Capricorn, representing dealings with your accountant and discovering once and for all where your money went and how it happened.

Monday, November 19 (Moon in Capricorn) A blend of Mars and Saturn relates to a possible journey in connection with a business transaction. You will provide energy and optimism, and this will coincide with a valuable lesson for someone who could be your partner or mate. Aries plays a creative role.

Tuesday, November 20 (Moon in Capricorn to Aquarius 4:54 a.m.) Someone who once played a major role in your life will be back, sooner than you think. Focus on direction, meditation, a decision about a fresh start in a new direction. Physical attraction will be much in evidence. Leo makes a creative contribution.

Wednesday, November 21 (Moon in Aquarius) The standing of your community is elevated. Confer with leaders about traffic, direction, the ultimate goal. Some people insist: "You can't do everything, so why not give someone else a chance!" Regard this as mild criticism, caused mainly by someone who is envious.

Thursday, November 22 (Moon in Aquarius to Pisces 4:51 p.m.) Fun and frolic on this Thanksgiving! There also will be metaphysical discussions about the fate of turkeys. However, that won't seem to disturb the appetites of the participants. Another Gemini is seriously involved in a senseless debate.

Friday, November 23 (Moon in Pisces) The Pisces moon relates to outstanding members of the community, some of whom express a desire to meet you. Pluto mixes with your Mercury, and emotional fireworks could ensue. Cooling water pours on fireworks, just in the nick of time. A Friday you won't soon forget!

Saturday, November 24 (Moon in Pisces) Today's scenario highlights your voice, singing, and reciting of delightful anecdotes. Takes a deep breath and proceed. This is likely to be one special Saturday night live. Take liberties with lyrics, if it will provide fun and laughter. Virgo and Sagittarius will play dynamic, memorable roles.

Sunday, November 25 (Moon in Pisces to Aries 5:20 a.m.) Someone intent on giving advice will finally decide, "I suppose you've heard enough from me!" Be polite, but firm; respond this way: "Free advice is never taken seriously, so I hope you understand!" Instead of a break in friendship, this will later be recalled as a subject of raucous laughter.

Monday, November 26 (Moon in Aries) Slow down on this Monday! The Aries moon in your eleventh sector relates to friends, fulfillment of desires, good fortune in finance and romance. Turn on your Gemini charm; make life more bearable for those who are confined to home or hospital. Virgo is in the picture.

Tuesday, November 27 (Moon in Aries to Taurus 4:04 p.m.) What you have been waiting for is "now." The spotlight is on overtime, added responsibility, the pressure of a deadline. On a personal level, a physical attraction will be followed by a serious talk about future plans. Be alert for the wisdom of pillow talk. Capricorn is involved.

Wednesday, November 28 (Moon in Taurus) Lucky lottery: 12, 16, 22, 28, 50, 51. A secret meeting concerns investments, dividing profits. Your popularity increases; you could be dispatched to a foreign country to introduce a product. Aries and Libra figure prominently, and have these initials in their names: I and R.

Thursday, November 29 (Moon in Taurus) Let go of preconceived notions. You will be in demand, careerwise and personally. A very daring Scorpio asks, "Are you available for private lessons?" Maintain emotional equilibrium, answer with aplomb, "Always, at five hundred dollars an hour!"

Friday, November 30 (Moon in Taurus to Gemini 12:02 a.m.) Your cycle moves up. Circumstances will fill your needs. You will be at the right place at a crucial moment. Creative juices stir. The spotlight is on love and marriage, business and money. Your search continues for Nirvana. Cancer and Capricorn persons will share culinary delights. You're invited!

DECEMBER 2001

Saturday, December 1 (Moon in Gemini) A lively, exciting Saturday, when you meet people who are original thinkers, creative, dynamic and who appreciate your unusual qualities. Go forth, be confident, and turn on your best charming smile! Leo and Aquarius play fascinating roles. Your lucky number is 1.

Sunday, December 2 (Moon in Gemini to Cancer 5:29 a.m.) Questions about your marital status loom large. The spotlight is on direction, motivation, selling and buying property. A dinner invitation comes from a Cancer—something to look forward to! A big financial deal is pending. Find out where money is and how to obtain it!

Monday, December 3 (Moon in Cancer) This could be the precursor to a winning streak. The moon in its own sign for you represents your income, locating lost articles, and finding ways to earn more money.

The spotlight is on diversity, versatility, humor, and intellectual curiosity. A Sagittarian plays a role.

Tuesday, December 4 (Moon in Cancer to Leo 9:14 a.m.) For racing luck at all tracks: post position special—number 8 p.p. in the fourth race. Pick six: 4, 2, 3, 8, 1, 1. Watch for these letters or initials in the names of potential winning horses or jockeys: D, M, V. Hot daily doubles: 4 and 2, 8 and 5, 7 and 6. Many favorites run out of the money. Taurus and Scorpio jockeys are subject to injury.

Wednesday, December 5 (Moon in Leo) Lucky lottery: 5, 10, 12, 17, 50, 51. Watch for a change of venue—read, write, report, and make others aware that you are doing double-duty. A flirtation is exciting, but it might be time to say, "Enough is enough!" Virgo is involved.

Thursday, December 6 (Moon in Leo to Virgo 12:10 p.m.) Music is featured. A guest in your home talks about the lives of composers, and keeps you informed of current events as they apply to music and musicians. The spotlight is on beautifying your surroundings, decorating, remodeling, and moving things around so that people have more room to walk.

Friday, December 7 (Moon in Virgo) Be analytical about this day in history. People consult you to verify information. The Neptune keynote tells you to avoid self-deception. It's very nice to be flattered, but do come up for air! Someone behind you wants you to fall flat. Don't give 'em the satisfaction!

Saturday, December 8 (Moon in Virgo to Libra 2:56 p.m.) Lucky lottery: 5, 6, 7, 8, 16, 45. The emphasis is on construction, a deadline, a relationship that begins as a mild flirtation, but could take a turn for more serious consideration. Deal gingerly with elements of time, distance, and language. Capricorn is involved.

Sunday, December 9 (Moon in Libra) People ask you to keep things simple. Your response: "I am not working for simple people and I will not talk or write down to them!" Aries and Libra figure in this exciting scenario, and will have these letters or initials in their names: I and R.

Monday, December 10 (Moon in Libra to Scorpio 6:08 p.m.) Emphasize independence, originality, and romance. The Libra moon is in your fifth house. Creative juices stir. You will be musing, "I am ready for love, so where is my lover?" Leo and Aquarius will play meaningful roles, and have these letters in their names—A, S, J.

Tuesday, December 11 (Moon in Scorpio) Strange occurrences! People whose names you cannot remember for the moment will suddenly appear, as if formerly invited as guests. Cancer, Leo, and Aquarius play amazing roles, and have these letters or initials in their names: B, K, T.

Wednesday, December 12 (Moon in Scorpio to Sagittarius 10:29 p.m.) Lucky lottery: 8, 12, 22, 33, 40, 50. The spotlight is on money, possible participation in an engineering project. An older person offers to share the benefit of experience. Avoid being haughty, but do announce, "Thank you, but no, thanks. I prefer to work alone!"

Thursday, December 13 (Moon in Sagittarius) Christmas is not that far away! Prepare your shopping list. Make purchases so that there will not be a last-minute rush. Within 24 hours, expect pressure connected with publicity, legal agreements, and your marital status. Taurus plays a dynamic role.

Friday, December 14—Solar Eclipse (Moon in Sagittarius)   The new moon, solar eclipse is in your house of public relations, legal arrangements, and marriage. What apparently was settled two weeks ago has sprung up again, requiring you to give the situation time and study. Written material must be attended to, pronto!

Saturday, December 15 (Moon in Sagittarius to Capricorn 4:47 a.m.)   For racing luck at all tracks: post position special—number 6 p.p. in the third race. Pick six: 2, 4, 6, 1, 5, 2. Be alert for these letters or initials in the names of potential winning horses or jockeys: F, O, X. Hot daily doubles: 2 and 4, 1 and 6, 4 and 2. Favorites give comfortable rides, but fail to show up in the winner's circle.

Sunday, December 16 (Moon in Capricorn)   Spiritual matters dominate. The Capricorn moon highlights mystery, intrigue, the necessity for checking accounting procedures. Learn the rules before agreeing to play in the game. Someone is pulling strings; be sure you are not the featured subject.

Monday, December 17 (Moon in Capricorn to Aquarius 1:43 p.m.)   All indications point to a down-to-business attitude. Don't brood over time wasted in the past. A failed love relationship is not the end of the world—don't act like it is! Powerful people take liking to you; their actions will verify it. Have luck with number 8.

Tuesday, December 18 (Moon in Aquarius)   An excellent day to make overseas contacts. A cruise would make for an exciting friendship, love relationship, or honeymoon. In your cycle high, with a Mars keynote you can make the most of this situation, whatever it might be. An aggressive Aries is involved.

Wednesday, December 19 (Moon in Aquarius) You make contact with an electrical engineer who explains why he does what he does and confides, "I would like to know more about astrology!" Make a fresh start, avoid brooding about the past, clear aside emotional debris. Your lucky number is 1.

Thursday, December 20 (Moon in Aquarius to Pisces 1:09 a.m.) A family member counsels, "Thank your lucky stars!" Focus on cooperative efforts, an assignment involving history, photography, or publishing. Lost references will be recovered. You'll feel more confident. You'll feel better about yourself. A Cancer is involved.

Friday, December 21 (Moon in Pisces) Climb up to a higher plateau. Participate in social activities. Your career gets a boost, so turn on your Gemini charm and smile, smile, smile. The moon position highlights the transformation of an obstacle into a stepping-stone toward your goal. A Sagittarian is in the picture.

Saturday, December 22 (Moon in Pisces to Aries 1:44 a.m.) Once again you are on solid ground! The Pisces moon represents your career, successful climb to the top. Your psychic vision should be taken seriously. Something or someone is trying to tell you something. Taurus, Leo, and Scorpio play dominant roles.

Sunday, December 23 (Moon in Aries) The emphasis is on communication, the ability to write articles or start a book or diary. Your creative juices stir. A flirtation is exciting and should not get out of hand unless you want to pay through the nose. Virgo and Sagittarius play dynamic roles.

Monday, December 24 (Moon in Aries) Be with your family, if possible. Christmas Eve gifts smack of originality. There's serious thought behind them, which could influence you to begin a marvelous, creative hobby. You'll win friends and influence people. Some of the presents involve money, investments, the stock market.

Tuesday, December 25 (Moon in Aries to Taurus 1:10 a.m.) The significance of this holiday hits home today. Neptune is involved, which means you will be musing, "What history behind this day; it is awe-inspiring!" Looking out in the world, you discern that the natives are restless. Pisces and Virgo are represented.

Wednesday, December 26 (Moon in Taurus) It is not too early to fill in the blank spaces in connection with New Year's Eve. Where will you celebrate and with whom? There are such things as gifts, reservations, as well as resolutions. You learned a lesson last year. Don't invite a heavy drinker who creates turmoil.

Thursday, December 27 (Moon in Taurus to Gemini 9:37 a.m.) Communication is received from someone who recently embarked on an adventure. Look beyond the immediate; pay attention to language and to the food and mores of people in other countries. A Libra makes a confession. Do not make accusations!

Friday, December 28 (Moon in Gemini) Look back to the past, realize you can dictate your future! A different, exciting love relationship is on the horizon. No matter what your chronological age, this will be inspiring and will stir your creative juices. Leo and Aquarius are ready to take charge.

Saturday, December 29 (Moon in Gemini to Cancer 1:38 p.m.) Lucky lottery: 3, 6, 10, 11, 22, 35. Your cycle is high, so circumstances turn in your favor. Be discriminating, choose the best, concentrate on quality. Cancer and Capricorn play dynamic, challenging, and creative roles.

Sunday, December 30—Lunar Eclipse (Moon in Cancer) The full moon and lunar eclipse fall in Cancer. Finances will be juggled, shaken-up, but ultimately you emerge not only a survivor, but a winner! Sagittarius and another Gemini play risky games, but the outcome is almost preordained. They emerge as big shots!

Monday, December 31 (Moon in Cancer to Leo 5:08 p.m.) Because you were alert to budget limitations, you will enjoy this day and evening. Taurus, Leo, and Scorpio play roles; one of these persons will make a proposal relating to business, career, or marriage. A business investment will be seriously discussed.

HAPPY NEW YEAR!

JANUARY 2002

Tuesday, January 1 (Moon in Leo) You get a pretty good idea of what the future holds by analyzing this day. You perceive, in varying degrees, the rhythm of the entire year. On this first day, one relationship could end, but another could be just beginning. Libra and Aries will figure prominently.

Wednesday, January 2 (Moon in Leo to Virgo 6:33 p.m.) Set an example for those who are sad and suffering the New Year blues. Highlight independence, freedom, originality, and the willingness to take a chance on romance. Leo and Aquarius will be in your corner offering valuable advice. Lucky lottery: 1, 7, 16, 25, 31, 40.

Thursday, January 3 (Moon in Virgo) There are many offers today, which should be properly labeled "proposals." The "proposals" relate to business, career, partnership, and marriage. For a time, you feared being alone. Now the realization hits home—you can be lonely in a crowd. Capricorn is involved.

Friday, January 4 (Moon in Virgo to Libra 8:23 p.m.) On this Friday, with the moon in Virgo, you will be concerned with where you live and the value of property. The key is to be versatile, to investigate various possibilities, and to keep an open mind and sense of humor. A Sagittarian is in the picture.

Saturday, January 5 (Moon in Libra) Details seem to pile up—and they will, unless you face facts and begin taking care of them. Taurus, Leo, and Scorpio figure in this scenario, and have these letters or initials in their names—D, M, V. You have been in and out of crucial moments and tight spots—you survive based on past experience.

Sunday, January 6 (Moon in Libra to Scorpio 11:41 p.m.) Show affection. Give a smile to get a smile. The Libra moon relates to sex appeal and personal magnetism—some bold member of the opposite sex will state, "I can hardly keep my hands off you!" Virgo and another Gemini are in this picture.

Monday, January 7 (Moon in Scorpio) Attention revolves around protecting your family. Focus on home, your domestic situation, and decisions relating to travel, investments, and budget. Strive for harmony, but do not abandon your basic principles. Taurus plays a significant role.

Tuesday, January 8 (Moon in Scorpio) You won't have as much time to arrive at important decisions as you first anticipated. The Scorpio moon in your sixth house means coworkers demand action; polite talk goes out the window. Pisces and Virgo will play extraordinary roles.

Wednesday, January 9 (Moon in Scorpio to Sagittarius 4:57 a.m.) On this Wednesday, you learn who is your ally and who just talks about it. You are given more responsibility and more money to go along with it. On a personal level, you'll be told you are too demanding when it comes to lovemaking. Have luck with number 8.

Thursday, January 10 (Moon in Sagittarius) Negotiations with someone from a foreign land can be completed. A communication block is removed. The result is greater understanding. Your prestige goes up. You are well thought of and you deserve it. Aries and Libra play fascinating roles.

Friday, January 11 (Moon in Sagittarius to Capricorn 12:18 p.m.) After initial confusion, you make a fresh start in a new direction. The Sagittarian moon represents your seventh house—law, public relations, reputation, and your marital status. You will not escape unscathed, but you will be victorious. Leo is in the picture.

Saturday, January 12 (Moon in Capricorn) The moon moves into your eighth house, which denotes interest in the occult and unusual ways to achieve a goal. Focus also on your home, family, and marriage. Tonight you'll be treated to a superb dinner. You might be asking yourself, "What did I do to deserve this?"

Sunday, January 13 (Moon in Capricorn to Aquarius 9:41 p.m.) On this 13th day of January, with the new moon in Capricorn, you get money that has been coming to you for a long time. For a reason you cannot fathom, people are paying more attention to what they owe you, money and otherwise.

Monday, January 14 (Moon in Aquarius) Maintain an aura of mystery and surprise. Don't tell all. Let others play a "guessing game." Those who care most about you will advise, "You've got them on the ropes, now keep them there!" Taurus, Leo, and Scorpio figure in this scenario and have these letters in their names—D, M, V.

Tuesday, January 15 (Moon in Aquarius) The lunar position emphasizes travel, drama, and communication with someone in a foreign land. Study the language and social habits of people who are different from you. You are preparing to do something big and important—know it, and maintain confidence and optimism.

Wednesday, January 16 (Moon in Aquarius to Pisces 9:01 a.m.) In matters of speculation, stick with number 6. A family member has a gift for you—it's supposed to be a surprise, so don't let on that you already heard about it here. Act surprised! Taurus, Libra, and Scorpio figure in this fascinating scenario.

Thursday, January 17 (Moon in Pisces) Focus on dealings with the government, your career, and ability to promote your own cause. Make your terms crystal clear. See people, places, and relationships in a realistic light. Pisces and Virgo figure in this scenario, and have these letters and initials in their names—G, P, Y.

Friday, January 18 (Moon in Pisces to Aries 9:34 p.m.) As you prepare for the weekend, realize you have made a favorable impact and thus people will expect more from you. In other words, it is a blessing in disguise. People look up to you, but they might expect you to say something brilliant or at least to hand them a five- or ten-dollar bill. Ah, sweet mystery of life!

Saturday, January 19 (Moon in Aries) What a Saturday night! Many people talk to you about distant lands, travel, and romance. Let it be known, "I know where I am and where I want to go and I know I want romance and love more than anything!" Keep a smile on your face as you say those words. Have luck with number 9.

Sunday, January 20 (Moon in Aries) The moon in your eleventh house coincides with a "lucky streak." Almost anything you do could turn out "just right." In choosing "lucky numbers" try these: 5, 7, 11, 12, 18, 22. Leo and Aquarius play sensational roles in your life today.

Monday, January 21 (Moon in Aries to Taurus 9:45 a.m.) In making a request for what you want, do not overlook what you need. Focus on your home, cooperative efforts, public appearances, and marriage. Someone close to you comments," I don't believe you know what you really want!" Cancer plays the top role.

Tuesday, January 22 (Moon in Taurus) The Taurus moon relates to secrets, confidential information, and behind-the-scenes agreements. Diversify, highlight versatility, and insist on top quality and the best. Sagittarius and another Gemini play extraordinary roles and have these letters in their names: C, L, U.

Wednesday, January 23 (Moon in Taurus to Gemini 7:26 p.m.) Lucky lottery: 4, 20, 26, 31, 40, 49. A secret is inadvertently revealed during a social gathering. If you don't want anyone to know, talk to no one about it. You learn some hard lessons of life and love—but you do learn, and that is all to the good.

Thursday, January 24 (Moon in Gemini) The moon is in your sign. Your cycle is high, so take charge of your own destiny. During this cycle, you exude personal magnetism, and an aura of sensuality and sex appeal. Don't break too many hearts! At the very least, offer tea and sympathy. Virgo plays a major role.

Friday, January 25 (Moon in Gemini) On this Friday, there could be a "reunion of hearts" with a family member. Don't let pride block your progress. It is true that pride goeth before a fall! A family member, a Taurus, has been wanting to end a foolish dispute. Now you can end it!

Saturday, January 26 (Moon in Gemini to Cancer 1:15 a.m.) Make no commitments this Saturday—as for promises, get them in writing. Most important, avoid self-deception. Someone has wagered that they can twist you around their little finger. Maintain your good humor. Enjoy the attention, but do not cooperate in making yourself look foolish.

Sunday, January 27 (Moon in Cancer) A power day, this Sunday! Don't take things too lightly, but at the same time refuse to be overwhelmed by incoming news. Capricorn and Cancer will play extraordinary roles, and have these letters or initials in their names—H, Q, Z. Have luck with number 8.

Monday, January 28 (Moon in Cancer to Leo 3:29 a.m.)   On this Monday there is a full moon in your third house. Translation: You'll have more to do with relatives and visitors than has been true in a month of Mondays. Let it be known you will have no part of a wild-goose chase. Aries dominates this scenario.

Tuesday, January 29 (Moon in Leo)   Although confused, you will make the right decision. Relatives and visitors continue to get involved. Take special care in traffic. Steer clear of a bibulous individual who insists, "I can drive!" Leo and Aquarius figure prominently, and have these initials in their names: A, S, J.

Wednesday, January 30 (Moon in Leo to Virgo 3:39 a.m.)   Lucky lottery: 1, 2, 6, 11, 16, 20. If patient, you learn where you stand in connection with the "arena of love." Otherwise, you could fall victim to wishful thinking. Attention revolves around direction, motivation, and your marital status. Capricorn is in this picture.

Thursday, January 31 (Moon in Virgo)   On this last day of the month, you could have something to celebrate! What you own, land or otherwise, turns out to be worth more than you originally estimated. You can be proud of yourself, without being arrogant. Maintenance is important; don't overlook it.

FEBRUARY 2002

Friday, February 1 (Moon in Virgo to Libra 3:44 a.m.)   On this Friday, the first day of February, you are getting ready to experiment, to travel, and to try a "new line" on someone who physically attracts you. Emphasize independence and creativity. Wear bright colors. Make personal appearances. Leo and Aquarius are involved.

Saturday, February 2 (Moon in Libra) Plan ahead. Schedule activities. The moon is in Libra in your fifth house—that section of your horoscope relates to creativity and sensuality. A child's words could transform your feelings. Capricorn and Cancer will play outstanding roles.

Sunday, February 3 (Moon in Libra to Scorpio 5:34 a.m.) The Libra moon coincides with a "stirring of your creative juices." You exude personal magnetism and an aura of sensuality and sex appeal. Don't break too many hearts! Sagittarius and another Gemini figure prominently. Give full play to your intuitive intellect.

Monday, February 4 (Moon in Scorpio) People comment, "Your timing is superb!" This comes about almost effortlessly—you do what comes naturally. Be willing to revise, review, and tear down in order to rebuild. Taurus, Leo, and Scorpio play roles, and have these letters in their names—D, M, V.

Tuesday, February 5 (Moon in Scorpio to Sagittarius 10:21 a.m.) You're in rhythm—what you do, say, and request rings a bell. Although you felt at first your love was unrequited, you now are sure and confident. Virgo, Sagittarius, and another Gemini figure in this exciting scenario. Have luck with number 5.

Wednesday, February 6 (Moon in Sagittarius) Racing luck—all tracks: post position special—number 2 p.p. in the fourth race. Pick six: 2, 4, 3, 2, 8, 7. Watch for these letters or initials in the names of potential winning horses or jockeys: F, O, X. Hot daily doubles: 2 and 4, 3 and 5, 6 and 7. Local jockeys win photo finishes.

Thursday, February 7 (Moon in Sagittarius to Capricorn 6:07 p.m.) Avoid self-deception. See people and relationships as they are, not merely as you wish they could be. Protect yourself from one who is free with flattery, but expects plenty in return. Pisces and Virgo play sensational roles, and have these letters in their names: G, P, Y.

Friday, February 8 (Moon in Capricorn) You'll be chosen to represent a unique group or organization. Activities border on politics. This could represent an opportunity for you to be on the national scene. Accept this chance. A love relationship will improve as a result. Capricorn is in this picture.

Saturday, February 9 (Moon in Capricorn) On this Saturday, you will realize you are attractive and desirable. At least three members of the opposite sex "make a play for you." This will be a lively Saturday night! Aries and Libra help you overcome obstacles and will prove loyalty. Your lucky number is 9.

Sunday, February 10 (Moon in Capricorn to Aquarius 4:14 a.m.) Your financial picture will be brighter within 24 hours. An unorthodox transaction works in your favor, and as a result, you'll be more secure where money is concerned. Leo and Aquarius play fascinating roles, and will support your efforts.

Monday, February 11 (Moon in Aquarius) The moon in Aquarius is in your ninth house—the focus will be on publishing, advertising, and spirituality. What you lost will be recovered—furthermore, you'll know where you stand and where you are going. Cancer and Capricorn, who seemed distant, will come close and become your valuable allies.

Tuesday, February 12 (Moon in Aquarius to Pisces 3:52 p.m.) The new moon in Aquarius, your ninth house, means you have decided to become involved in a transaction that includes a foreign nation. Give full play to your intellectual curiosity, to social activities, and to charm. Good humor and charm will win for you friends, hopes, and financial gain.

Wednesday, February 13 (Moon in Pisces) Steps seem made to order for you to climb. Your career is emphasized; prestige is on the rise. You could gain new heights, if you take those steps. Taurus, Leo, and Scorpio play major roles, and have these initials in their names: D, M, V. Have luck with number 4.

Thursday, February 14 (Moon in Pisces) On this Valentine's Day, more people are thinking of you. You will receive more cards than in the previous years. By coincidence, you exude sex appeal and members of opposite sex wonder why they failed to notice this before today. Virgo is represented.

Friday, February 15 (Moon in Pisces to Aries 4:24 a.m.) Attention revolves around your home, family, security, insurance, and the sale or purchase of property. You are going strong, so don't stumble due to lack of confidence. Focus on charm, diplomacy, and the willingness to fight when cause is right. Libra is involved.

Saturday, February 16 (Moon in Aries) The Aries moon is in your eleventh house—that section of your horoscope represents hope, wishes, luck, and timing. You win friends and influence people, and could be ultrasuccessful as a fund-raiser. Lucky lottery: 7, 11, 18, 23, 45, 51.

Sunday, February 17 (Moon in Aries to Taurus 4:57 p.m.) This could be your power play day! Whatever venture you embark upon, you succeed in. Past experience and training helps assure success. Capricorn and Cancer play outstanding roles, and will serve as your cheering section. Have luck with number 8.

Monday, February 18 (Moon in Taurus) Strive for universal appeal. Become aware of how people in other nations live, their love and food habits. Give some study to language. Open lines of communication. Aries and Libra play instrumental roles and should be included in your immediate plans.

Tuesday, February 19 (Moon in Taurus) In answer to your question: "Yes, a fresh start, a new kind of love are all part of this dynamic scenario." Imprint style; don't follow others; highlight originality, daring, and your pioneering spirit. Above all, put aside preconceived notions. Leo will play a dramatic role.

Wednesday, February 20 (Moon in Taurus to Gemini 3:48 a.m.) Focus on partnership, cooperative efforts, your marital status, and being at the right place at a crucial moment. The moon in your sign represents your high cycle—this means take the initiative, imprint style, and be where the action is. Cancer and Capricorn will be in your corner.

Thursday, February 21 (Moon in Gemini) Diversify; accent versatility. Circumstances move in your favor, so be selective and insist on quality. Be positive that everything sold to you has your stamp of approval. Display your sense of humor, and give full play to your intellectual curiosity. Have luck with number 3.

Friday, February 22 (Moon in Gemini to Cancer 11:13 a.m.) Money comes to you, whether or not you expect it. You also locate lost articles. Your cycle is high where valuables are concerned. People look to you for guidance, and some want to borrow money. Say "no" in a diplomatic way. Scorpio plays the top role.

Saturday, February 23 (Moon in Cancer) Your cycle remains high where finances are concerned. If you feel you have a good deal, don't back down. Those who tell you it cannot be done are themselves failures. Take risks; take a chance on romance. Lucky lottery: 5, 12, 15, 18, 25, 50.

Sunday, February 24 (Moon in Cancer to Leo 2:34 p.m.) Attention revolves around domesticity, family, home, and insurance. There's music in your life, so dance to your own tune. Someone in a pugnacious mood attempts to start a fight. Laugh and walk away. Taurus, Libra, Scorpio play memorable roles.

Monday, February 25 (Moon in Leo) On this Monday, you will know without knowing. This means you'll have instinctive knowledge—do not be afraid to act on a hunch. Follow your instincts and your heart. A relative tells a tall story. Be polite, but have none of it. Pisces is in this picture.

Tuesday, February 26 (Moon in Leo to Virgo 2:48 p.m.) The moon in Leo represents your third house—that section of your horoscope tells of relatives, short trips, and ideas which require further development. Avoid getting involved in a wild-goose chase. Also avoid driving with a heavy drinker.

Wednesday, February 27 (Moon in Virgo) Racing luck—all tracks: post position special—number 8 p.p. in the first race. Pick six: 8, 2, 1, 3, 5, 8. Watch for these letters and initials in the names of potential winning horses or jockeys: I and R. Hot daily doubles: 8 and 2, 1 and 5, 1 and 8. Foreign horses do well, but could suffer injuries. Aries jockeys win.

Thursday, February 28 (Moon in Virgo to Libra 1:46 p.m.) It seems you've been here before. You ask yourself, "Could this be déjà vu?" The scenario on this last day of February features familiar faces and places. Shake off a tendency to be afraid of "something new." Leo and Aquarius play key roles and will support your cause.

MARCH 2002

Friday, March 1 (Moon in Libra) As you prepare for the weekend, aspects point to attractiveness, humor, and sexuality. The focus is also on cooperative efforts along with serious questions about marriage. Capricorn and Cancer will play outstanding roles. Your lucky number is 2.

Saturday, March 2 (Moon in Libra to Scorpio 1:52 p.m.) On this Saturday, your feelings are ambivalent: at one time favoring partnership and marriage, at other times being repelled by the prospects. With the moon in Libra, your fifth house, you emit personal magnetism, sensuality, and sex appeal. Have luck with number 3.

Sunday, March 3 (Moon in Scorpio) On this Sunday, you begin to know for sure what your priorities are, and you realize which are the important ones. Taurus, Leo, and Scorpio play major roles, and have these letters or initials in their names: D, M, V. A mathematical puzzle will be solved!

Monday, March 4 (Moon in Scorpio to Sagittarius 4:54 p.m.) On this Monday, you are alive, alert, and willing to experiment and learn. Do some writing, if you can. Take note of dreams. You are especially attractive, even though you say, "That is hard to believe!" The dry spell is over!

Tuesday, March 5 (Moon in Sagittarius) You lovingly view your home and property as you sigh, "At last, it is mine!" You know what is meant now when the term "pride of ownership" is used. Focus also on music, design, and color coordination. Domestic harmony can be restored, if you are so determined.

Wednesday, March 6 (Moon in Sagittarius to Capricorn 11:48 p.m.) This day is bittersweet—fun, because people are mystified; frustrating, because you can't seem to get major points across. Pisces and Virgo play leading roles and could have these letters or initials in their names—G, P, Y. Have luck with number 7.

Thursday, March 7 (Moon in Capricorn) Within 24 hours, the main opposition you face will be erased. The moon has left your opposite sign, so actions now can be based on your decisions, not fate. Capricorn and Cancer play instrumental roles, and have these letters in their names: H, Q, Z.

Friday, March 8 (Moon in Capricorn) On this Friday, you have access to "privileged information." Much of what you learn is confidential and involves foreign nations. Be broad-minded; avoid decisions based on narrow or preconceived notions. What a Friday!

Saturday, March 9 (Moon in Capricorn to Aquarius 9:56 a.m.) Today you make a fresh start in a new direction. You delve into arcane literature, you discover there are other areas of interest, and you determine to investigate. Opportunities exist for romance and participation in creative projects. Your lucky number is 1.

Sunday, March 10 (Moon in Aquarius) With the transitting moon in your ninth house, you are exploring the possibility of publishing, advertising, and travel. On this Sunday, you also make an effort to remedy problems at home, including your marital status. A Cancer is involved.

Monday, March 11 (Moon in Aquarius to Pisces 9:56 p.m.) A very social Monday! A visitor from a foreign land livens the scene and lends spice. Learn what you can, and give full play to your intellectual curiosity. Before the day is finished, you could receive an invitation to visit. A Sagittarian is involved.

Tuesday, March 12 (Moon in Pisces) Grab an opportunity to learn more about how people in other nations live and love. You are gaining practical lessons and knowledge about sociology. Taurus, Leo, and Scorpio figure prominently, and have these letters and initials in their names—D, M, V.

Wednesday, March 13 (Moon in Pisces) A mysterious stranger becomes part of your social scenario. Sex and the creative urge are involved—the relationship is exciting and dramatic, and success or failure depends upon your mature approach. Written material is more important than you might have assumed.

Thursday, March 14 (Moon in Pisces to Aries 9:01 p.m.) The new moon in Pisces is in your tenth house. That section of your horoscope represents promotion, career, and more money and prestige. Attention also revolves around your home, the security of your family, and your marital status. Taurus, Libra, and Scorpio will play major roles.

Friday, March 15 (Moon in Aries) This is the "Ides of March." Your numerical cycle is 7-Neptune. Thus, beware of deception, especially self-deception. Don't believe everything you hear, unless you hear it from me! Perfect techniques, streamline procedures, and rely on your "inner feelings."

Saturday, March 16 (Moon in Aries to Taurus 10:59 p.m.) On this Saturday you will concede, "It sure is lively!" The moon in your eleventh house means you obtain hopes and wishes. You also are successful in obtaining funding for an unusual project. Lucky lottery: 5, 6, 8, 11, 18, 22.

Sunday, March 17 (Moon in Taurus) On this St. Patrick's Day, the moon is in Taurus, your twelfth house. You will have fun, but there will be a tinge of guilt if you ignore basic issues. Someone you promised to help will hold you to it. Aries figures prominently.

Monday, March 18 (Moon in Taurus) On this Monday, you examine ideas of ghosts and goblins. Your interests will be piqued along unorthodox lines. Your thoughts will be original and dynamic, and with the moon in Taurus, look behind the scenes. Leo and Aquarius encourage you and are part of today's exciting scenario.

Tuesday, March 19 (Moon in Taurus to Gemini 10:18 a.m.) You learn once and for all that there is nothing to fear, except that you make it so. Another Gemini could be involved in "playing tricks." The focus is on marriage, partnership, and cooperative efforts. A valuable article that had been missing will be found—close by.

Wednesday, March 20 (Moon in Gemini) In your high cycle, the moon is in your sign, the emphasis is on personality and physical attraction. A Libra wants to hear your story and encourages you to write. Social activities accelerate. You could be the "party giver." Have luck with number 3.

Thursday, March 21 (Moon in Gemini to Cancer 9:05 p.m.) Your cycle continues high, so hurdle obstacles, and don't be afraid of what is on "the other side." You possess magical elements. People ask, "What is your secret?" Take all this in stride; be quietly modest. Taurus and Scorpio play outstanding roles.

Friday, March 22 (Moon in Cancer) You are asked to "find money." You are not dreaming—it is real, and when you bend to pick it up, you'll realize this is your lucky day. Virgo, Sagittarius, and another Gemini play major roles, and have these letters or initials in their names—E, N, W.

Saturday, March 23 (Moon in Cancer) This Saturday could be the start of a winning streak. A Cancer asks you, "Why aren't you laughing or at least smiling? Luck seems to be riding with you!" Your answer: "I guess it's because I can hardly believe it!" Your fortunate number is 6.

Sunday, March 24 (Moon in Cancer to Leo 12:10 a.m.) On this Sunday, you might want to be alone, but a family member insists on tagging along. It is best to speak out, something like this—"I love you, but I feel I want to be alone for a little while!" If spoken in this way, Pisces will understand.

Monday, March 25 (Moon in Leo) This can be a powerful Monday! Dig deep, explore, and discover. Someone close to you may have been "holding your money." Avoid threatening tones. Make it clear: "I don't want something like this to ever happen again!"

Tuesday, March 26 (Moon in Leo to Virgo 1:42 a.m.) What seemed a catastrophe 24 hours ago will now be cause for laughter. A journey is arranged. You will see for yourself that this is a big, round world. Aries and Libra figure in this exciting scenario. Have luck with number 9.

Wednesday, March 27 (Moon in Virgo) On this Wednesday, you could win a contest, especially with these numbers—1, 5, 6, 11, 18, 22. A dynamic, dramatic Leo offers to "guide your destiny." Response: "Thanks, but no, thanks. I feel I can control my fate!" Hot weather!

Thursday, March 28 (Moon in Virgo to Libra 1:03 a.m.) The full moon in Libra, your fifth house, coincides with a stirring of creative juices. Be ready for change, travel, and a variety of sensations. Some people ask in a belligerent way, "Who do you think you are?" Response: "I am me and that is all I can or hope to be!"

Friday, March 29 (Moon in Libra) A social Friday night! You'll be complimented. Your ego swells. Try to maintain balance, but do show appreciation for kind or exciting remarks by a Libran. Focus on diversity, versatility, advertising, and publishing. Sagittarius plays a role.

Saturday, March 30 (Moon in Libra to Scorpio 12:21 a.m.) Compared to recent days, you might consider this Saturday dull. Maintain balance and a steady pace. You are closer to a major achievement than might be anticipated. Taurus, Leo, and Scorpio figure in this scenario. You'll be asking, "What can I do to prove I know where I am and where I'm going?"

Sunday, March 31 (Moon in Scorpio) On this last day of March, you could be engaged in a "creative process." You'll be asked to write your résumé, suggestions, and aspirations. Don't back down! This could be your turn at the "big time." Members of the opposite sex find you attractive and say so in no uncertain terms.

APRIL 2002

Monday, April 1 (Moon in Scorpio to Sagittarius 1:49 a.m.) Forces are scattered; fun and games prevail. No one can really fool you, but you can deceive yourself. Sagittarius and another Gemini engage in "April Fool" jokes. Watch for typos, proofread, and be ready to rewrite if necessary. Have luck with number 3.

Tuesday, April 2 (Moon in Sagittarius) Someone you thought had gone out of your life makes a dramatic return. Scorpio is involved. The major player is Sagittarius. Protect your belongings. Someone wants something for nothing, and expects you to be the "fall guy." An offer includes an overseas journey.

Wednesday, April 3 (Moon in Sagittarius to Capricorn 6:58 a.m.) Lucky lottery: 9, 13, 15, 23, 28, 51. The moon in your seventh house spotlights partnership, cooperative efforts, and your marital status. An excellent time for investigation, research, reading and writing, and the stirring of creative juices. Virgo figures in this scenario.

Thursday, April 4 (Moon in Capricorn) Racing luck—all tracks: post position special—number 2 p.p. in the sixth race. There are many close calls in traffic. Be a careful driver, and avoid heavy drinkers. Attention revolves around your home, family, insurance payments, and the sale or purchase of an art object.

Friday, April 5 (Moon in Capricorn to Aquarius 4:06 p.m.) Someone attempts to sell you a "bill of goods" relating to the occult. Be informed and skeptical. Let people know you did not recently fall off the turnip truck. A Pisces declares, "I want to be your friend and I wish you would stop being cool toward me!"

Saturday, April 6 (Moon in Aquarius) The lunar position relates to distribution, production, advertising, and publishing. A discussion of theology with an Aquarian proves fruitful and inspiring. Dig deep for information. You will have the tools necessary. This could be your power play day—make it so!

Sunday, April 7—Daylight Saving Time Begins (Moon in Aquarius) You might feel as if you are in another dimension. This follows an additional discussion concerning theology and metaphysics. You come to the realization, "I am not earthbound. I am free to explore, and to arrive at my own conclusions." Aries plays a role.

Monday, April 8 (Moon in Aquarius to Pisces 4:57 a.m.) On this Monday, you feel as if "something strange is happening." In the sky, the moon is leaving Aquarius and will be in Pisces. Stress originality and independence. You will advance in your career, if you don't hold back. The moon in your tenth house relates to authority and promotion.

Tuesday, April 9 (Moon in Pisces) Focus on a different kind of relationship with your family. Purchase a gift; call it a peace offering or anything you wish. It will bring smiles to faces and resulting happiness. The numerical cycle highlights cooperative efforts, public appearances, and the ability to almost read minds.

Wednesday, April 10 (Moon in Pisces to Aries 5:39 p.m.) You attend a social gathering that includes "the boss." Be yourself, relate anecdotes, and encourage others to write, advertise, and publish. By giving a smile, you also receive a smile. Show sincere interest in the outside activities of coworkers. Have luck with number 3.

Thursday, April 11 (Moon in Aries) The moon in your eleventh house portends a "lucky streak." Elements of timing and luck ride with you. You can afford to take a chance on romance. Taurus, Leo, and Scorpio play unique roles and could have these letters or initials in their names—D, M, V.

Friday, April 12 (Moon in Aries to Taurus 5:54 a.m.) The new moon in your eleventh house "speaks well of you." The emphasis is on hopes, wishes, and desires—ask for what you need, as well as frivolous material. This day is very good for writing, and for tracking down clues in connection with dreams and impressions. A Sagittarian is involved.

Saturday, April 13 (Moon in Taurus) Sightings will be reported concerning UFOs and some religious experiences will be noted in connection with apparent visions of the "Virgin Mary." People will be busy on all fronts promoting theories and beliefs. Libra plays a top role.

Sunday, April 14 (Moon in Taurus) On this Sunday, there will be multiplicities of religious experiences. Some experiences will prove inspiring; others could be frightening. The moon is in your twelfth house, so you will be dealing with institutions, churches, and researchers.

Monday, April 15 (Moon in Taurus to Gemini 4:55 p.m.) Your happy Monday has finally arrived! You locate lost articles and could find ways of considerably increasing your income. You are provided with secret information that is very private. Keep a promise to be discreet. Capricorn is involved.

Tuesday, April 16 (Moon in Gemini) Your cycle moves up. You learn where you stand (quite high!) and what you can do about it. Finish what you start. Get a look behind the scenes. Your judgment and intuition are on target. A burden you've been carrying will be lifted from your shoulders.

Wednesday, April 17 (Moon in Gemini) With a new outlook, you will feel refreshed. Your vigor and optimism return. Be original; don't follow others. Place your Gemini stamp on whatever you do. Leo and Aquarius will play outstanding roles. Lucky lottery: 1, 7, 10, 15, 42, 44.

Thursday, April 18 (Moon in Gemini to Cancer 1:59 a.m.) Attention revolves around your home, family, security, and insurance payments. Your cycle continues high, so act now—don't wait for your luck to run out. Cancer and Capricorn will play leading roles. Focus on direction, motivation, and how to deal with a surprise announcement from a family member.

Friday, April 19 (Moon in Cancer) Arrange a social gathering; include someone who lately has been disenchanted. Your role today is to bring laughter and to use your intellectual curiosity. Explore and discover! A Sagittarian could become your valuable ally, if you so permit.

Saturday, April 20 (Moon in Cancer to Leo 8:19 a.m.) The moon moves into Cancer, your "money house." During this cycle, you recover lost articles and could make profitable investments. A Cancer will show the way, if you are willing to listen and learn. Absorb knowledge, distill it, and then act.

Sunday, April 21 (Moon in Leo) Get ready for quick changes and short trips. A relative visits unannounced. Maintain your emotional equilibrium and sense of humor. A flirtation that begins as a joke could become serious. Know when to say, "Enough is enough!" Virgo is in the picture.

Monday, April 22 (Moon in Leo to Virgo 11:33 a.m.) Attention revolves around your home, family, and protection of assets. Remember recent resolutions about exercise, diet, and nutrition. You can look very good and attractive if you take care of yourself. Libra will play an outstanding role.

Tuesday, April 23 (Moon in Virgo) Carefully examine all real estate offerings and opportunities. There is an aura of deception present—remember, you get nothing for nothing. No one is ready to give you something of value free. Pisces and Virgo will figure in this exciting scenario.

Wednesday, April 24 (Moon in Virgo to Libra 12:20 p.m.) The moon in Virgo, your fourth house, represents security requirements, land, and home. Capricorn and Cancer play major roles, and could have these letters or initials in their names—H, Q, Z. Be persistent in digging for information—money and power are involved. Your lucky number is 8.

Thursday, April 25 (Moon in Libra) Look beyond the immediate. Be willing to take a chance on romance. The moon in your fifth house stirs your creative juices. There is more to you than you might realize. Tonight, you get the idea—you are special and vulnerable. Aries and Libra figure in this scenario.

Friday, April 26 (Moon in Libra to Scorpio 12:15 p.m.) You have waited for this day. It is a time to break free, to express yourself, and to make a fresh start in a new direction. Leo and Aquarius play memorable roles, and have these letters or initials in their names—A, S, J. In matters of speculation, stick with number 1.

Saturday, April 27 (Moon in Scorpio) The full moon in Scorpio represents your sixth house—which means you could get involved with someone in your workplace. The focus will be on basic issues, work methods, and ability to get things done despite the odds. Capricorn and Cancer are in this picture, and will be on your side.

Sunday, April 28 (Moon in Scorpio to Sagittarius 1:13 p.m.) Tonight you'll have reason to celebrate—a reunion takes place with someone who had played an important role in your life. Accent self-expression and an appreciation of the arts. Let it be known that you are multidimensional. Sagittarian plays a top role.

Monday, April 29 (Moon in Sagittarius) The emphasis is on proposals of business, career, or marriage.

Highlight public relations, legal affairs, your reputation, and prestige. Taurus, Leo, and Scorpio play major roles, and could have these letters or initials in their names: D, M, V. A mystery will be solved!

Tuesday, April 30 (Moon in Sagittarius to Capricorn 5:02 p.m.) You could discover today that you are in love with your mate. If single, you are drawn to an individual who has attracted you from the start. Logic tends to take a backseat. Emotions rule, so protect yourself in close quarters. Another Gemini asserts his or her beliefs, some of them amusing.

MAY 2002

Wednesday, May 1 (Moon in Capricorn) On this first day of the month, with the moon in Capricorn, you'll be paying more attention to your diet and nutrition. The pressure is on. You will be up to it. People depend upon you to a greater extent, including your writings and opinions. Scorpio is involved.

Thursday, May 2 (Moon in Capricorn) Investigate claims others make concerning the "supernatural." Focus on change, travel, and a variety of sensations. The numerical cycle number 5 equates to Mercury, planet of information. Don't be satisfied to know something happened—find out why it occurred.

Friday, May 3 (Moon in Capricorn to Aquarius 12:44 a.m.) There will be better days ahead! Prepare for travel, education, advertising, and publishing. Look beyond the immediate. Predict your future and make it come true. Attend an auction, if possible—a genuine bargain will be made available. The focus will be on rhythm, sound, and music.

Saturday, May 4 (Moon in Aquarius) On this Saturday, you should separate fact from illusion. An envious person wants you to tear down everything you have built. The reason: jealousy, and a feeling of worthlessness. Look up to the sky. The answer is there.

Sunday, May 5 (Moon in Aquarius to Pisces 11:45 a.m.) This is your kind of day! Forces of creativity, responsibility, and results will be featured. You gain friends, allies, and possibly a new love. Capricorn and Cancer will play major roles, and have these letters or initials in their names—H, Q, Z.

Monday, May 6 (Moon in Pisces) Let go of preconceived notions, and pay respects to someone in a position of authority who has suffered hard times healthwise. The more you give today, the more you will receive. Golden Rule: To get a smile, give a smile. Aries is in this picture.

Tuesday, May 7 (Moon in Pisces) Choose with care—people who want you to do things "the old way" are sincere, but sincerely mistaken. Do things your way, the new way. Imprint style; let others follow you, if they so desire. Maintain independence; also maintain creative control of any project.

Wednesday, May 8 (Moon in Pisces to Aries 12:21 a.m.) Within 24 hours, your cycle moves up, you obtain funding for a project, and you win friends and perhaps a new love. For now, however, fulfill duties at home and again show regard for someone who once was among the high and mighty.

Thursday, May 9 (Moon in Aries) Accent humor and curiosity, examine priorities, and find out which is first. This could be the start of a winning streak—

in matters of speculation, stick with number 3. Sagittarius and another Gemini will "fill in the spaces." Diversify!

Friday, May 10 (Moon in Aries to Taurus 12:30 p.m.) Your goal is in sight—Taurus and Scorpio seem somehow to interfere with the completion of a project. Don't force issues. Let it be known: "I will be back and I will finish." During this scenario, you once again learn that "all that glitters is not gold."

Saturday, May 11 (Moon in Taurus) You get help from "backstage." A Taurus has vital information, and wants to share it. Upon awakening, take notes and write down your dream. You are both teacher and student today—so speak and learn. No matter how things appear on the surface, dig deep for further data.

Sunday, May 12 (Moon in Taurus to Gemini 11:02 p.m.) An area of your life that had been dark will receive the benefit of greater light. The new moon in your twelfth house reveals that you are on the right path, despite some "frightening" intervals. Sound and music play roles. A Libra will become your valuable ally.

Monday, May 13 (Moon in Gemini) Your knowledge of sports and other subjects will be tested. If you don't know the answers, admit it. If you do know, don't keep everybody waiting—give the answer in a confident, cool manner. Be near water, if possible— Pisces and Virgo play memorable roles.

Tuesday, May 14 (Moon in Gemini) This is one Tuesday you won't soon forget! The moon is in your sign, and circumstances are turning in your favor, even as you read these lines. Stress independence and originality, and imprint your own style. Capricorn and Cancer play major roles.

Wednesday, May 15 (Moon in Gemini to Cancer 7:32 a.m.) On this Wednesday, you are provided with an opportunity to cash in on a special collection. The moon is leaving your sign and entering your money and personal possessions sector. You continue to be "riding high"—do not be discouraged by negative responses from others.

Thursday, May 16 (Moon in Cancer) Make a fresh start. In matters of speculation, stick with number 1. Leo and Aquarius play important roles, and they want you to succeed. At the track: number 3 post position in the seventh race. Be aware of these letters or initials in the names of horses or jockeys destined to win—A, S, J.

Friday, May 17 (Moon in Cancer to Leo 1:50 p.m.) The spotlight is on cooperative efforts, public relations, special appearances, and proposals of partnership and marriage. Your popularity is on the rise. People want you here, there, and everywhere! Cancer and Capricorn play sensational roles, and have these initials in their names: B, K, T.

Saturday, May 18 (Moon in Leo) What a Saturday night! Your wit and wisdom ride forth. People will be fascinated, especially members of the opposite sex. Some will be bold enough to let you know, "I find it difficult to keep my hands off you!" Lucky lottery: 3, 15, 18, 22, 30, 45.

Sunday, May 19 (Moon in Leo to Virgo 6:00 p.m.) On this Sunday, attend to details. Impress others by your skill with crossword puzzles. Solve mathematical problems. Make this your "makeover" day. Look and feel different. Your vigor returns; balance rest and energy. Scorpio is involved.

Monday, May 20 (Moon in Virgo) You'll be sighing, "At last, I feel free and capable of doing almost anything I want!" The numerical cycle number 5 equates to Mercury, which means you can write, read, and teach. Meeting with a special member of the opposite sex will prove satisfying, a boost to your ego.

Tuesday, May 21 (Moon in Virgo to Libra 8:17 p.m.) Attention revolves around general work, health, domestic "situation." Decorate, fix things at home, beautify your surroundings. You are due to be visited by a person you want very much to favorably impress. Taurus, Libra, and Scorpio play major roles.

Wednesday, May 22 (Moon in Libra) Avoid self-deception. See people and relationships in a realistic light. You do possess "psychic energy" and you will know it for sure by tonight. In matters of speculation, stick with number 7. Pisces and Virgo figure in this scenario.

Thursday, May 23 (Moon in Libra to Scorpio 9:37 p.m.) You have been waiting for this day! Pressure will be on. You will be up to it. The moon in that section of your horoscope relating to creativity and sexual attraction makes this a day to remember. Don't break too many hearts! Offer tea and sympathy!

Friday, May 24 (Moon in Scorpio) Look beyond the immediate. Examine the possibility of visiting a foreign land to promote your product or talent. Aries and Libra will play featured roles. Ignore a person who is negative, envious, and at times evil. Have luck with number 9.

Saturday, May 25 (Moon in Scorpio to Sagittarius 11:21 p.m.) Your cycle is such that you can be successful in a new environment. Do not follow others. Let them follow you, if they so desire. Turn on your Gemini charm. Let it be known that you intend to finish what you start. Lucky lottery: 1, 10, 12, 18, 40, 50.

Sunday, May 26 (Moon in Sagittarius) The full moon in your marriage house obviously relates to cooperative efforts, partnership, and your marital status. Focus on legal affairs, public relations, your prestige, and reputation. Cancer and Capricorn figure in this dynamic scenario.

Monday, May 27 (Moon in Sagittarius) Although there will be confusion, make it work for you. You will have time to choose, to be selective, to insist on quality. Someone who is "grumpy" wants to complain because of jealousy. Have none of it! Say what you mean, and mean what you say!

Tuesday, May 28 (Moon in Sagittarius to Capricorn 2:54 a.m.) Your attention will turn to accounting methods within 24 hours. Someone you trust will confide, "I do not know all I am supposed to know!" Take charge of your own business, career, and destiny. The wise person controls his own fate!

Wednesday, May 29 (Moon in Capricorn) Get ready for change and a variety of sensations—open lines of communication. Read, write, and teach—share information, put pieces together, and come up with the complete story. Someone of the opposite sex tosses modesty aside, declaring, "You make me feel giddy!"

Thursday, May 30 (Moon in Capricorn to Aquarius 9:35 a.m.) Attention continues to revolve around your home, insurance, and the protection of family and property. During this cycle, you will hear "the sound of music." People comment favorably on your voice, and encourage you to go further and to study and practice. A Sagittarian is involved.

Friday, May 31 (Moon in Aquarius) On this last day of May, you are tempted to take too much for granted. Instead, test the waters—be sure of the temperature, and that you can handle "bigger waves." A Pisces, though not evil, nevertheless does not enjoy your success. Time is important!

JUNE 2002

Saturday, June 1 (Moon in Aquarius to Pisces 7:36 p.m.) A lively Saturday night! You meet someone who is "clever with words." A physical attraction results; maintain your emotional equilibrium. Prepare a list of questions, if you meet a "lively Virgo." This meeting comes about sooner than you anticipated. Your lucky number is 5.

Sunday, June 2 (Moon in Pisces) Many wishes come true for you this Sunday. Be near water, if possible. Encourage a Libra friend to emerge from an emotional shell. By helping others, you also aid yourself. Know it, and act accordingly. You will receive a gift.

Monday, June 3 (Moon in Pisces) On this Monday, lie low if possible. Consider your views to be private, not yet ready to be exposed to the public. Protect yourself in emotional clinches. A love partner will not fight fairly. Know it, and prepare your own plan of battle accordingly.

Tuesday, June 4 (Moon in Pisces to Aries 7:50 a.m.) Within 24 hours, the lunar position enables you to win friends and influence people. If you wait, time is on your side. Tonight, you learn how serious or otherwise is a relationship. Capricorn and Cancer will play exciting roles. Your lucky number is 8.

Wednesday, June 5 (Moon in Aries) You could succeed in almost anything you do. Fame and fortune awaits your "arrival." Look beyond the immediate; maintain a universal perception. Avoid anything narrow, especially a narrow mind. There are more things in heaven and earth than fit your philosophy.

Thursday, June 6 (Moon in Aries to Taurus 8:05 p.m.) Make a fresh start. Highlight versatility. Give full play to your intellectual curiosity. You are very attractive. A member of opposite sex confides, "I can hardly contain myself!" Be kind; offer tea and sympathy at the very least. An Aquarian is involved.

Friday, June 7 (Moon in Taurus) You receive proposals of business, career, or marriage. Be selective; choose the best. A Cancer could play an exceptional role. You'll be invited to dine out—accept this invitation; be gracious and hungry! Capricorn plays a top role.

Saturday, June 8 (Moon in Taurus) On this Saturday, request that promises be put in writing. People talk about practical things, including money. Your cycle moves up, so you'll get what you want, if persistent. Social activities accelerate; you receive lots of compliments, some of them sincere. Your lucky number is 3.

Sunday, June 9 (Moon in Taurus to Gemini 6:28 a.m.) Be aware of red tape and obstacles. You will overcome, and you'll win. Let others know you are not without allies. Taurus, Leo, and Scorpio figure in this exciting scenario. Face the music early, present a format, deal with superiors, and be confident. Don't walk with your hat in your hand!

Monday, June 10 (Moon in Gemini) The new moon in your sign makes this a different, creative Monday. Begin a project, if possible. Be sociable to Leo and Aquarius. Read, write, and teach. Realize the importance of the written word. Take notes about dreams. Start a diary. Reread a love letter.

Tuesday, June 11 (Moon in Gemini to Cancer 2:13 p.m.) On this Tuesday, you win the cooperation of key people in beautifying your surroundings, especially your home. Remember, give a smile to get a smile. Be diplomatic, but firm. Taurus, Libra, and Scorpio figure in this "amazing" scenario. Don't reveal a secret!

Wednesday, June 12 (Moon in Cancer) Twenty-four hours ago, you had a bright idea—don't tell how it is done! Let others play the guessing game. Maintain an aura of intrigue and mystery. Do not wear your heart on your sleeve. Define terms, and listen to a proposition about real estate. Don't believe everything you hear!

Thursday, June 13 (Moon in Cancer to Leo 7:38 p.m.) Money comes from a surprise source. Previously, you put pressure on it—but it did not seem to do any good. However, today you get money that has been coming to you, a very pleasant surprise. Capricorn and Cancer will play outstanding roles.

Friday, June 14 (Moon in Leo) Focus on drama, communication, and expressions of love. If you open your mind, you'll perceive future trends. Don't worry about whether it is possible, just do it! Aries and Libra will play mysterious roles. Have luck with number 9.

Saturday, June 15 (Moon in Leo to Virgo 11:22 p.m.) Focus on drama, entertainment, color coordination, and showmanship. You'll be very impressive, especially in dealing with the opposite sex. A Leo will be bold enough to say, "I can hardly keep my hands off you!" Stress independence, originality, and a fresh start in a new direction.

Sunday, June 16 (Moon in Virgo) Give special consideration to your mate or partner. An illness could strike in the form of indigestion. Know it, and be patient and sympathetic. Capricorn and Cancer figure in this dynamic scenario. Tonight features food, gifts, and trading recipes and compliments.

Monday, June 17 (Moon in Virgo) Your property value is discussed. Be perceptive. Don't give up something of value for nothing. Ask questions, and get estimates in writing. Let others realize your time is valuable and you do not expect to "play games." A Sagittarian is in the picture.

Tuesday, June 18 (Moon in Virgo to Libra 2:10 a.m.) What appears to be an illusion will turn out to be "the real thing." A conflict of interest is involved. People close to you disagree and this makes you uncomfortable. Taurus, Leo, and Scorpio figure in this quixotic scenario.

Wednesday, June 19 (Moon in Libra) Your creative juices stir. Imprint your own style. Don't follow others. There's an exciting reunion tonight. Virgo, Sagittarius, and another Gemini will play leading roles. A project started three months ago is due to become a reality. Lucky lottery: 3, 4, 6, 10, 18, 22.

Thursday, June 20 (Moon in Libra to Scorpio 4:41 a.m.) Attention revolves around your home. A young person confides, "I want to be like you!" Get ready for a change of plans; have alternatives at hand. Taurus, Libra, and Scorpio will figure prominently. Refuse to be discouraged by someone who lacks faith.

Friday, June 21 (Moon in Scorpio) Someone who shares your interest lacks ability, and wants you to shoulder responsibilities. Have none of that—don't be taken for granted. Libra plays a top role. Define terms, outline boundaries, and do not fall victim to self-deception.

Saturday, June 22 (Moon in Scorpio to Sagittarius 7:41 a.m.) A healing process is under way. An emotional bruise taught you a valuable lesson. Pressure, responsibility are featured. You not only will be up to it, but you will overcome and succeed. Capricorn, Cancer figure in this exciting scenario. Lucky number is 8.

Sunday, June 23 (Moon in Sagittarius) A relative could arrive unannounced. Maintain your equilibrium. Be courteous, but make crystal clear that you would like to have advance notice before visits. Aries will play a "mysterious" role. It's important that you finish what was started two months ago.

Monday, June 24 (Moon in Sagittarius to Capricorn 12:01 p.m.) The full moon position equates to a short trip involving a relative who seeks to recover legal documents. Be cooperative, but avoid a wild-goose chase. Look beyond the immediate; maintain a universal outlook. Leo and Aquarius will play outstanding roles.

Tuesday, June 25 (Moon in Capricorn) Check accounting figures. A computer error could cause a mixup. Remember that figures don't lie, but liars figure. Protect yourself at close quarters; don't give up something of value for nothing. Plan ahead for a possible journey. A Cancer is involved.

Wednesday, June 26 (Moon in Capricorn to Aquarius 6:35 p.m.) If attending the track, choose the number 3 horse in the third race. You will be popular during social activities tonight. Sagittarius and another Gemini will play featured roles. Give full play to your intellectual curiosity—ask questions, and demand answers.

Thursday, June 27 (Moon in Aquarius) The moon position "reminds" you of a long-ago and faraway commitment. Someone who once played a major role in your life will make a surprise appearance. This helps you to maintain your emotional equilibrium. A Scorpio pushes for completion of a story.

Friday, June 28 (Moon in Aquarius) An exciting time, as you prepare for a lively weekend. Virgo, Sagittarius, and another Gemini will pay dominant roles. Get ready for change, travel, and a variety of experiences. In matters of speculation, stick with number 5. You exude personal magnetism and an abundance of sex appeal.

Saturday, June 29 (Moon in Aquarius to Pisces 4:02 a.m.) Lucky lottery: 1, 2, 5, 6, 12, 20. Attention revolves around your home, family, and income potential. Focus on a possible change of residence or marital status. Be diplomatic, not weak. People comment,

"Your voice is different—very pleasant." Sing with enthusiasm.

Sunday, June 30 (Moon in Pisces) Don't be impatient. See people and relationships in a realistic way. Above all, avoid self-deception. A Pisces wants something for nothing from you. Protect yourself in emotional clinches. Learn the difference between generosity and extravagance.

JULY 2002

Monday, July 1 (Moon in Pisces to Aries 3:48 p.m.) Obtain a family agreement on how to celebrate the holiday. The "Fourth" this year will be of vital importance. Find out whom you want to be with, and where. Take notes, especially of your dreams. Properly interpreted, dreams could be the guideposts to the future.

Tuesday, July 2 (Moon in Aries) Be realistic in making plans for the upcoming holiday. People who make grandiose promises may not be capable of fulfilling them. Be self-reliant; don't disappoint young persons who look up to you. Pisces and Virgo play extraordinary roles.

Wednesday, July 3 (Moon in Aries) Be positive of material, food, and beverages. Become familiar with historical facts relating to the holiday. Do not be shy about being patriotic! Capricorn and Cancer figure in this scenario. An older family member deserves special consideration.

Thursday, July 4 (Moon in Aries to Taurus 4:15 a.m.) Happy Fourth! Maintain a universal outlook. Absorb information concerning Independence Day. This could be a memorable time, if you are determined to make it so. Open lines of communication. Someone in another city wants to tell you something.

Friday, July 5 (Moon in Taurus)   The holiday is over and you did well! This is a new day and could feature creative projects, love, romance, and style. Emphasize originality, derring-do. Others follow you, and rely upon your leadership. Leo and Aquarius figure in this exciting scenario.

Saturday, July 6 (Moon in Taurus to Gemini 2:59 p.m.)   On this Saturday, you make discoveries about "certain people." You may not be completely happy, but you will be informed. Questions will be asked about commitments and marriage. An individual behind the scenes wants to know too much, too soon.

Sunday, July 7 (Moon in Gemini)   What a Sunday! The moon is in your sign. You will be at the right place at a special moment. Your vitality returns; optimism replaces gloom. As you read these lines, circumstances are turning in your favor. Be selective and critical; insist on quality.

Monday, July 8 (Moon in Gemini to Cancer 10:34 p.m.)   Your cycle remains high, despite slight impediments. Scorpio attempts to bully, but will not succeed in shaking your beliefs. Many rely upon you; don't let them down! Proofreading is necessary, along with some research. You'll be engaged in a debate.

Tuesday, July 9 (Moon in Cancer)   Your financial picture is bright, despite a minor setback. A flirtation could get more involved than you originally anticipated. A trip out of town may be necessary. Know when to say, "Enough is enough!" Virgo and Sagittarius figure prominently in this scenario.

Wednesday, July 10 (Moon in Cancer to Leo 3:06 a.m.) A new outlook on profits and losses is necessary. You could be more affluent than you originally estimated. Taurus, Libra, and Scorpio are in this picture, and could have these letters or initials in their names—F, O, X. Lucky lottery: 6, 13, 16, 18, 19, 24.

Thursday, July 11 (Moon in Leo) On this Thursday, "lie low," if possible. Someone wants something for nothing. You could be the prime target. A Cancer is persuasive, flatters you, and does have a motive. Define terms; do not fall victim to self-deception.

Friday, July 12 (Moon in Leo) On this Friday, you feel vigorous, creative, and sexy. The Leo moon coincides with sociability, popularity, and the renewal of a relationship with a sibling. Capricorn and Cancer will play surprising roles, and can help cut through red tape.

Saturday, July 13 (Moon in Leo to Virgo 5:39 a.m.) On this Saturday, you complete a project. Communication from someone overseas elevates your morale. Maintain a universal outlook. Avoid narrow-minded people. Your sense of prophecy is heightened—predict the future; make it come true. Have luck with number 9.

Sunday, July 14 (Moon in Virgo) Avoid a wild-goose chase. Do not be a passenger in an automobile driven by a heavy drinker. Make a fresh start; don't become enthralled by one who talks big but does not have two nickels to rub together. This message will become crystal clear by tonight.

Monday, July 15 (Moon in Virgo to Libra 7:38 a.m.) The spotlight is on cooperative efforts, public appearances, and dealings with city officials. People are willing to listen, if you actually have something important to say. Where you live and marriage—these things figure prominently.

Tuesday, July 16 (Moon in Libra) Highlight versatility, be selective, make inquiries, and realize you are influential, perhaps in your own way. Favors are returned. This means those you helped in the past will return the kindness. Your popularity is on the rise. Participate in a political-charitable campaign.

Wednesday, July 17 (Moon in Libra to Scorpio 10:12 a.m.) On this Wednesday, do some rewriting and research, and attend to basic issues. The Libra moon relates to the "stirring of your creative juices." You have plenty of sex appeal, and could be involved in a relationship that provides pleasure but nothing else. Scorpio is involved.

Thursday, July 18 (Moon in Scorpio) The focus is on the area of your chart relating to work and health—reports in all areas are favorable, if not extraordinary. A friendship ensues with someone you previously felt was dull or inconsequential. An excellent day for reading, writing, and learning by teaching others.

Friday, July 19 (Moon in Scorpio to Sagittarius 2:01 p.m.) A low-key approach brings the desired results. Don't reveal your ace-in-the-hole. Be confident within; let others know you will fight if the cause is right. Taurus, Libra, and Scorpio play "amazing" roles. Decorate, remodel, and beautify your home—domestic issues dominate this scenario.

Saturday, July 20 (Moon in Sagittarius) Define terms; locate missing legal papers. See people, places, and relationships as they really are, not merely as you wish they could be. A temporary delay works in your favor—time is on your side, and becomes your tremendous ally. A Pisces is in the picture.

Sunday, July 21 (Moon in Sagittarius to Capricorn 7:27 p.m.) Spiritual values surface. Questions arise concerning morality, character, honor, partnership, and marriage. Do your own thing; don't follow others. Do things your way, whether or not it makes you popular. Leo and Aquarius will figure in this scenario.

Monday, July 22 (Moon in Capricorn) A universal outlook proves beneficial. Avoid anything that is "narrow-minded." Communicate with someone from another land. Find out how your talent or product would "fit." A reunion tonight proves dramatic, romantic, and satisfying. Aries plays a role.

Tuesday, July 23 (Moon in Capricorn) You've waited for this day—it is here now, so make the most of it by taking the lead, and displaying your pioneering spirit. Someone who claims, "I love you," should be asked to "prove it." Leo and Aquarius will be a major part of your scenario.

Wednesday, July 24 (Moon in Capricorn to Aquarius 2:39 a.m.) Accent cooperative efforts. Investigate travel plans. Look beyond the immediate. Peer into the future, where answers reside. Attention during part of this day will revolve around food, recipes, and restaurant management. Lucky lottery: 2, 3, 5, 18, 20, 21.

Thursday, July 25 (Moon in Aquarius) At the track: post position special—number 5 p.p. in the seventh race. Your popularity is on the rise. More people want to be with you, to read what you write. The focus is on publishing, advertising, showmanship, and design. A Sagittarian plays a fantastic role.

Friday, July 26 (Moon in Aquarius to Pisces 12:04 p.m.) Be methodical and thorough. Check accounting and computer figures. Within 24 hours, you will have more responsibility and authority. You'll earn more money, and at times during the day, you wish for peace and quiet as in the past. Scorpio plays a top role.

Saturday, July 27 (Moon in Pisces) Be ready for a change of scene. Realize that today you exude personal magnetism and sex appeal. Be aware, daring, and confident, but don't break too many hearts. You will be approached by a Virgo who has something of value to relate—listen, but avoid being naive.

Sunday, July 28 (Moon in Pisces to Aries 11:38 p.m.) A relative who has been "in hiding" will make an appearance. All in all, this will prove to be a pleasant experience. You will obtain cooperation in making your surroundings more beautiful, especially at home. Focus on emotional security, financial advantages, and a decision regarding where you will live.

Monday, July 29 (Moon in Aries) Get your second wind! Your cycle moves up. Within 24 hours, a major wish will be fulfilled. In matters of speculation, stick with number 8. Define terms, play the waiting game, but know when to say, "Enough is enough!" Pisces and Virgo play exciting roles.

Tuesday, July 30 (Moon in Aries) Following an initial delay, a promise made to you by an executive will be fulfilled. Exude confidence; state your case and then leave matters as they are. Focus on promotion, production, and extra responsibility. You'll be up to it, no matter what the pressure.

Wednesday, July 31 (Moon in Aries to Taurus 12:15 p.m.) Lucky lottery: 1, 9, 10, 12, 39, 44. Look beyond the immediate. Let go of a burden not your own in the first place. Someone you helped in the recent past will return the favor, albeit reluctantly. Be creatively selfish; let others know your time and efforts are valuable.

AUGUST 2002

Thursday, August 1 (Moon in Taurus) A blend of practicality and imagination is featured. Time is on your side; you can afford to play the "waiting game." Wait for the right offer. Don't force issues. Pisces and Virgo will be featured. At least one will ask, "What am I doing here?"

Friday, August 2 (Moon in Taurus to Gemini 11:44 p.m.) As you prepare for the weekend, remember obligations to someone who was there when you needed him. Focus on business-career pressure. You will be up to it. You get the green light from a legal counselor. Capricorn and Cancer will play sensational roles.

Saturday, August 3 (Moon in Gemini) Your cycle is moving up. You could receive a "stunning" offer. Circumstances are turning in your favor, so be selective and choose quality. Wear brighter colors; make personal appearances. A Libra helps you gain recognition. Lucky lottery: 7, 12, 18, 22, 30, 50.

Sunday, August 4 (Moon in Gemini) Make a fresh start. Take the initiative. Realize that you are exuding personal magnetism and sex appeal. Don't break too many hearts—at the very least, offer tea and sympathy. Within 24 hours, one of your original concepts "catches on."

Monday, August 5 (Moon in Gemini to Cancer 8:00 a.m.) The focus is on cooperative efforts, public relations, legal affairs, and your marital status. A Cancer will be bold enough to tell you, "You are so attractive, I would like to know you better!" Home economics are discussed.

Tuesday, August 6 (Moon in Cancer) Show off your sense of humor. You are on the verge of earning more money. Collect and research data—those who think you could be a "pushover" will suffer a rude awakening. Know your subjects. Plunge into a debate. You can win big!

Wednesday, August 7 (Moon in Cancer to Leo 12:25 p.m.) The feeling of entrapment is temporary. People want to be with you, and have questions to ask. Be pleasant, but know when to announce, "Enough is enough!" Taurus, Leo, and Scorpio will play major roles. Revise, review, line up your schedule, and set priorities.

Thursday, August 8 (Moon in Leo) The new moon in Leo coincides with different friends and an unusual course of action. Don't start anything that you cannot finish, including a love relationship. A relative is restless and needs you to buoy confidence. Virgo plays an "interesting" role.

Friday, August 9 (Moon in Leo to Virgo 2:02 p.m.) Attention revolves around your family and home. A visitor from another state says, "I knew you wouldn't mind my coming unannounced." Be pleasant, but state, "I am always happy to see you but please no more unannounced visits!" Taurus, Libra, and Scorpio figure in this scenario.

Saturday, August 10 (Moon in Virgo) Your keywords should be, "Wait and see!" You do not have the necessary facts. They will be forthcoming within 3 days. Meanwhile, deal gingerly with Pisces and Virgo. A mystical experience last night could be interpreted as a "prophetic dream."

Sunday, August 11 (Moon in Virgo to Libra 2:37 p.m.) Evaluate your property. Decide what you want to do in connection with sales and purchases. You hold the trump card. Legal authorities are on your side. Move ahead in a confident, direct way. Capricorn and Cancer will play outstanding roles.

Monday, August 12 (Moon in Libra) On this Monday, look beyond previous experiences. Focus on imagination, prophecy, and the ability to look past the obvious. Aries and Libra will play major roles and they want to be helpful. Let go of an obligation you had no right to carry in the first place.

Tuesday, August 13 (Moon in Libra to Scorpio 4:00 p.m.) Get off to a fresh start. Replace gloom with optimism. The lunar position emphasizes the "stirring of creative juices." There have been self-doubts, but put them aside. You are doing the right thing at the right time. A love relationship prospers.

Wednesday, August 14 (Moon in Scorpio) Work methods are reviewed. A passionate Scorpio says, "You can do this much better if you do it my way!" Maintain your emotional equilibrium and then "do things" your way. You'll be dealing intensely with persons born under Cancer and Capricorn.

Thursday, August 15 (Moon in Scorpio to Sagittarius 7:25 p.m.) Your sense of humor is your ally. Laugh at your own foibles. Focus on versatility, diversity, intellectual curiosity, and the determination to select quality. Sagittarius and another Gemini figure in today's exciting scenario. Your lucky number is 3.

Friday, August 16 (Moon in Sagittarius) Focus on reviewing, rewriting, and rebuilding—you can renew a friendship with a temperamental Scorpio. Be willing to tear down in order to rebuild—make intelligent concessions without abandoning your basic principles. Taurus is also in this picture.

Saturday, August 17 (Moon in Sagittarius) Focus on public appearances, legal affairs, your reputation, and marital status. Do what you know must be done, then "be done with it." Examine various aspects of a project without scattering your forces. You possess "winning ways," and tonight you'll know this is a fact.

Sunday, August 18 (Moon in Sagittarius to Capricorn 1:15 a.m.) Some of your legal questions and problems will be answered in a positive way. Focus on home ownership, romantic issues, and the ability to beautify your surroundings. Someone who is knowledgeable about art, music, and literature could come into your life. Be receptive, but not naive.

Monday, August 19 (Moon in Capricorn) An aura of deception exists, deliberate or otherwise. Accounting procedures require revision. A computer error is not unlikely. Pisces and Virgo will play outstanding roles, and could have these letters or initials in their names—G, P, Y.

Tuesday, August 20 (Moon in Capricorn to Aquarius 9:16 a.m.) You can have things "your way"—the rub is, "What *is* your way?" Tonight will be time for greater self-discovery. Are you taking too much for granted? Capricorn and Cancer play leading roles, and have these letters or initials in their names—H, Q, Z.

Wednesday, August 21 (Moon in Aquarius) Look beyond the immediate. Plan ahead for a journey that could take you overseas. You actually require representation in another nation. Know it, and do something about it. Aries and Libra play fascinating roles, and have these letters in their names—I and R. Your lucky number is 9.

Thursday, August 22 (Moon in Aquarius to Pisces 7:10 p.m.) The full moon in your ninth house, in Aquarius, indicates clearly that through an innovative process you will create a profitable enterprise. Emphasize originality, daring, adventure, and new fields to conquer. On a personal level, you could fall madly in love with a Leo.

Friday, August 23 (Moon in Pisces) Focus on cooperative efforts and activities connected with City Hall. You'll receive proposals that include career and marriage. If married, the spark that brought you together in the first place reignites. Accent direction, motivation, where you are going and why.

Saturday, August 24 (Moon in Pisces) Focus on your ability to accept more leadership responsibility. The emphasis is on social activities, and political and charitable campaigns. A Sagittarius and another Gemini will figure prominently, and have these letters in their names: C, L, U. Your lucky number is 3.

Sunday, August 25 (Moon in Pisces to Aries 6:47 a.m.) Solve a mathematical problem. By doing this, you display skill and knowledge. A Pisces helps you overcome difficulties in reaching the top. You know inwardly that you belong in an elevated position—the key now is to act as if you are aware of it.

Monday, August 26 (Moon in Aries) The moon in Aries relates to your eleventh house—your popularity is on the rise. You win friends and influence people. This will be one of your most exciting, creative days. The number 5 numerical cycle relates to change, a variety of sensations, and a display of writing skills.

Tuesday, August 27 (Moon in Aries to Taurus 7:30 p.m.) Attention revolves around your home, family, domesticity, and the ability to beautify surroundings. Music will be in your life, as you strive for harmony. You will be complimented on your appearance and voice. A gift is received from a Libran who genuinely does care for you.

Wednesday, August 28 (Moon in Taurus) The Taurus moon relates to your twelfth house—you've been keeping a secret, and now you can come out in the open. Define terms; state who you are and why you are here. Pisces and Virgo will play outstanding roles, and have these letters or initials in their names: G, P, Y.

Thursday, August 29 (Moon in Taurus) A power play day. You begin to "feel your oats" as August winds down. Focus on investments, production, and dealings with executives. Before this day is finished, you will have "revealed" much of your itinerary: why you are here and how you intend to accomplish goals.

Friday, August 30 (Moon in Taurus to Gemini 7:44 a.m.) Questions and pressures relating to marriage will be much in evidence in the next 24 hours. Check travel plans. Look beyond the immediate. Let go of a burden not really your own in the first place. Aries and Libra will play "sensational" roles.

Saturday, August 31 (Moon in Gemini) On this last day of August, your inventive capabilities surge forward. The moon in your sign relates to your high cycle—this means you will be at the right place at a special moment. Leo and Aquarius play outstanding roles. Have luck with number 1.

SEPTEMBER 2002

Sunday, September 1 (Moon in Gemini to Cancer 5:13 p.m.) On this Sunday, you will surprise many with a display of confidence. The moon in your sign, plus the number 8 numerical cycle, coincides with important contacts, projects, and accomplishments. Capricorn and Cancer will play outstanding roles.

Monday, September 2 (Moon in Cancer) Look beyond the immediate. Check with a travel agent about a possible journey overseas. A love relationship is at a standstill—but only temporarily. Refuse to be taken for granted, and almost before you know it, you'll be regarded in a different, more positive way.

Tuesday, September 3 (Moon in Cancer to Leo 10:34 p.m.) The money situation will show much improvement. Stress independence; show off your pioneering spirit. What had been held back from you will be released. Do your own thing; do not follow others. Leo and Aquarius will play dramatic roles.

Wednesday, September 4 (Moon in Leo) Within 24 hours, you could be embarking upon a "short journey" in connection with a relative. Stick to a sensible pace. Let it be known you do not intend to become part of a wild-goose chase. A Cancer has your best interests at heart and will prove it.

Thursday, September 5 (Moon in Leo) Social activities accelerate. Forces tend to be scattered. Questions arise: "Which invitations to accept?" You will be consulted about color coordination, design, entertainment, and showmanship. Have luck with number 3.

Friday, September 6 (Moon in Leo to Virgo 12:14 a.m.) You have a definite path to follow, despite minor obstacles. This is your "makeover" day. Revise, review, rewrite—and remember that hard writing makes easy reading. Tear down in order to rebuild. You will be rewarded for extra time spent in the "rebuilding process."

Saturday, September 7 (Moon in Virgo to Libra 11:56 p.m.) Your possessions, including property, turn out to be worth more than you originally estimated. Check the facts and figures. Do your own investigating. A Pisces means well, but lacks well-researched conclusions. Virgo will also play a role. Have luck with number 5.

Sunday, September 8 (Moon in Libra) On this Sunday, if possible, remain on familiar ground and reestablish connections with your family. Beautify your surroundings. Make a decision about design and architecture associated with where you live. Taurus, Libra, and Scorpio play outstanding roles.

Monday, September 9 (Moon in Libra to Scorpio 9:48 p.m.) Define terms, outline boundaries, and do not drive with a heavy drinker. Avoid self-deception. See people, places, and relationships in a realistic light. Pisces and Virgo play major roles, could have these letters or initials in their names—G, P, Y.

Tuesday, September 10 (Moon in Scorpio) This could be your power play day! The moon position relates to the stirring of creative juices. The number 8 numerical cycle coincides with added responsibility, a leadership role, production, promotion, and a greater degree of financial security.

Wednesday, September 11 (Moon in Scorpio) Finish what you start. Realize that your original idea is ready to "take off." Emphasize universal appeal. Open lines of communication. Aries and Libra will play constructive roles. One relationship is running its course—another is on the way. Be receptive.

Thursday, September 12 (Moon in Scorpio to Sagittarius 1:44 a.m.) Make a fresh start. Exercise independence of thought and action. The numerical cycle number 1 equates to the sun. This combines with your Mercury—your ideas, formats, and other contributions will be appreciated and will pay you handsomely. Leo is in this picture.

Friday, September 13 (Moon in Sagittarius) Not an unlucky day for you! Separate superstition from fact. Focus on your family, partnership, cooperative efforts, and your marital status. You might be wondering, "Why are things happening so fast?" People you associate with could be temperamental and lack patience.

Saturday, September 14 (Moon in Sagittarius to Capricorn 6:47 a.m.) Questions about partnership, legal affairs, and marriage loom large. Lie low. Don't start a debate or a fight, but don't run away either. Social activities accelerate. Somehow people feel it is their duty to introduce you to someone who could play an important role in your life.

Sunday, September 15 (Moon in Capricorn) Be receptive, not naive. Keep both feet on the ground; find out what you are getting into before progressing too far. People, especially Sagittarius, will compliment and flatter you. Taurus, Leo, and Scorpio also play roles and have these initials in their names: D, M, V.

Monday, September 16 (Moon in Capricorn to Aquarius 2:54 p.m.) On this Monday, investigate where angels fear to tread. A computer error is likely; accounting procedures require review. You exude personal magnetism, and an aura of sensuality and sex appeal. At least one member of the opposite sex confides, "I can hardly keep my hands off you!"

Tuesday, September 17 (Moon in Aquarius) A short trip involves a relative. Make crystal clear, "I don't want to be involved in any wild-goose chase!" Taurus, Libra, and Scorpio figure prominently, and could have these initials in their names—F, O, X. The Aquarius moon relates to travel, spirituality, and gaining self-recognition.

Wednesday, September 18 (Moon in Aquarius) Lie low; play the waiting game. Travel is involved, as well as advertising, publishing, and showmanship. Use your Gemini wit and wisdom. You are going places. You are in charge of your own destiny. Pisces and Virgo will play major roles.

Thursday, September 19 (Moon in Aquarius to Pisces 1:17 a.m.)   Within 24 hours, you receive news that a project, long delayed, is given the green light. Deal with people in other cities and lands. Don't wait to be told—take the initiative, and contact higher-ups. Capricorn and Cancer will figure in this scenario.

Friday, September 20 (Moon in Pisces)   The Pisces moon relates to your career, promotion, production, and a work assignment that includes a sea resort. You have proven yourself; there's no need to keep an appointment hat in hand. Speak up, and assert your views. Do not back down from your principles. Aries is in this picture.

Saturday, September 21 (Moon in Pisces to Aries 1:10 p.m.)   A love relationship fills you with magnetic appeal. Maintain your self-esteem. Begin a project. Let love lead the way in many areas. Leo and Aquarius figure prominently, and could have these initials in their names: A, S, J. Have luck with number 1.

Sunday, September 22 (Moon in Aries)   A family member makes a surprise announcement, and it's very favorable. You can hardly believe your "good luck." The moon in Aries, your eleventh house, coincides with your ability to win friends and influence people. Excellent for obtaining funding, and for displaying Gemini wit and wisdom.

Monday, September 23 (Moon in Aries)   Racing luck—all tracks: post position special—number 3 p.p. in the fifth race. People question you about participation in political-charitable campaigns. Be pleasant, but avoid definite commitments. Sagittarius plays a role.

Tuesday, September 24 (Moon in Aries to Taurus 1:53 a.m.)   On this day, attend to details. Realize that within 24 hours, secrets will be exposed—to your advantage. You could be in the midst of a winning streak. Deal with facts and figures; research subjects which you might be called upon to debate.

Wednesday, September 25 (Moon in Taurus) Lucky lottery: 2, 5, 12, 13, 18, 25. Read, write, and learn by teaching. What you once took for granted will require additional study. A flirtation is more serious than you originally anticipated—know when to say, "Enough is enough!"

Thursday, September 26 (Moon in Taurus to Gemini 2:25 p.m.) Focus on "backstage." The answers will be found, if you look in areas previously covered. What you discover will have a "stunning effect." Don't make a federal case out of minor infidelity. Voice, sound, design, and a domestic relationship all figure prominently.

Friday, September 27 (Moon in Gemini) In your high cycle, you can put across ideas and concepts previously rejected. You get the proverbial "second chance." Pisces and Virgo will play major roles, and could have these letters or initials in their names: G, P, Y. Maintain an aura of intrigue and mystery.

Saturday, September 28 (Moon in Gemini) What you have been waiting for is here. A powerful individual announces, "I will back you!" Focus on production and a financial transaction that definitely is not minor league. Capricorn and Cancer will play dynamic roles, and have these letters in their names—H, Q, Z.

Sunday, September 29 (Moon in Gemini to Cancer 12:59 a.m.) Spiritual values surface. More money will become available. You will wonder, "What did I do that was right? I would like to find out and do it again!" The best answer is: It was in your stars, planets, and numbers. Libra plays a sensational role.

Monday, September 30 (Moon in Cancer) On this last day of September, with the moon in its own sign, Cancer, your concentration will be on locating lost articles and increasing your earning power. Your prestige moves up. You are due to gain recognition. Leo and Aquarius figure in this dramatic scenario.

OCTOBER 2002

Tuesday, October 1 (Moon in Cancer to Leo 7:56 a.m.) On this Tuesday, you learn where you stand and how far you can go. The moon position accents your earning power and ability to locate lost articles and to improve your income potential. You'll be asked questions about a foreign land, possible investment.

Wednesday, October 2 (Moon in Leo) You'll conclude, "October could be my lucky month!" It could be, especially if you make a fresh start in a new direction—details are forthcoming by tonight. Leo and Aquarius play top roles, and sincerely want to be your valuable allies. Your fortunate number is 1.

Thursday, October 3 (Moon in Leo to Virgo 10:50 a.m.) Focus on cooperative efforts, partnership, and marriage. A Leo relative who seems to have all the answers is himself in a quandary. Be cooperative to a certain point and then say, "Thanks, but no, thanks!" Cancer and Capricorn will now bow out of the picture.

Friday, October 4 (Moon in Virgo) Highlight diversity and versatility, and become knowledgeable about the value of your property. Sagittarius and another Gemini will play fascinating roles, and have these letters or initials in their names: C, L, U. Have luck with number 3, tonight!

Saturday, October 5 (Moon in Virgo to Libra 10:50 a.m.)   You'll be tested and challenged. Many people ask questions in the hope that you will be embarrassed. Maintain your emotional equilibrium. Answer truthfully; that is all anyone can ask of you. Taurus, Leo, and Scorpio play memorable roles, and have these initials in their names—D, M, V.

Sunday, October 6 (Moon in Libra)   The new moon in Libra in your fifth house relates to children, challenge, variety, and a stirring of creative juices. An upstart Leo attempts to goad you into losing your temper. Have none of it! In matters of speculation, stick with number 5.

Monday, October 7 (Moon in Libra to Scorpio 9:57 a.m.)   Attention revolves around your home, family, security, and property values. You look different and your voice is unusual—people comment; accept this as a compliment. If there is music in your life tonight, dance to your own tune. Libra is represented.

Tuesday, October 8 (Moon in Scorpio)   Time is on your side—wait and see. Focus on work methods, and winning the friendship of someone who shares your basic interests. You'll be asked to participate in an enterprise that is due to become profitable. Pisces and Virgo play outstanding roles.

Wednesday, October 9 (Moon in Scorpio to Sagittarius 10:21 a.m.)   You missed an opportunity 24 hours ago—today you get the proverbial second chance. You'll be on the inside of a proposition that has been built to acquire a profit. Consult familiar friends, including a Cancer and a Capricorn. Your lucky number is 8.

Thursday, October 10 (Moon in Sagittarius)   On this Thursday, questions loom large, such as, "What are you going to do about cooperative efforts, partnership, and marriage?" Have the answers at hand. Be sure others realize you could at any moment take off for a trip overseas.

Friday, October 11 (Moon in Sagittarius to Capricorn 1:45 p.m.)   The moon in Sagittarius, your seventh house, relates to long-term commitments, including marriage. You meet new people, and emphasize originality, entertainment, and romance. Shake off lethargy. Refuse to be a prisoner of preconceived notions.

Saturday, October 12 (Moon in Capricorn)   Financial questions are answered. A review is agreed upon. Focus on direction, motivation, and a decision relating to your partnership and marital status. Cancer and Capricorn play outstanding roles, and could have these letters or initials in their names—B, K, T.

Sunday, October 13 (Moon in Capricorn to Aquarius 8:51 p.m.)   The lunar position coincides with an interest in the occult. There are some mysteries you want to solve—it won't matter if you try so go ahead. To repeat a line from Shakespeare, "There are more things in heaven and earth . . . than are dreamt of in your philosophy, Horatio!"

Monday, October 14 (Moon in Aquarius)   Before this day is finished, you'll have the feeling of more freedom. Plan ahead in connection with a possible journey. Financial pressures are due to be relieved within 24 hours. Taurus, Leo, and Scorpio will play outstanding roles.

Tuesday, October 15 (Moon in Aquarius) The moon in Aquarius relates to advertising, travel, publishing, and a recognition of spiritual values. People who previously took you for granted will now take a "second look." A Virgo member of the opposite sex confides, "I find you so attractive that at times I can hardly keep my hands off you!"

Wednesday, October 16 (Moon in Aquarius to Pisces 8:51 p.m.) Look beyond the immediate. Take advantage of a "publishing opportunity." The highlight is also on your home, loved ones, insurance, and protection of your property. Taurus and Libra will play outstanding roles. A family member compliments you on your voice. Be happy about it!

Thursday, October 17 (Moon in Pisces) Transform a tendency to brood into a positive meditation. Bring forth your psychic abilities. Trust your inner feelings. Do not equate delay with defeat. What you are waiting for will arrive within 3 days. Pisces and Virgo will be active in your scenario and helpful, too.

Friday, October 18 (Moon in Pisces to Aries 7:12 p.m.) Be ready for a "powerful" weekend. The emphasis is on promotion, production, and added recognition and prestige. Some people ask, "To what do you attribute your success?" Take time to smile and modestly state, "I didn't figure I had that much success!"

Saturday, October 19 (Moon in Aries) Your wishes will be fulfilled! The Aries moon represents your eleventh house—that section of your horoscope represents your hopes, wishes, and ability to win friends and influence people. Look to the future. Design a product so that it will meet the requirements of the future. Your lucky number is 9.

Sunday, October 20 (Moon in Aries) Spiritual values surface in a dramatic way. Spirited discussion revolves around Charles Darwin and Alfred Russell Wallace. It will be stated that Wallace and Darwin were on the same wavelength, except that Wallace claimed a man had spiritual values. Leo dominates this scenario.

Monday, October 21 (Moon in Aries to Taurus 7:55 a.m.) The full moon in your eleventh house coincides with romance, speculation, and personal magnetism. In continuation of a debate, you point out that Alfred Russell Wallace stunned colleagues by publishing his book *Scientific Developments in Modern Spiritualism*.

Tuesday, October 22 (Moon in Taurus) You gain followers today by exhibiting your charm, personality, and sense of humor. Those you once sought guidance from will now return the compliment. Give full play to your intellectual curiosity, and investigate the practicality of travel in connection with a unique project.

Wednesday, October 23 (Moon in Taurus to Gemini 8:16 p.m.) Lucky lottery: 2, 13, 20, 22, 24, 42. A secret meeting takes place. You might not be invited, but don't make a federal case of it. You are needed more than you need others. Maintain your emotional equilibrium. Laugh at those who take themselves too seriously.

Thursday, October 24 (Moon in Gemini) Your cycle moves up. Within 24 hours, you'll name your own ticket and price. A voluble Taurean talks sense and you must listen carefully to understand. Read, write, teach, and go slow on that flirtation—it could be getting out of hand.

Friday, October 25 (Moon in Gemini) The moon in your sign equates to your high cycle. Accent your personality. Be with people who are bright and at times controversial. Take the initiative. You will be at the right place at the right time. It is possible that you might change your residence and marital status.

Saturday, October 26 (Moon in Gemini to Cancer 7:09 a.m.) Avoid making commitments that you know will be difficult to fulfill. See people, places, and relationships as they are, not merely as you wish they could be. This means avoid self-deception. Pisces and Virgo will play active roles.

Sunday, October 27—Daylight Saving Time Ends (Moon in Cancer) On this Sunday, you will obtain a correct evaluation of your possessions. You will know "the cost of things." A Cancer-born family member pleads, "You can trust me and I wish you would confide in me. It would make me feel much better." Your lucky number is 8.

Monday, October 28 (Moon in Cancer to Leo 2:18 p.m.) A project that has been long delayed can be completed. Travel overseas is a distinct possibility, which could include special dealings with Aries and Libra. For some time, you've complained, "Not enough excitement." Today you get your fill of exciting developments.

Tuesday, October 29 (Moon in Leo) A relative, previously quiet, engages in colorful verbiage. Maintain your own balance. Realize that sticks and stones can break your bones, but words hurled at you need not do damage. An Aquarian, who has been out of sight, will play a marvelous role.

Wednesday, October 30 (Moon in Leo to Virgo 6:58 p.m.) Proposals are received concerning business and career, partnership and marriage. Take time to be selective. Choose what you can handle and let the others go until "next time." Cancer and Capricorn will participate in putting across a dynamic, exciting project.

Thursday, October 31 (Moon in Virgo) For most people, it will be Halloween. For magicians around the world, it will be "National Magic Day." It is a day when magicians and others remember Harry Houdini. There will be inquiries concerning whether or not he "came back." Mrs. Houdini told Walter Winchell, "Houdini did come back to me during a séance."

NOVEMBER 2002

Friday, November 1 (Moon in Virgo to Libra 8:27 p.m.) On this Friday, the first day of November, you feel revitalized. Display your pioneering spirit. Make a fresh start in a new direction. Leo and Aquarius figure prominently, and will serve as inspiration. Work methods improve. You are more valued, and those in authority will let you know it.

Saturday, November 2 (Moon in Libra) With the moon in your fifth house, you exude personal magnetism and creativity. A flirtation that started innocently could be getting "complicated." Focus on children, challenge, change, and variety. Have luck with number 2.

Sunday, November 3 (Moon in Libra to Scorpio 8:09 p.m.) You will relax today. You also will laugh at your own foibles. With the moon remaining in Libra, your fifth house, you will be active in connection with children and creative projects. Sagittarius and another Gemini figure prominently.

Monday, November 4 (Moon in Scorpio) The new moon in Scorpio is your sixth house—which relates to your general health, impassioned pleas, and contacts with people who share your basic interests. This will not be an easygoing day. But you'll overcome obstacles and objections. Taurus is represented.

Tuesday, November 5 (Moon in Scorpio to Sagittarius 8:01 p.m.) Be ready for swift changes. Read, write, teach, and study yourself in connection with whom you want to spend the rest of your life. Focus on getting your thoughts on paper. Spend time analyzing your dreams. Tonight will be significant!

Wednesday, November 6 (Moon in Sagittarius) Lucky lottery: 6, 13, 18, 40, 42, 51. The lunar position emphasizes cooperative efforts in connection with City Hall. The emphasis is on public relations, legal affairs, and your marital status. There will be a reunion tonight. Tears will flow—give logic equal time!

Thursday, November 7 (Moon in Sagittarius to Capricorn 10:00 p.m.) On this Thursday, you separate fact from fancy without losing the valuable ingredient of imagination. Define terms: pay attention to real estate, to boundaries and basic costs. Pisces and Virgo will play "astounding" roles.

Friday, November 8 (Moon in Capricorn) You've waited for this day! Focus on accounting, royalties, and banking totals. An older person wants to help and is sincere, but can't quite keep up with the times. The pressure is on due to added responsibility. Capricorn is in the picture.

Saturday, November 9 (Moon in Capricorn) On this Saturday, look forward with anticipation. Open lines of communication. Someone in a faraway land has information to give you. Look beyond the immediate. Maintain an aura of universal appeal. Have luck with number 9.

Sunday, November 10 (Moon in Capricorn to Aquarius 3:27 a.m.) On this Sunday, spiritual values rise. The numerical cycle number 1 relates to the sun and blends with your Mercury. Original thoughts and presentations will pay dividends. Don't wait to be told. Go your way. Stress independence and creativity.

Monday, November 11 (Moon in Aquarius) You emerge from an aura of confusion. You are fit and in fighting form. Blend this "action cycle" with humor. You'll be asked important questions about partnership, cooperative efforts, and marriage. A Cancer plays a major role.

Tuesday, November 12 (Moon in Aquarius to Pisces 12:41 p.m.) Forces are scattered. Nevertheless, you can select the best—emphasize quality. Remember resolutions about exercise, diet, and nutrition. Someone of the opposite sex will sidle up to you and whisper, "I can hardly keep my hands off you!"

Wednesday, November 13 (Moon in Pisces) Racing luck—all tracks: post position special—number 4 p.p. in the fourth race. Someone in a position of authority seeks to confer with you. It's not strictly business. Be open-minded, without being naive. Scorpio is involved.

Thursday, November 14 (Moon in Pisces to Aries 12:37 a.m.) The lunar position accents promotion, production, and leadership. Get ready for quick changes. Maintain your sense of direction. A flirtation could be getting too hot not to cool down. Virgo, Sagittarius, and another Gemini play featured roles. Your lucky number is 5.

Friday, November 15 (Moon in Aries) Focus on harmony, especially at home. With the moon in your eleventh house, you win friends and influence people. You obtain funding for a favorite project. You'll have luck in matters of speculation, especially with these three numbers: 2, 9, 8.

Saturday, November 16 (Moon in Aries) You will be "called in" for a consultation. The emphasis will be on the future, discarding old methods and concepts. Your pioneering spirit surfaces to your advantage. Do research on language, numbers, and symbols. During a heated debate, insist that you know what it is all about and will do something to prove it.

Sunday, November 17 (Moon in Aries to Taurus 1:22 p.m.) On this Sunday, relax with the knowledge that you did your best and favorably impressed executives. You will be told about a fresh start, a new project which will bring you more independence. Leo, Capricorn, and Cancer play spectacular roles.

Monday, November 18 (Moon in Taurus) You sense, properly so, that something is being hidden. Look behind the scenes. You are not being told the complete story. Let it be known that you are not pleased with efforts to deceive. Aries and Libra will figure in this dramatic scenario.

Tuesday, November 19 (Moon in Taurus) Leo and another Gemini have something to tell you—listen! Get ready for a fresh start. Accept new concepts. Don't ridicule ideas which appear to be "fantastic." Recall Shakespeare's lines: "There are more things in heaven and earth, Horatio, than are dreamt of in your philosophy."

Wednesday, November 20 (Moon in Taurus to Gemini 1:23 a.m.) The full moon, lunar eclipse is in Taurus which represents your twelfth house. There is a rumble and stumble and you know for sure that something is going on backstage. Keep your emotional equilibrium, and hold off on accusations.

Thursday, November 21 (Moon in Gemini) Your cycle is high, so you put forth personal magnetism and sex appeal. Your popularity increases. A Sagittarian declares, "You have got it today!" Another Gemini asserts, "If we stick together on this, it will turn out well for both of us!"

Friday, November 22 (Moon in Gemini to Cancer 11:46 a.m.) A day made to order for you—obstacles placed in your path will be "easily" overcome. Your cycle is such that help comes from surprise sources, along with additional funding. Taurus, Leo, and Scorpio figure in this unusual scenario. Keep an open mind!

Saturday, November 23 (Moon in Cancer) Relatives and money blend during this cycle. You will receive a "vote of confidence." A valuable article lost ten days ago will mysteriously reappear. Don't look a gift horse in the mouth. Don't ask too many questions. Lucky lottery: 5, 15, 20, 25, 35, 40.

Sunday, November 24 (Moon in Cancer to Leo 8:01 p.m.) On this Sunday, stick close to your family, if possible. There is talk of expense in design, architecture, and further steps in beautifying your surroundings, especially at home. Keep abreast of what is happening, so that you are not off balance.

Monday, November 25 (Moon in Leo) A well-meaning relative suggests a trip. Your response should be negative, unless you want to be caught up in a wild-goose chase. Say thanks but no thanks, perhaps next time. Make crystal clear that your time is valuable and you must receive proper, advance notice.

Tuesday, November 26 (Moon in Leo) Results you have been hoping for will surface—this is your power play day, so take advantage of it! On a personal level, a relationship is warm at present, but could ultimately get too hot not to cool down. A Cancer is involved.

Wednesday, November 27 (Moon in Leo to Virgo 1:40 a.m.) Have answers ready for a critical analysis likely to be put forth by Virgo. Stick to your principles, but also make intelligent concessions. A long-range forecast is involved, which could include a weather report. Aries declares, "You are the person for the job!"

Thursday, November 28 (Moon in Virgo) On this Thanksgiving, you might be opening the door to an exciting new relationship. Be calm, but express enthusiasm for ideas and thoughts presented by a Leo. On this Thanksgiving, express gratitude for all the opportunities you had throughout the year.

Friday, November 29 (Moon in Virgo to Libra 4:53 a.m.) Out of confusion will arise definite opinions.

Trust your instincts and your heart. Those who attempt to overanalyze will be wrong. Trust your hunch. Give full play to your intuitive intellect. Cancer and Aquarius will play "sensational" roles.

Saturday, November 30 (Moon in Libra) On this Saturday, the last day of November, the Moon is in Libra. That is your fifth house, the section of your horoscope relating to creative and sexual activities. Avoid being fixed in your views. Don't insist on the answers which will reassure your ego. Have luck with number 3.

DECEMBER 2002

Sunday, December 1 (Moon in Libra to Scorpio 6:14 a.m.) This is the last month of the year. Christmas is on the way, along with New Year's Eve. On this first day of December, there will be much soul-searching. You will be considering resolutions relating to your home, family, and marriage.

Monday, December 2 (Moon in Scorpio) Nothing happens halfway today! Your "health problem" can be resolved if you practice moderation. This is not always easy during the holiday season. However, you have the intelligence, wit, and wisdom to do it and you will.

Tuesday, December 3 (Moon in Scorpio to Sagittarius 6:57 a.m.) Check your details. A computer error is a distinct possibility. Double-check your bank balance, insurance, and telephone payments. Taurus, Leo, and Scorpio will play dramatic roles. Some have these letters or initials in their names—D, M, V.

Wednesday, December 4 (Moon in Sagittarius) The new moon, solar eclipse is in Sagittarius, in your seventh house. There could be plenty of action, including upsets in connection with legal affairs, public relations, and your marital status. Take notes, start a diary, and be especially aware of dreams and their symbols. Your lucky number is 5.

Thursday, December 5 (Moon in Sagittarius to Capricorn 8:38 a.m.) Attention continues to emphasize cooperative efforts and participation in a public recognition of past and present heroes. You will be directly concerned with your public image, your legal rights and permissions, and marriage. A Libra is involved.

Friday, December 6 (Moon in Capricorn) You will feel as if "something ominous" is in the air, and could happen at any time. Focus on hospitals, institutions, and the fall from favor of a distinguished citizen. Maintain your emotional equilibrium. Be open-minded, without being naive.

Saturday, December 7 (Moon in Capricorn to Aquarius 12:54 p.m.) History lessons are reviewed, as you and the nation remember "Pearl Harbor Day." Check the facts and figures involved. Organize your priorities. You have much to offer. There is no reason to downplay contributions. Lucky lottery: 8, 18, 24, 35, 48, 51.

Sunday, December 8 (Moon in Aquarius) Travel to a foreign land should not be dismissed. There is a distinct possibility. Look beyond the immediate; your sense of prophecy is heightened. Predict your future. Make it come true! Aries and Libra figure in this dynamic, dramatic scenario.

Monday, December 9 (Moon in Aquarius to Pisces 8:46 p.m.) Racing luck—all tracks: post position special—number 7 p.p. in the first race. Throughout the day, wear bright colors and make personal appearances. A love relationship might get too hot not to cool down. Avoid making demands. Ride with the tide. Leo plays a top role.

Tuesday, December 10 (Moon in Pisces) You have a decision to make which involves your family or career. A secret meeting takes place. You are the subject of a discussion. Do what must be done. Be gracious about it. Cancer and Capricorn are directly involved, and feel you should follow their counsel.

Wednesday, December 11 (Moon in Pisces) By using charm and wit you get your way, which is the "right way." Feature humor. Keep plans flexible. Make intelligent concessions. Sagittarius and another Gemini will play featured roles. Lucky lottery: 3, 7, 10, 30, 46, 50.

Thursday, December 12 (Moon in Pisces to Aries 7:57 a.m.) Attend to details. Someone attempts to take your attention away from the essentials. Be polite, but indicate, "Thanks, but no, thanks, not today!" Scorpio and Taurus are involved, and might attempt to "bully you." Rebuild and rewrite. Your lucky number is 4.

Friday, December 13 (Moon in Aries) You will be excellent at obtaining funding for a unique project. You win friends and influence people. Don't hold back! This is your kind of day. You will have luck despite "Friday the 13th." Another Gemini is in the picture.

Saturday, December 14 (Moon in Aries to Taurus 8:42 p.m.) A family member deserves attention, even if the scheme is half-baked. Avoid being accusatory. Listen with an expression of "I want to hear more!" This helps relieve pressure. Taurus and Libra figure in this scenario and make contributions.

Sunday, December 15 (Moon in Taurus) Grab an opportunity to express your desires. In matters of speculation, you might find number 7 to be lucky. Visit someone temporarily confined to home or hospital. It could have been you, so be thankful! Pisces and Virgo figure in this scenario.

Monday, December 16 (Moon in Taurus to Gemini 8:41 a.m.) Make this your power play day! You gain access to privileged information. Let it be known: "I'll use it if necessary!" Capricorn and Cancer will play instrumental roles. You will be provided with the material necessary to carry out a project.

Tuesday, December 17 (Moon in Gemini) Maintain a universal outlook. Representatives of another nation could contact you. Be careful what you say. Say very little of consequence. Aries and Libra figure in this dramatic scenario, and have these letters in their names—I and R.

Wednesday, December 18 (Moon in Gemini) You might be hitting yourself with sledgehammer words concerning yesterday. Today start fresh; imprint style; do not follow others. The moon in your sign represents your high cycle. Don't back down. Stand tall for your principles. Have luck with number 1.

Thursday, December 19 (Moon in Gemini to Cancer 6:29 p.m.) Racing luck—all tracks: post position special—number 5 p.p. in the fifth race. The full moon in your sign represents the completion of a family dispute over money. Be receptive without being weak. You'll be at the right place at a special moment.

Friday, December 20 (Moon in Cancer) Diversify; highlight your intellectual curiosity. Insist on all information, not just bits and pieces. Somehow others bend to your will. Perhaps it is due to the sincere expression you maintained for the past three days. A Sagittarian plays a major role.

Saturday, December 21 (Moon in Cancer) On this Saturday, you get the "facts of life." Be practical where money is concerned. A Cancer family member moves to your side in an argument. Missing papers are located. This helps you put across your concepts and desires. Be a gracious winner!

Sunday, December 22 (Moon in Cancer to Leo 1:47 a.m.) Get ready for a change of scene and policy. If you are aware and move with the times, you win another major victory. A short trip is necessary to appease a family member who, if made angry, could cause trouble. A Sagittarian renders a fair decision.

Monday, December 23 (Moon in Leo) Relatives and the protection of your property at home figure prominently. Flowers, music, and gifts are a major part of this scenario. Music plays, so dance to your own tune. A domestic adjustment is just what you want and need. Libra is in this picture.

Tuesday, December 24 (Moon in Leo to Virgo 7:04 a.m.) Spiritual values of your holiday will be much in evidence. The Leo moon represents showmanship, gifts, and expressions of good will. Avoid being materialistic. State your beliefs in a "believable way." If you wait, you win. Do not force issues.

Wednesday, December 25 (Moon in Virgo) Much to your pleasure, you receive a practical gift and hear up-to-date counsel. People look to you for approval.

In actuality, you are in a powerful position. Don't abdicate, despite pressure. This will be one of your most enjoyable, profitable of Christmas Days.

Thursday, December 26 (Moon in Virgo to Libra 10:52 a.m.) You feel like you are "back home again." You are on your own turf. Others note difference in your attitude and actions. Those who once took you for granted will change their minds. Aries and Libra will play meaningful roles.

Friday, December 27 (Moon in Libra) Your creative juices stir. Give of yourself through reading and writing. Exciting changes are made at your behest. The holiday spirit prevails; be kind, but insist on the truth. Begin a project; highlight originality. Leo will play a dramatic role.

Saturday, December 28 (Moon in Libra to Scorpio 1:40 p.m.) The emphasis is on partnership, cooperative efforts, and marriage. If single, that might not be for too long. If married, the spark that brought you together in the first place will reignite. Cancer and Capricorn will play memorable roles. Your lucky number is 2.

Sunday, December 29 (Moon in Scorpio) If you don't know what to do, do nothing. You are currently in an aura of confusion. Don't rationalize. Face facts as they exist. An Aquarian means well, but advice is not valid. Sagittarius and another Gemini figure in this dynamic scenario.

Monday, December 30 (Moon in Scorpio to Sagittarius 4 p.m.) A Scorpio could overturn your work schedule. Maintain your emotional equilibrium. Let it be known: "I won't scare easily!" Continue to handle details; do proofreading. Be willing to tear down in order to rebuild. A Taurus voluntarily provides vital information.

Tuesday, December 31 (Moon in Sagittarius) Don't be in a car driven by a heavy drinker. It's a lively New Year's Eve, when many will make resolutions and promises. Don't believe everything you hear. Someone of the opposite sex, perhaps full of adult beverages, says, "I can hardly keep my hands off you!"

HAPPY NEW YEAR!

ABOUT THE AUTHOR

Born on August 5, 1926, in Philadelphia, Sydney Omarr was the only person ever given full-time duty in the U.S. Army as an astrologer. He also is regarded as the most erudite astrologer of our time and the best known, through his syndicated column (300 newspapers) and his radio and television programs (he was Merv Griffin's "resident astrologer"). Omarr has been called the most "knowledgeable astrologer since Evangeline Adams." His forecasts of Nixon's downfall, the end of World War II in mid-August of 1945, the assassination of John F. Kennedy, Roosevelt's election to the fourth term and his death in office . . . these and many others are on the record and quoted enough to be considered "legendary."

ABOUT THIS SERIES

This is one of a series of twelve
Day-to-Day Astrological Guides
for the signs of 2002
by Sydney Omarr.